Glimpses into the World of Verrier Elwin

Glimpses into the World of Verrier Elwin

Edited

Krishna Mohan Sinha Roy

GYAN

ISBN: 978-81-212-1991-4

Published, 2021

Published by

Gyan Publishing House
5, Ansari Road
Daryaganj, New Delhi-110002
Phone: 011-47034999, 9811692060
www.gyanbooks.com
E-mail: books@gyanbooks.com

and

Anthropological Survey of India
27 Jawaharlal Nehru Road,
Kolkata - 700016, (West Bengal)
Tel.: (033) 22521698
www. ansi.gov.in

Printed at: Gyan Press, Delhi.

Cataloging in Publication Data—DK
Courtesy: D.K. Agencies (P) Ltd. <docinfo@dkagencies.com>

"Tribal World of Verrier Elwin" (Workshop-cum-seminar) (2017: Jagdalpur, India)
Glimpses into the world of Verrier Elwin / edited, Krishna Mohan Sinha Roy.
pages cm
Five papers in Hindi.
Papers presented at a three day workshop-cum-seminar entitled "Tribal World of Verrier Elwin" held from 21-12-2017 to 23-12-2017 in Jagdalpur, Bastar District, Chhattisgarh, organized by Anthropological Survey of India.
Includes index.
ISBN 9788121219914

1. Elwin, Verrier, 1902-1964—Congresses. 2. Tribes—India—Bastar (District)—Social conditions—Congresses. 3. Tribes—India—Bastar (District)—Social life and customs—Congresses. 4. Ethnology—India—Bastar (District)—Congresses. I. Sinha Roy, K. M., editor. II. Anthropological Survey of India, organizer, publisher. III. Title.

LCC GN635.I4A17 2017 | DDC 305.800954137 23

Contents

Foreword

The collection of papers, both in Hindi and English, edited by K.M. Sinha Roy, resulted from a Seminar that the Sub-Regional Centre of the Anthropological Survey of India (henceforth AnSI or the Survey) at Jagdalpur (Chhattisgarh) held on 22 and 23 December 2017. On 21 December, a day before the seminar, the officials of the AnSI and the invitees (many of them retired from the AnSI) to the Seminar proceeded to the village of Binjli (Narayanpur) where the village authorities had expressed their wish to request the Survey to build a memorial at the site (behind the present-day school building) where Verrier Elwin had lived during the days of his fieldwork for the book on the Muriya. A meeting inaugurating the plan of building the Elwin Memorial, as the AnSI thought of naming it, was to take place on 21 December, in which, and it was an exciting part, the residents of Binjli were to narrate what they had learnt about Elwin from their parents and grandparents, or anyone alive in the village who had seen and interacted with Elwin. The town of Jagdalpur had a couple of people who had vivid memories of Elwin visiting their school or seeing him in the bazar speaking to the local people. What touched these people, a handful of them in their nineties, was that Elwin wore the Indian dresses (long kurta and pyjama) and had a gentle and smiling face. They also recalled visiting his hut (made with mud and thatched with straw) built near Chitrakote waterfalls where he lived whenever he was in Bastar.

Today, these notables from Jagdalpur have faint memories of Elwin. What they remember about him are the snippets of Elwin's persona. For instance, Elwin's wife distributed toffees and other sweets to children, Elwin used to stay in the *ghotul*, and he had got a temporary toilet constructed near it, he used to generously give his 'foreign liquor' to the villagers and in reciprocation, drink the locally-brewed spirit, he used to go to the forest for hunting and brought the game to be distributed among people, and that he was perpetually asking questions on people's lifestyles, rituals, and customs, and writing the answers he received in his notebooks. They knew that Elwin was a writer, and his books had already been published. Some also claimed to have read these, finding them useful in their work with the tribal communities they were carrying out.

Similar were the memories of the Binjli dwellers. A nonagenarian woman remembered that it was for the first time in her life (when she was 10-12 years of old) she saw a 'white-complexioned, tall man'. She said those days every one observed distance from him, because he looked different and unpredictable, but soon his 'gentle smile' and the fact that he was venturing out to speak to people, and also offering toffees and balls to children, made people feel comfortable in his presence.

Listening to this I was instantly reminded of Malinowski's account of his stay with the Trobriand Islanders. When the children would come closer to his tent which he had pitched in the village of Omarakhana, and peep inside to see what that 'strange' man was doing, and Malinowski would lift his eyes to see them, they would quickly run away. Gradually, the same children started coming inside Malinowski's tent, sit and observe him for hours, and then strike a little conversation with him. Initially when Malinowski went out of his tent, people would try to go away, avoiding him, clearing his way, but with the passage of time, they stopped attending to him and continued with the errand they were busy with. The phase of what anthropologists say 'dis-attending' had begun. No more was Malinowski unusual to the local eyes.

The same process was witnessed in Elwin's case, and soon he was participating along with the people in hunting expeditions, marriage functions, where he danced, sang, and made merry. He also joined the *ghotul*, where he was given a new name Maliaru. Lovingly, people called him 'Sahabji', and the mango tree he planted closer to the place where he had built his house was known as 'Sahab Marka'.

These memories have become a part of the people's collective heritage. We could not come across more than a couple of people in Binjli who had seen Elwin, and they only remembered isolated incidents, some of which are described in this volume, and some I have dealt with in my paper published in *Man in India* (2018, 98[1]: 231-53). However, there were scores of them who had heard from their elders the stories of Elwin which they repeated to the others, and in this way, these stories were descending from one generation to the next. The common understanding, they all shared was that Elwin wrote books on their community, and because of his writings, the outside world (the state and its bodies) came to know about it. What was unimportant to them was what he wrote and how it is being evaluated now, how far that information holds veracity, and whether his work is being read today.

Elwin is judged not in terms what he wrote or what he did for the people of Binjli or the Muriya, but in terms of the relations he cultivated with the ancestors of the contemporary people; the facts of great significance to them are that he was respectful towards people and so were they, and he lived in their midst with sincerity and commitment, and extended assistance whenever it was needed. Yes, they also knew that once he left their village, he did not return, and they came to know later that he had written books on them, but then, they said his exit is not to be mourned, because it is the 'truth of life', the 'cycle of life'. We are all 'travellers' (*pathik*), said a school teacher. Till the 'journey is completed, we are together', and after that 'we go our own ways'. Elwin was not an exception. The Binjli people want the memorial to be built in his name since it would remind them of the sweet relations their ancestors had with him, and 'one who chose their village worthy of traversing through'. As I learnt, the memorial would be a symbol of their past and their ancestors.

In his life of sixty-two years, Elwin produced detailed ethnographic accounts on the lives of not less half a dozen communities. Not only that, he collected the folktales and songs of these communities, which he published separately. Besides this he took thousands of photographs of tribal people and collected their material artefacts. In his obituary on him, David Mandelbaum said that "[Elwin] produced the largest corpus of data on Indian ethnography which has come from a single hand." He further said that Elwin made tribal people, who were 'relatively invisible' and 'socially submerged', known to the world as 'real people, rather than tiresome savages, and their cultures as worthy of study.' In this process, Indian leaders came to know of the predicaments of tribal communities.

Elwin's love for the tribes was beyond the pale of doubt. This idea runs through his *The Tribal World of Verrier Elwin*, which is an autobiographical account, for which in 1965 he was honoured with the Sahitya Academy Award, given by the India's National Academy of Letters. In his autobiography, he wrote: "When I am no longer in a tribal village, I spend much of my time and most of my thought among the tribal people." He was one of the architects (along with Pandit Jawaharlal Nehru) of the policy of integration of tribes with the mainstream of Indian society, a policy which still is the sheet-anchor of our approach towards tribes. For his 'absorbed and concerned attachment' to India's tribes, in 1961, he was bestowed with one of the civilian awards, Padma Bhushan.

In our repeated meetings with the people of Binjli, we realized that Elwin left an indelible impact on them, and this impact has been carried forward over generations, with the result that he has become one of the emblems of their self-description and identity. 'Elwin lived in my village', is one of the epithets by which they describe their village; and I am certain it must be the case in other villages also where he lived and the communities of people with whom he spent his time. People cherish his demeanour, his manners, his smile, his geniality, and the landmarks of his stay.

Vinay Kumar Srivastava

Preface

From the time I visited Jagdalpur, I had realized one thing and it was that 'Bastar means Verrier Elwin'. He was a real friend of the tribal people in whose midst he had lived for many years. He was in Binjli village of Narayanpur district of Chhattisgarh. The villagers conveyed the importance of this site which had a mango tree and had a small hut occupied by Verrier Elwin. The mango tree was referred by the villagers as *Sahab Marka*. Here *Sahab* refer to Elwin and *Marka* means a mango tree. From the community people of Binjili, a letter was also received by Anthropological Survey of India officials, which stated the communal willingness of the villagers to construct a building on that place where Elwin used to live during his research work. Our honorable Director V.K. Srivastava accepted their wish to construct a building in memory of Elwin which would be a Library-cum-Museum. During that period, one of the principals of Narayanpur District, had confided that Elwin was the only 'white man' in those days who wore only *kurta* and *pyjama*, when other foreigners wore only western dresses. Elwin was unlike other westerners, he lessened the gap between the 'colonized' and the 'colonizers'.

The more I heard and read about Elwin, the more I felt the desire to bring all the people who knew Verrier Elwin's contribution, so that the present generation may know more about his involvement for India.

The Anthropological Survey of India held a three-days workshop-cum-seminar from 21-12-2017 to 23-12-2017 in the tribal land of Bastar, Chhattisgarh. The workshop which aimed at highlighting the great contribution made by the renowned Anthropologist Verrier Elwin was based on the theme of, "*Tribal World of Verrier Elwin*" and was hosted by the Anthropological Survey of India, Sub-Regional Centre, Jagdalpur, Bastar. It was attended by various eminent anthropologists.

The editor expresses his heart-felt thanks to all the contributors of the paper for their constant co-operation towards completion of this volume. The volume consists of some selected papers contributed in a seminar entitled ***'Tribal World of Verrier Elwin'***.

K.M. Sinha Roy

Introduction

The Anthropological Survey of India held a three days workshop-cum-seminar from 21-12-2017 to 23-12-2017 in the tribal land of Bastar, Chhattisgarh. The workshop which aimed at highlighting the great contribution made by the renowned Anthropologist Verrier Elwin was based on the theme of, "Tribal World of Verrier Elwin" and was hosted by the Anthropological Survey of India, Sub-Regional Centre, Jagdalpur, Bastar. It was attended by eminent anthropologists.

The venue of the Inaugural session was Binjli village, Narayanpur where Verrier Elwin had spent a major part of his time during his stay in Bastar. The programme started at 10:00 a.m. on 21-12-2017. K.M. Sinha Roy welcomed the guests after which, "Lighting of the lamp," was done by Chief Guest Smt. Santi Salam (who is herself a tribal lady and hails from this area) and by other distinguished guests. The Welcome Address was read by K.M. Sinha Roy, Head of Office, Sub-Regional Centre, Jagdalpur, office. After which Vinay Kumar Shrivastava, Director, Anthropological Survey of India, Kolkata, in his introductory key note Address informed the invited distinguished guests and the tribals who had gathered there in large number and informed that the AnSI was going to construct a traditional house in memory of Verrier Elwin and that it was starting the process by organizing the first day event and Foundation of the New Building (Library-cum-Museum). He also told that the AnSI was also going to share the experiences of villagers about Verrier Elwin. The Guest of Honour at this function was R.K. Bhattacharya, Ex. Director, AnSI, who also spoke on the occasion. Other distinguished guests present at the function were Jayanta Sarkar, Ex. Director-in-Charge, AnSI, and Umesh Kumar, Ecologist, AnSI, Kolkata. The Chief Guest Smt. Santi Salam in her address thanked the AnSI for their commendable work in Bastar and for their resolve to construct a library-cum-museum in Binjli village in order to commemorate and preserve the memory of Verrier Elwin.

After the cultural programme and tea break Messrs Meghnath Kumeti, Shiv Kumar Pandey, Ramlal Dugga, Bindeswar Mahair, Ram Singh Thakur,

Harihar Vaishnava and Kiran Niruti shared their experiences with the audience. After which there was a break for High Tea. In the Afternoon Session Shri Ashok Elwin, son of Verrier Elwin and Messrs Megani Dugga, Ganga Ram Kashyap, Miss Ratni Salam, Lachhu Ram Dugga and Devnath Usendi spoke about Verrier Elwin. After Tea Break there was Valedictory Session which was addressed by Vinay Kumar Shrivastava. The function concluded with the vote of thanks proposed by P. R. Sahoo, Anthropologist (C), AnSI, Sub- Regional Centre, Jagdalpur.

The Anthropological Survey of India held a Two Day National Seminar on the, "Tribal World of Verrier Elwin" on 22 and 23 December, 2017 in the conference hall, AnSI, Jagdalpur. The Chief Guest at the Inaugural function of the Seminar was Dr. Shailendra Kumar Singh, Vice Chancellor, Bastar University, C.G. K. M. Sinha Roy, Head of Office, AnSI, Jagdalpur welcomed the chief guest and other distinguished guests. Shailendra Kumar Singh, the chief guest, speaking on the occasion praised the effort of the AnSI and showered his blessings to the Seminar. Guest Honour Umesh Kumar, Sr. Ecologist also spoke on the occasion.

Inauguration of Photographic exhibition based on the, "Life and Culture of Bastar, was done by Shailendra Kumar Singh, V.C., Bastar University. After which there was Tea Break. The Session after the Tea Break started with Jayanta Sarkar in the Chair, Keynote Address was presented by Amitava Sarkar and Gautam Bera and Mitashree presented their research papers.

The next Session started after the Lunch Break. R.K. Bhattacharya was to preside this Session but owing to his indisposition B. L. Jha was made the Chairperson. Special lecture was delivered by Jayanta Sarkar. The scholars who presented their research papers were Samira Dasgupta, Sukrita Kujur, Rajendra Singh, Bhuneswar Sahoo, Anand Murty Mishra. Ram Kumar B. spoke about Verrier Elwin and Ambedkar on Hindu religion. After which there was Tea-Break. In the evening the Bison-Horn Maria tribals presented their fantastic Bison-Maria dance, which captivated the spectators.

The Chairperson for the Morning Session of the Seminar on 23-12-2017 was B.L. Jha. R. K. Bhattacharya delivered the special lecture who spoke about Verrier Elwin's Diary and about his graphic description of tribals and their life among whom he lived for many years. Then Swapan Koley spoke about, "Muria/Maria and Their Ghotul". Elwin's son Ashok Elwin spoke about his father's many faceted lives and about the activities in which he was very fruitfully engaged throughout his life which benefited anthropological findings immeasurably. The next speaker was Rajesh

Roshan who presented a critique of, "Maria Murder and Suicide Cases". Shashi Pandy, a scholar of Gondi, spoke about the salient features of Gondi language. Palash Jalani spoke about the rapidly changing conditions taking place in the Muria communities of Bastar. The next Session started after the Tea Break with Amitava Sarkar as the Chairperson. Special lecture was delivered by Kanchan Mukhopadhyaya who spoke, about Elwin's philosophy and its contemporary relevance. Ranju Hasini Sahoo related her experience of about 15 years as an anthropologist. Shri Rameshwar Parsad Pandey and B. L. Jha are the two persons who claim to have seen Verrier Elwin and his wife. B. L. Jha who was presented in this session, read out the article written by Rameswar Pandey about Ewin and his wife and then he read about his own article.

The Chairperson of the Final Session was Kanchan Mukhopadhyay. Many scholars presented their papers notable whom were Piyush Ranjan Shahoo and Sukrita Kujoor.

At the Valedictory Function Vinay Kumar Shrivastava in his magnificent speech enumerated the various fields in which the Anthropological Survey of India was engaged in carrying out studies and during work.

The workshop came to a close with the Vote of Thanks proposed by Piyush Ranjan Sahoo, Anthropologist(C), AnSI, Sub-Regional Centre, Jagdalpur.

Public judgements: not ignore nor deny regarding Verrier Elwin

Some scholars appeared in the soil of India in different times as social, economic and religious reformers like - Ishwarchandra Vidyasagar, Raja Rammohan Roy, Bapuji, Sister Nivedita, Annie Basant, Mother Teresa etc. Their great contribution towards our society is memorable forever.

In this connection, it is an opportunity to write a few lines about Verrier Elwin, a British who contributed most of his life to assess life and culture of the people of Central and North-East India. He was a student of Oxford University and later on was influenced by philosophy of Mahatma Gandhi which was reflected in his famous books, journals, publications, etc. He was one of the best friends of Pandit Jawaharlal Nehru who was influenced by his Philosophy.

It is not an easy task for anthropologists to study any community which is unknown in aspects like their culture and different ecological set-up.

Similarly it reminds our Jarawa study during 1990 by the team of Anthropological Survey of India. At that time we had applied so many method, tools and techniques for our study which would enable us to meet with Jarwa people. Finally we learn about them but still so many things are unknown to us.

Elwin, as a self trained anthropologist and whatever he studied about the tribal people of Central (Bastar) and North-East India, give a base line for understanding the communities. There are so many debates going on about his writings but none can deny his contribution in development and welfare activities of India.

Due to his above mentioned contribution, Government appointed him as Deputy Director of Anthropological Survey of India for some years. Besides, some age-old information was also gathered from Binjli villagers of Narayanpur own those who were closely associated with Verrier Elwin, like Ratni Salam, Rameswar Pandey, and the their present family members like Ram Lal Dugga, Devnath Usendi and others.

Remembering memories by individuals

Ratni Salam:
Wife of Late Sundar Salam
Village Bakulbahi in Narayanpur district

Ratni Salam, resides at Bakulbahi village of Narayanpur district in Chhattisgarh. She could not remember her actual age due to her seniority. As per her family members she has crossed the boundary of 100 years. Though she has lost the power of eye sight and hearing but she never forgot the memories of her childhood at Binjli village. From her failing memory she was only able to explain some hazy picture of Sahab ji (Verrier Elwin).

During her childhood she loved very much to travel with her elder uncle (*pepi*) Rupji Manjhi, the *head man* of Duggal pargona. It was the first time when she had seen a white colour man with tall figure in her Binjli village at the age of 10-12 years.

In the beginning she and her friends maintained distance from him because his colour was entirely different from them. But after a few days they saw that the white man mixed-up with her uncle and other elders of the village and was called "Sahab Ji".

Note: Sinha Roy collected and compiled the views of some tribals of Bastar about Verrier Elwins who were very intimate to him for a prolonged period which are produced herein.

Their shyness gradually faded out when Sahab Ji offered toffee (*peppier goti*) and ball (*gande*). Most of the time he used to put on half-pant, *kurta* and a pair of boots.

His reddish face was always full of gentle smile and tried to communicate with the villagers in his language. They could not understand his words and it became very amusing (*Kandy Forenar*) for them. He took active participation in hunting, marriage functions, dances, singing, ritual and social performances, etc. She saw him in their Ghotul at the age of 13-14 years when she joined there as per social tradition. Her friends gave him a new name Maliaru at *Ghotul*. He visited their *Ghotul* and observed the activities of *Ghotul* members.

He liked their traditional liquor (*darang*) like salfi (*gorga*), and mahuwa (*irum daranga*), and enjoyednon-vegetable food very much, like flesh (*hobing*) of cow, pig (padar), and fish (*mink*). Amarjit, a local man, prepared food for him. He also participated in hunting with the villagers. He maintained cordial relations with their king (Raja) of Poral kotia.

Her uncle, Rupji manjhi, was the best friend of Sahab Ji. Once her uncle went to Delhi with him.

He lived at Binjli village with his wife (*dhonda*) in a traditional hut. It was looked like *Ghotul* which was made by the villagers. The roof of the hut was thatched by *khaddar* (one type of grass) and walls were made of wooden poles. There were two rooms in the hut. He slept on *machan* (the place with little bit height) which was located in the one corner of a room. The *machan* was made of wooden poles and bamboo splits. There was a wooden box in his room in which he kept his clothes and other materials. He planted a mango tree (*marka*) there beside his hut. The villagers called the tree as Sahab Marka in the memory of Verreir Elwin.

Ram Lal Dugga
Son of Late Magduram Dugga
Kotwar of Binjli village

Ram Lal Dugga, the son of Late Magduram Dugga and resident of Binjli village informed that he served as kotwar of Binjli village after his father. During his childhood his father brought one pair of boots and gave to his mother to keep safely. Then he enthusiastically asked his mother about the boots. She replied that it was the boot of Sahab ji who stayed here for a long time. Your father took care of him as a kotwar. One day he went to the market with his father at Narayanpur and noticed a Sahab at Banaglow who was wearing shirt, half pant and similar type of boot in his foot. Then he asked his father about the Sahab Ji. His father told him that the Sahab was not the earlier Sahab.

He also told that previously the whole area was full of jungle and wild animals like tigers, wild pigs, bears etc. Sometimes tigers also attacked their domestic animals. The Sahab Ji took initiative to kill the tigers. They divided themselves into some groups to hunt the tigers with drum, musical instruments and other hunting implements. All groups moved together from different sides by beating drums and other musical instruments, while Sahab Ji was waiting with his gun (bonduk) outside the village i.e. near to Binjli dam. After attempted several times the villagers lose their hopes but one day Sahab Ji shot a tiger with his gun.

He preferred to stay in our village and finally he prepared a hut to gossip with us. Even he did not hesitate to share his food and drink with us. He learned about preparation of *mohuwa* liquor from the villagers. At that time Kosi, a Abujh Maria girl, took care of him.

During some monetary urgency Magduram asked for his help. He gave the money and joked that if you are unable to repay the amount, your elder daughter will be kept with me.

He attended their village meetings and observed how elders took decisions to solve village level disputes. He participated in dances and festivals and captured the memorable moments in his camera. He gave toffee (*peppier goti*) and ball (*gande*) to the children.

I never saw him but came to know about him when some foreigners and the researchers of different parts of India came to our village, who asked about Sahabji. They visited our home because my father was known to Sahab Ji. It gives me a chance to know about the relationship between my father and Sahab Ji.

Devnath Usendi
Grandson of Rupji Manjhi (daughter's son)
Binjli village

Devnath Usendi, son of Late Raghunath Usendi and grandson of Rupji Manjhi, lives in Binjli village. He informed us that his grandfather (dada) was Rupji Manjhi, the Manjhi (Head Man) of Duggal parogona and under his jurisdiction there were 28 villages during that time. From his childhood he heard from his father and grandfather about Sahab Marka (mango tree) and at that time he was in primary school. He thought that the mangos of the tree were very sweet and tasty and for that the villagers called the Mango tree as Sahab Marka. So in a summer season he collected some ripe mangoes of that tree for realising taste. But he found that the mangoes were very sour. Then he became very upset. He asked his father, why he called the mango tree "Sahab Marka". Then his father laughed and replied that the mango tree was planted by a Sahab named Verrier Elwin and that time he resided in our village just beside the mango tree. So in the memory of Sahab Ji we call the tree "Sahab Marka".

Devnath Usendi also told that his grandpa recalled some stories about Sahab Ji. His grandpa told that Shahba Ji stayed here during the childhood of his father. At that time Sahab Ji made a hut which looked like a *Ghotul* with the help of villagers and he took him as a local guide during his field work. Sahab Ji observed each and every incidence of their village. He did not hesitate to offer his food and liquor to the villagers. While the villagers offered anything the Shabji whole heartedly accepted those things. Elwin Sahab always wanted to learn their language though they laughed at him due to his different pronunciation.

When the children played in the field which was near to his hut, he used to come from his hut and enjoyed the game. If they stopped their playing due to shyness then he gave them toffee (*peppier goti*) or ball to continue it. Sometimes few children of his father's group observed him what he did in his hut.

When Devnath Usendi was in middle school at that time two foreign people came to their village. They themselves introduced that they were relatives of Sahab ji and took him as their local guide. They gave him *peppier goti* and in the evening played a musical instrument. Due to Sahab Ji so many foreigners came at Binjli which made them proud.

From the description of the above persons it is found that Verrier Elwin had no formal training in anthropological research but the methods he applied during his field work indicate his interest in anthropology which reflected in his famous monograph, books, articles, journals etc.

Rameshwar Prasad Pandey

About 80 years ago my classmate Mustak told me that one Indian lady, wife of an English man was casually giving chocolates and some sweets to him. In those years his father was an officer in Land Settlement department of Bastar state. His contact was with Verrier Elwin and he was known to the family. Verrier Elwin with his wife an Indian lady was residing in the out-house of Circuit House, Jagdalpur.

I with my two friends were going to play hockey in the nearby ground of the swimming pool. We saw the lady in big frock like dress, walking in front of their residence. At that time there was no compound wall or any type of protection of the Circuit House (guest house). We used to see this lady walking daily and decided to meet her in exception of some sweets as my friends had told. As we went near the lady she gestured us to come and to wait for some time. In the mean time she went inside her house and came with some sweets (chocolate-Peppermint) and distributed among we three players. She asked about the class which we attended in the school. We separately replied. She asked us to come again. She asked about our festivals and rituals etc. I came to know that Verrier Elwin also strolling in front of the house in which he lived.

In the year 1947, I graduated in Arts and I was appointed as a teacher in Grigbon High School, Jagdalpur. Two years later when I passed B.T., I was transferred to Kondagaon as Asst. District Inspector of School in the year 1953. I was ordered to go to Binzali village in Narayanpur tahsil to complete 40 days on Social Education, i.e. Adult Education. I went to Binli and resided in Ghotul as it was used a guest house in the village. There was no school in the Binzali village. Here in the Ghotul Shahab Verrier Elwin used to stay for many days as villagers told me. They had constructed a temporary toilet nearby the Ghotul. I learned from the villagers that Elwin was very friendly among the youth and old. He tested the local wine and distributed his foreign wine to the villagers. Sometimes he went for hunting in the forest and when dead animals were brought to eat and he was taking his share. He used to ask about the culture and rituals of the villagers. He collected information of all the then Bastar State though his translator.

I was sent to Ranchi for three months' training meant for, "For working in Tribal Areas". From all India development blocks in the first batch I was sent. Ghuha was the director of the training centre.

During the training one Asst. Professor from Orissa Mahapatra was asked to prepare for tribal of Bastar. He directed me to read the books of Verrier Elwin which were in the library of the training centre. I came to know about Bastar from their books. I was working in the past as Social Education Organizer. The information collected from his book was very valuable in my working. I realised that he was a very famous Anthropologist.

Chapter - 1

Verrier Elwin in Bastar

B.L. Jha

At this distance of time, I have rather a hazy memory of Verrier Elwin. I was a school student when I saw Verrier Elwin for the first time at Jagdalpur, perhaps either in 1941 or 1942. I remember to have seen him near the Gol Bazar of Jagdalpur. I was quite surprised and amused when I saw a white man wearing kurta and pyjama and moving about in chappals, because I had never before seen a Gora Sahib, a white man move about Indian attire. Here I would want to mention that this was not the first time when I had seen a European, because we used to see many English men with their women and children here. It appears that the English people seemed to like the climate of Bastar, and particularly of Jagdalpur, because the summer month here were not very hot, there was ample rainfall in the rainy season which kept the atmosphere cool and the winter months were much colder than they were at many other places of Madhya Pradesh. Therefore almost all the top administrative posts of Bastar which was then a Princely State were manned by Englishmen and I had seen all of them moving about in European dress. Therefore I was vastly amused and surprised when I saw Verrier Elwin moving about in Indian attire. Verrier Elwin, as I remember him, was a man of medium stature, perhaps 5 ft. 8 or 9 inches tall and he always seemed to wear a smile on his face.

I saw him for the second time in our school where he had been invited as chief guest to address us at our annual function by our head master i.e. Principal M. N. Deo who had himself obtained a Teachers' Diploma from Edinburgh University, Scotland. I do not now remember what all Verrier Elwin said on the occasion but he was attired in the same Indian style. Later on, I saw the hut at Chitarkote waterfalls where he had lived for some time when he was in Bastar. This hut which overlooked the waterfalls was built as I remember now, in pure tribal style with stone and mud and was thatched with straw. It had stone benches and stone table and also some other things made of stone. This is all I remember about Verrier Elwin. I had also seen his tribal wife once. She was wearing Sari and probably she had bob-cut hair.

Later on, I came to know more about Verrier Elwin that he was born at Dover, U.K. on 21 August 1902. He was educated at Oxford. He did not possess any degree in Anthropology but he was sincerely interested in the tribal people which made him a self-trained anthropologist, ethnologist and a tribal activist. He came to India, his adopted country for the first time when he was only 25. Although Verrier Elwin came to India as a Christian Missionary for propagating Christianity among the tribals, but he got immensely interested in the tribal people of India. He left the job of a clergy and became deeply involved in studying the lives of the tribal people of India. He wrote many books on the tribal people of India. He is considered a controversial figure who first abandoned the clergy to work with Mahatma Gandhi and the Indian National Congress, then converted to Hinduism in 1935 after staying in a Gandhian Ashram. Elwin is best known for his early work with the Bigas and Gonds of Orissa and Madhya Pradesh. He later also wrote on the tribal of several North-East Indian states, especially North East Frontier Agency (NEFA) and settled in Shillong. Elwin was a close friend and advisor of Pandit Jawahar Lal Nehru and his idea and research had a great influence on Nehru's vision of the tribals and on framing the policy for the tribals.

I have read some of Elwin's books, among them, "The Muria and Their Ghotul", Maria Murder and Suicide Cases". Although I read these books long back yet I remember that, "The Muria and Their Ghotul" has been written in picturesque language and gives an intimate account of the life of the Ghotul Murias. While the other book goes deep into the simple yet volatile psyche and irascible temperament of the Maria tribals of Bastar. I do not know what other writers have written about Verrier Elwin but from the brief glimpses I had of him and from some of his writings and from the description of the kind of life he lived and the work he did, I am led to the conclusion that he was a versatile genius, that he was unassuming yet quite colourful and that he was an unconventional and therefore a controversial personality. He had all the traits of a great man in him. He loved to walk the un-trodden path; rather he loved to make his own path. He had been trained to convert but he got converted himself. He fell briefly under the spell of Mahatma Gandhi and then turned to the tribal. He wrote volumes of literature. He dared to experiment and experience. I am led to believe that in his rather brief sojourn through life he savoured it to the full.

I pay my humble homage to such a great soul who has left a lasting imprint in the field of anthropological and ethnological studies.

The building of a library-cum-museum in Binjali village of Narayanpur where Elwin lived for some time and a two-days seminar based on his life and work by the Jagdalpur Centre of the Anthropological Survey of India and by the Anthropological Survey of India itself is a fitting tribute to such great scholar of Anthropology I thank them all for this very commendable effort.

Chapter - 2

वेरियर ऐलविन

किरणनुरुटी

वेरियर एलविन का जन्म 29 अगस्त 1902 में इग्लैण्ड में हुआ था। उनके पिता अफ्रिका के बीहड़ों के खोजी थे। माता को आदमखोर शेर ने खा लिया था। उनकी शिक्षा दीक्षा आक्सफोर्ट यूनिवर्सिटी में हुई। वे शिक्षा के पश्चात अक्सफोर्ट यूनिवसिर्टी में प्राध्यपक बनना चाहते थे, किन्तु शिक्षा के दौरान भारतीय मित्रों से महात्मागांधी के अहिंसावादी मित्रों से एवं उनके अहिंसावादी आर्दशवाद एवं रविन्द्रवाद के उन्नयाक प्रदीरवाद पर चर्चा ने आपको भारत के प्रति आकर्षित किया।

उनका आगमन मिशनरी के माध्यम से 1927 में भारत में हुआ। उन्होंने सर्वप्रथम पूना में एक आश्रम खोला। वे भारत में इग्लैड के एक पादरी बनकर आये थे। इस समय उनका उद्देश्य ईसाई एवं हिन्दु धर्म के संबंधों का अध्ययन करना था। 1928 में महात्मागांधी के सम्पर्क में आये। भारत के राष्ट्रीय आन्दोलन ने उनके जीवन में क्रांतिकारी परिवर्तन ला दिया अब वे अधिकांश समय साबरमति आश्रम में बिताने लगे। यहीं पर उनकी मित्रता शामराव हिवाले से हुई वे उच्च शिक्षित महाराष्ट्र सम्पन्न परिवार के थे, समाज सेवा को अपनी जीवन शैली में स्वागत करे किन्तु इसे दूसरों पर क्यो लादे। चर्च से झगड़े का मूल कारण यही था कि उन्होंने भारतीयों का धर्म परिवर्तन करने से मना कर दिया और क्राइस्ट सेवा संघ से नाता तोड़ लिया। जब शामराव को इस बात की जानकारी हुई तो उसने भी पादरी बनने की अपनी योजना त्याग दी।

एल्विन ने स्पष्ट लिखा है, कि चर्च ऑफ इग्लैड और ब्रिटिश साम्राज्यवाद में मिली भगत थी। दोनों की नीति भारतीय राष्ट्रीय आन्दोलन के प्रति दमनकारी थी। आज भी साम्राज्यवाद के साथ धर्म को थोपने का सिलसिला जारी है। यही कारण था कि वह मिशनरी कार्य से दूर होने लगे। इसका परिणाम यह हुआ कि उन्होंने 1936 में इग्लैंड जाकर आर्करे लिक्विसमेन्ट पर हस्ताक्षर करके औपचारिक रूप से चर्च ऑफ इग्लैड से संबंध विच्छेद कर दिया।

सन् 1936 में वे करंजिया से दूसरे गांव गये, वहां चर्च नही था। अपनी छोटी सी संस्था का नाम भी बदल दिया। इस क्षेत्र के आदिवासी गौड़, बैगा, अगरिया, लोगों की शिक्षा एवं स्वास्थ्य सेवाओं पर कार्य किया। इसके साथ 1935 से 1942 तकबस्तर के मुरिया क्षेत्र में बराबर जाते रहे। 1940 में उनको जनगणना अधिकारी नियुक्ति किया गया, यहां रहकर उन्होंने घोटुल का अध्ययन किया। उन्होने लगभग 347 घोटुल का अवलोकन किया। दण्डामी माड़िया गोड़ों में किए जाने वाली हत्याओं पर भी गहन शोध कर प्रत्येक कारण को सटीक ढंग से प्रस्तुत किया। उन्होंने छत्तीसगढ़ की अगरिया जन जाति का भी गहन अध्ययन किया तथा उडीसा की रमणीय पहाड़ियों पर भी उन्होने काफी समय व्यतीत किया।

मुरिया एण्ड देयर घोटुल में मुरियाओं की सामाजिक आर्थिक एवं सांस्कृतिक पहलुओं पर प्रकाश डाला। उन्होंने जन्म से लेकर मृत्यु तक के संस्कार, धर्म, गोड़ो के देवी देवता को बखूबी बताया है। अपने अध्ययन में बताया कि घोटुल उनका सांस्कृतिक आधार भी होता है।

एल्विन का पूरा जीवन आदिवासियों की सेवा एवं उनकी जीवन शैली पर अध्ययन में बीता। चूकि वे उनके बीच ही रहते थे एवं उन्हें निकट से जानने एवं उनकी भावनाओं को समझने का मौका मिला जो हमें अमूल्य पुस्तकों के रूप में प्राप्त हुए।

1953 में उन्हें ट्राइबल अफेयर्स टू द नार्थ ईस्ट फ्रंटीयर एजेन्सी के सलाहकार के रूप मे उनको रूचिकर कार्य मिला और तभी वे कानूनी रूप से भारतीय नागरिक बन गयें वे जो आत्मा से पहले से जुड़े थे। 22 फरवरी 1964 को भारत की धरती पर ही उन्होंने अंतिम सांस ली। ऐसे महान व्यक्ति जिन्होंने मानवविज्ञान के अध्ययन को नई दिशा दी, यहां के आदिवासियों के अध्ययन की कल्पना ही नहीं की जा सकती। आज हम उनके द्वारा किए गए शोध का एकांश भी कर पायें तो उन्हें सच्ची श्रद्धान्जली होगी।

Chapter - 3

On Verrier Elwin

Ashok Elwin

At the onset I must admit that I am neither a scholar nor academic but the only surviving son of Verrier Elwin, and it is an honour for me, to be given a chance, to speak a little about my father and also to recollect some of my faint memories of him. What I am going to speak a little about are taken from his books and writings by other great scholars, to whom will refer.

Verrier Elwin (1902-1964) was unquestionably the pioneering scholar and friend of India's tribal people. An Anglican priest and Oxford Don, he came to India as a missionary. He became an active supporter to the National movement and then lived an intense three decades amidst the wilds of India's tribal world. His anthropological studies and popular books on tribal customs, myths and folklore were path-breaking, both for anthropology and the awareness of the rich cultural diversity in our nation. Most importantly, his book's brought about a keener awareness of the need to do justice to the poor and deprived tribal people living in the remoteness of India's hills and forests.

Friends and associates of such luminaries of his age from Mahatma Gandhi, Sardar Vallabhai Patel and Pandit Jawaharlal Nehru to Romain Rolland and Arthur Koestler, J.R.D TATA, he was once described as a "freakish Englishman whose eccentricities even Oxford could not dim but who had been able to discover poetry and art in strange places".

For Elwin, anthropology did not mean field-work but "it meant his whole life". His method was to settle down among the people, live with them, share their life as far as an outsider could and generally do several books on them.

According to him "there is nothing whatever hostile to scientific inquiry in having an intense and affectionate interest in the people one studies, in desiring their progress and welfare and in regarding them as human beings rather than as laboratory specimens".

Initially as a missionary with the Christian Seva Sangh, he was deeply moved by Mahatma Gandhi's philosophy of Ahimsa and supported the national movement whole-heartedly. This of course did not go down well with the power of that time and when my father went back to England, he was refused a visa to come back to India and finally had to sign an undertaking that he would not get involved with the freedom struggle. A gentle suggestion by Sardar Vallabhai Patel and Seth Jamnalal Bajaj to work among the Gonds of central Provinces set him to "plunge into the dark. We had no idea what our new country would be like. We knew nothing about the tribes". The austerity which he observed as a monk of the Christian Seva Sangh and also at the Sabarmati Ashram probably prepared him for the years ahead.

Along with his missionary colleague and friend Shamrao Hivale, Elwin started his life's work at Karanjia, a Gond village in Mandla district of the Central Province. Having apprehensions of his first day of arrival in the tribal village he writes "Oh why did I leave the lovely books and libraries of Oxford and London". He continues, "As I lay down to sleep on that mud floor, the doubts and fears of the previous day vanished, never to return. In that little goat shed, I realized that I was caught, that never would I be able to escape the call of the primitive world; for better or worse I was committed".

From 1931 to 1953 he continued to spend most of his time in houses of mud and thatch all over the tribal villages of central India, Bastar, Orrisa and Bihar, living and working amongst them and above all, writing a series of fascinating ethnographies of tribes on the margin of survival. He also compiled authoritative collection of tribal myths and art and even wrote two novels with aboriginal theme.

From his shift as an active supporter of the national movement to working among the tribals, he writes "my belief in India's right to independence never changed". However, he adds, "in the long run, I am sure that I have been able to serve India better as a "tribal man" than I could have done as an amateur politician".

His ethnographies were enthusiastically received both in India and abroad, and his notes indicated that he planned at least another half a dozen studies of individual tribes. In the event however, these were never written, for in 1953, he was invited by Prime Minister Pandit Jawaharlal Nehru as advisor to the government on administrative policy towards the tribals of the North East Frontier Agency (now called the state of Arunachal Pradesh) to be based at Shillong, the then capital of Assam. This ended a phase when he wrote such acknowledged anthropological masterpieces as 'The Muria and their Ghotul' and 'The Religion of an Indian Tribe'. An American Anthropologist described his 'Myths of Middle India' as a 'Landmark in the exploration of the intellectual history of mankind'.

In the concluding phase of his work, he restless as ever, travelled widely in the frontier tracts of North-East India, continuing his collection of tribal art and folklore. He wrote in his autobiography "I covered about two thousand miles, of which two hundred and fifty were on elephant and pony and the rest on foot". The steep mountainous region of NEFA did not deter him "the difficulties were great but the splendor of the countryside and the charm of the people were altogether exhilarating". Comparing the North Eastern frontiers and Central India, he reminiscences "I sometimes thought it might have been better if I had come to NEFA when I was thirty and spent the later years among the indulgent hills of Orissa or Baster. And yet had I done that, I should not have been able to write the books I did about Central Indian tribes, for soon afterwards they changed".

Elwin became an Indian citizen in the middle of June 1954. In 1961 he was awarded the Padma Bhushan for his lifelong work and contribution to the welfare of the tribals of India.

Nari Rustomji, a former adviser to the governor of Assam in his foreword to a collection of Elwin's work published by the North Eastern Hill University, entitled very aptly "Philanthropologist", speaks of his friend and colleague's last phase of work "from 1955 until his death in 1964, Elwin was mainly pre-occupied in helping to implement the policy of promoting deeper and wider respect for the culture and way of life of the tribes of India in general and of the North Eastern frontier in particular. Although he enjoyed no statutory powers, his influence and inspiration permeated the entire administrative fabric".

Elwin emphasized attitudes that should be taken towards the tribal and the psychological and social adjustments that had to be made. He cautioned on the danger of overwhelming the people and also sensitized the administration of the anxieties and fear inherent among the tribes about their land and culture. He writes "it is more a problem of introducing changes without being destructive of the best values of the old life". Elwin's writings also largely influenced the then Prime Minister Jawaharlal Nehru, who admitted in the Foreword to 'A Philosophy for NEFA' – "I have learnt much from him". On the other-hand Elwin in all his humbleness called himself a missionary of Nehru's principles and formula of developing the tribal people along the lines of their own tradition and genius".

Pandit Nehru also laid down his famous Panch Shila (five principals) for the tribal people of India in the said Foreword, convinced that a national tribal policy should be on the general lines indicated by Elwin and that avenues of development for the tribes be pursued within the framework of these fundamental principles.

The extent of Verrier Elwin's many sided contribution to the tribal cause through his writings "soaked with love and imagination" (Hindustan Times) and his "burning enthusiasm and unflagging efforts" (Nari Rustomji), is still felt today and his philosophy's relevance is timeless.

Yet another aspect of Elwin's multi-faceted personality was his keen interest in photography which he used extensively, so as to present lavishly, a fresh and exciting concept of the remote tribes with which he came in contact in the pre and post-independence era. He had built an excellent collection of thousands of rare photographs.

In an article published in the Sunday Statesman dated the 1st of March 1942, titled 'WITH A CAMERA IN THE INDIAN JUNGLE' Elwin wrote:

"Not even the hunter with his gun can get such thrills or endure such arduous and exhausting days as the anthropologist with his camera in the jungle. The difficulties and dangers of shooting big game with a camera are well known. My own experience is that of a hunter of men. When the men pursued are wild and timid, there may be quite as much excitement from the chase as from going after animals. The camera to many aboriginal people is an object of not only of embarrassment but of fear. The mysterious aperture which points in their direction in so sinister a manner, the almost inevitable fuss and preparation that precedes the taking of even the simplest photographs, cannot fail to alarm them".

I was born in Shillong on the 31 October 1954, ten months after my father assumed office at Shillong. In fact a birthday party for my father's friend, Victor Sassoon, a photographer from Calcutta, was being celebrated in our house, when my mother was rushed to the Welsh Mission Hospital where I was born.

My father had rented a large house called "Sridham" situated in the then outskirts of Shillong. A portion of this house was used as his office.

His personal staff consisted of a stenographer, Someswar Lahiri, two Khasi Typists, Higher Land Syiemlieh and Lockhart Jyrwa, his field-assistant, Sundarlal Narmada, who was with him for over thirty years and his two chaprasis – Haricharan and Bhajan, members of the Pradhan tribe from Patangarh, for over twenty-five years. The major portion of the house consisted of his large library and museum, a portion of which was also used as a living room. His study room where he spent most of his time was adorned with statues of Lord Buddha, Tribal Masks and artifacts, which he had collected during his stay in Central India and on his tours in the North East and during his visits to Ceylone (Sri Lanka), Africa and Thailand. The rest of the house was used as our residential quarters.

I recollect there used to be a stream of visitors to the house, politicians, government servants, officials from the armed forces and Indian Frontier Administration Services, delegations of tribal people and many interesting people, one of the earliest and most important being, Pandit Jawaharlal Nehru on the 28 August 1955. Of course I don't remember this visit as I was still a baby, but came to know of it later on. There were others like Shri G.D. Pant, the then Union Home Minister, Shri Jayaprakash Naryan, C. v on Fürer Haimendorf, the Austrian expert on Indian tribes, Arthur Koestler, the Hungarian born Englishman and writer and many more. My mother, Lila, who came to Shillong almost direct from a remote tribal village, had adapted herself well to being an admirable hostess to those who visited our house.

My father used to be on tour for weeks together and when he was in Shillong he would be busy either in the NEFA Secretariat or in his office at home, with official work, or writing his books and articles for newspapers and magazines or cataloguing his enormous collecting of rare photographs of tribes of Central India and the North East Frontier track.

He was also a stamp collector and one of his stamp albums was titled "POSTAGE STAMS AND THE TRIBAL PEOPLE OF THE WORLD". It is worthy to mention that the 'first tribal' stamp ever to be issued in India shows a woman of NEFA at her loom. This stamp was designed from a photograph taken in 1947 by my father of a Konyak woman in Totok village. Unfortunately this stamp is missing from the album.

Because of his busy schedule he was not able to spend much of his time with us. However he would take us out whenever he could, to the movies, which would be the late night show, carrying flasks filled with tea or coffee and blankets to keep warm during the winter months. He would also take us out for a Chinese meal quite regularly and the occasional picnics which we always looked forward to.

My eldest brother Kumar from his previous marriage had accompanied my father on two long tours on foot, in northern Siang and Tirap, covering a couple of hundred miles each time. Wasant, my elder brother, also went on two tours with him and once he took all of us to Lungleh, in the then Lushai Hills, now the State of Mizoram. I remember this trip very vividly as I was bitten by a monkey and had to take anti-rabies injection in my stomach for fourteen days.

I fondly recollect my father's friends who would visit the house quite frequently, alone or with their families such as Nari Rustomji, the Advisor for Tribal Areas, including the North East Frontier Agency, Brig. D.M. Sen, Formerly Judge-Advocate in the army, Major-General Ajit Guraya, of the Assam Rifles, Diying Ering, Member of Parliament of NEFA, Pran Luthra, who succeeded Nari Rustomji as advisor and officers of the Indian Frontier Administration (IFAS) who all stood with our family long after my father passed away. Today most of them are no more but I am in touch with some of their children.

I was just over nine years old when my father passed away, while on an official trip to Delhi. It was a stormy night, with thunder and lightning, when at around two or three in the night, there was frantic knocking on our bedroom window where my mother and I were sleeping. We both got up and my mother went to open the front door while I stayed on in the bedroom, peeping from the door. I saw my father's friends Maj. Gen. Guraya and Col. Sharma along with their wives enter the house and then speak to my mother after which she swooned and collapsed on the floor. I realized that something was wrong and it was only the next day that I was informed that father was no more and just before his body was brought home from Delhi. The next day, as was his wish, he was cremated amidst the chanting of Buddhist hymns, and I preformed the last rites. Parts of the ashes were taken to Tuting by Kumar where they were immersed by him in the Siang river, and the rest in the Bhramaputra river.

It was a difficult period for my mother especially to bring us up and also to look after the legacy left behind by my father. Nari Rustomji and B. Das Shastri who worked as Philologist in the NEFA administration arranged for the sale of the museum and library to the National Museum in Delhi and the National Library, Calcutta. The proceeds from this sale enabled my mother to purchase a house in Shillong. In 1952 my father had made a will bequeathing most of his assets to Shamrao and then in 1959 had made another will cancelling the previous will and bequeathing ninety percent of his assets to my mother and ten percent to Kumar which was given to him around 1966.

In 1968 a case was filed in the Madhya Pradesh High Court by Shamrao Hivale against my mother who being the legal heir had inherited what my father had left and this case carried on till 1970 when the judge disposed of the case in favour of my mother. Then in 1971, Kosi, my father's first wife, filed a fresh suit in the M.P. High Court naming as respondents my mother, myself, Shamrao Hivalae and others, claiming that my father had never divorced her and that she and her children had claim over all my father's proprieties. This case carried on for years the only people to benefit, being the lawyers, until in April 1980, Justice B.C. Varma of the M.P. High Court, in his order found that my father and mother were legally married, that my father and Kosi, had been legally divorced and that the will of 1959 was legitimate. Kosi then filed a special leave petition in the Supreme Court of India, but was also unsuccessful. These cases, resulted, in that, none, of my father's books could be reprinted and published and over the years his name was also almost forgotten. It was only in 1991 that a few books, namely *The Muria and their Ghotul, Maria Murder and Suicide, Leaves from the Junbgle, The Agaria and Myths of Middle India*, were especially reprinted for Vanya Prakashan, a publication enterprise of Madhya Pradesh Government, and published by The Oxford University Press.

Shortly after the North East Hill University was created, my mother had made a contribution to the university, for holding the Verrier Elwin Endowment Lectures, to which eminent persons were invited to deliver these lectures, such as Nari Rustomji, Professor Christopher von Furer-Hainendorf, Professor Binod C. Agarwal, Dr. Daniel O'Conner, Dr. Ramachandra Guha, Dr. Gautam Kumar Bera, Professor A.C. Bhagabati, etc., to name a few. Unfortunately these lectures have not taken place for the last several years for reasons best known to the university.

A small book entitled "28 Poems" by my father was released in Shillong on the 22 February 2012 by my mother and me, although my father had first printed this booklet for private circulation in 1956. The publication of this book was facilitated by the North East Zone Cultural Centre Dimapur. In the last three years I have been able to organize several exhibitions of some rare photographs from his collection of the tribes of the North East Frontier Agency in collaboration with the Adivasi Arts Trust, London, the Indian National Trust for Art and Cultural Heritage, Delhi, and the Indira Gandhi Rastriya Manav Sangralaya, Bhopal. More recently an exhibition of his photographs of tribes of Central India, again, in collaboration with the Adivasi Arts Trust and the Indira Gandhi Rastriya Manav Sangrahalaya, (IGRMS) Bhopal, was held at my mother's village, Patangarh. These rare collections of photographs and documentaries now need to be digitized and preserved and I have done this to the best of my ability. This is extremely important as the negatives and films, although still in good condition, will definitely get spoiled due to weather conditions and fungal attacks.

My eldest brother Wasant passed away in 2013, followed by the death of my mother three months later. My youngest son Larry also passed away a year and a half later, followed again by the death of my elder brother, Nakul, after three and a half months. I am married to a tribal lady from the Garo tribe of Meghalaya and have three surviving children, two daughters and a son, who stay with me and are employed in Shillong.

To conclude, I refer to Ramachandra Guha's biography of Verrier Elwin, titled "Savaging the Civilized" where in the concluding paragraph in his introduction to the second edition he writes: "Finally there is the charm of Elwin's life itself, the thematic and geographical range he travelled, and the grand themes he touched and illuminated. He was a serial bridge-builder between Christianity and Hinduism, the forest and the city, India and England, elite and subaltern, the locality and the globe. His remarkable, incident-filled life is a window into the history of modern India and perhaps the history of the modern world itself".

Chapter - 4

Anthropology of Verrier Elwin: Stray Observations

R K Bhattacharya,

It gives me immense pleasure to be a part of this seminar on the Tribal World of Verrier Elwin organized by the Sub-Regional Centre of the Anthropological Survey of India, situated in Jagdalpur, Chattisgarh. It is a fitting tribute to a man who made Chattisgarh and the surrounding areas his home for over decades and from where he found his two brides.

I

There are many extraordinary people in the world and surely Verrier Elwin, baptized as Harry Verrier Holman Elwin (Elwin 1998: 1; Guha 1999: 1) was one of them. The volume and nature of Elwin's works, the depth of his understanding and the immense range of tribes that he interacted with over prolonged periods of time firmly established him among the important anthropologists of India that also brought him world-wide fame. Elwin stayed among a number of tribes of India for different periods of time and his writings on them were based on his direct observations and interactions. His felicitous work on the tribes is filled with affection and sympathy.

Elwin's formal academic career can be summed up very briefly – he shone as a brilliant graduate student of English literature and Theology in the prestigious Merton College of Oxford University securing first class in both these subjects. His profound appreciation and knowledge of English literature reflected strongly in his writings while he seemed to have abandoned Theology altogether as he also refused to accept the robe. I am tempted to quote some lines from his autobiography testifying to his abiding love for poetry when he expresses the inner turmoil between his work among the tribes and his 'mission' as a missionary:

But through the water pale and thin
Still shine the unoffending feet (Elwin 1988: 339).

I may mention here how D.K. Bhattacharya quoted a poem by Elwin on our past preceptors of anthropology in his key-note address on the occasion of the foundation day of AnSI in December this year (for reference to the poem, see Guha 1999: 210-211).

Obviously, Elwin's writings do not allow any drab mediocrity; rather his writings have a strong sense of wit and satire filled with tongue-in-cheek humour. The other quality that abounds vividly in his writings is the depth of poetry, use of allusions and a soul-touching humility. Sir Francis Young husband considered Elwin as 'a man of extreme sensitivity' (Hivale 1935:7) and on reading Elwin's work on tribes, one would fully agree with the above. We may remark on the range of his reading – we find references to the ancient tribes and their traditions as described in the *Ramayana*, *Mahabharata*, *Vishnu Purana* and *the Katha Sarit Sagara* in *A Philosophy for NEFA* (1960: 29-31). All these qualities make his writings readable and enjoyable; reading his works carefully richly stimulates academic interest and insight. Elwin's personal emerges through his writings, giving us a two-way reading experience - one Elwin's detailed account of the tribes and two, the perception of the tribes about Elwin especially his endearing aspects that brought him close to those whom he interacted with. I cite the paper of Vinay Srivastava (1991) that further elucidates the nature of Verrier Elwin's fieldwork on the Baigas. Elwin's qualities appeared to have impressed a great number of luminaries of his time including Gandhi and the other leaders of this country. Elwin steeped in classical music, poetry, literature and art (Elwin 1998:339) and could readily express his admiration and respect for the lives of the tribes; their strengths and capacities – a view that is a diametric departure from what many of us (I refer to my 'tribe' of anthropologists) have with respect to the tribes or those considered the 'others'. There may be a lesson for us here to learn to value and cultivate the experience of being intensely embedded in the appreciation of culture, even if it is different from ours.

Elwin's introduction to the *Songs of the Forest* (1935: 13-47) jointly written with Shamrao Hivale, Elwin's lifelong friend and researcher living and sharing life together among the Gonds and a few other tribes of central India provides the geographic spread of these tribes as well as their history in a nutshell, especially of the Gonds. Elwin gives us an emic view of life and culture of the Gonds and Baigas. He recorded the narration of his informant, Panda Baba, of the creation myth and about the gods and spirits of these tribes; such as Thakur Deo, husband of Mother Earth; Annadeo, the God of Food; Cow-mother; Pawan Dassorie, Spirit of the Wind and description of epic characters – Rama, Sita and Lakshman including his *nimmat-kingri,* a stringed musical instrument. The tribes consider Lakshmanjati as the most revered character whose 'body is purity itself' and he is a 'true celebrate'.

Most anthropologists and ethnographers talk volumes about the importance of insider's views but seldom are able to shun their own rationale and outlook that somehow permeates in their reportage; culture-specific reasoning is often bypassed or not heeded to. Elwin, I find is a departure from the general kind of anthropologists and ethnographers. I appreciate and recommend to the anthropologists and ethnographers to try and emulate the example of Elwin.

Reading quite a few of Elwin's books one feels that one has entered the kind of a world created in the literary style of magic-realism rather like that of Garcia's *One Hundred Years of Solitude* (1972). He is convinced that to completely understand lives, one has to take into account the perceptions of the informants, however subjective and inexplicable they may be.

Elwin wrote, 'the real culture of the Gonds and the Baigas is to be found in their songs and dances'. I would say that this is true for many other tribes living in the plains of India. In all these tribes songs are usually composed by women and the women are the reservoir of tunes and songs. One more common aspect that I have noted is that these tribes are witty, patient and have quite a *joie de vivre* (Elwin describes this as 'merriness of spirit'). According to Elwin, all these characteristics help the tribes to triumph over their poverty. I take liberty to cite a few of Elwin's lines in his inimitable style of translation of a Gond song describing the Gond's outlook on nature's 'disquieting and stimulating inhumanity', where she is ferocious,

Huge and mighty forms that do not live
Like living men, moved slowly through the mind
By day, and were a trouble to my dreams.

II

Elwin's writing on Gond children from their birth to growing up is remarkably evocative. This I take from Elwin's first monograph on 'Life in a Gond Village' written in the form of a diary in which Elwin very neatly presented the mythology and folklore, almost an oral history without any formal training in the discipline of anthropology (Elwin, 1936: 11-53).

Besides, the book portrays characters such as Panda Baba, or themes that pre-date the subaltern studies of contemporary times. The 'Introduction' of the diary contains the Gonds' version of Hindu epics. The book was published by John Murray, a well-known publishing house of London, which also published quite a few of his other monographs successively.

Children are named with awkward names so as to ward off evil eye including any threat of premature death. Mothers during their day-to-day visits to the nearby forests for fuel strap their children on their backs and this is the first initiation of the children to their natural environment. As the children become a little self-assured they in a small group are sent for herding cattle and they explore nature walking around jungles, mountains and streams collecting berries, digging up edible roots and whatever other available food items they can find. They also learn to be careful about snakes, tigers and such other predatory animals. Elwin broke the monotony of his description by taking refuge in small beautiful poems appropriately portraying the scenes. I get tempted to quote two lines:

Where little footpaths sweet to see
Go seeking sweeter footpaths still (Elwin ibid: 29).

Children play all sorts of games imitating old people, their fathers, grandmothers and others; they are extraordinarily fond of repeating riddles. Along with all this, the children learn to take responsibility, like sleeping alone all night in the wheat-fields to drive away wild pigs, etc.; working the bellows in smithys; plastering the floors and walls of their huts with cow-dung; and minding their younger siblings. I may mention here of a recent publication on Tribal Children and their Childhood (Behera 2015;) that is devoted to the understanding of children. It is indeed remarkable that Elwin realized the value of children as a source of significant anthropological research so many years ago. From personal experience I may add that the childhood of Santal children in the villages I have studied or visited, is in many ways, a mirror-image of the Gond children (Bhattacharya, K and R.K. Bhattacharya 1999: 303-304).

III

'There are many elements in the Gond ethos which should be conserved – their simplicity and freedom, their love of children, the position of their women, their independence of spirit…, their freedom from many of the oriental inhibitions. I think the primitive has a real message for our sophisticated modern world which is…threatened with disintegration, as a result of its passion for possession' (Elwin 1936: 37-38).

Elwin noted the shortcomings too – disease, scarcity of potable water, provision of enough food and illiteracy (Ibid: 42-43), and accordingly suggested measures for overcoming these. The measures are prevention of disease with timely inoculation, proper sanitation, cleaning of villages and supplying drinkable water, providing education to both girls and boys, improvement of agriculture by demonstration and supplying good, healthy seeds to be sown, proper cooking of food, banishing the dull conservatism and the attitudes of abject humility of the poor and frustrated by creating a new spirit with a desire for the fullness of life. These were not his empty words (or Father Elwin's mere sermons) but were executed by setting up the Gond Seva Mandal at Karanjia; and later on a few more branches of the Mandal in other villages.

I feel an inner urge to refer to you that all of the above seems to echo Rabindranath Tagore's concept of Rural Reconstruction out of which grew Sriniketan (1922), the other significant extension of the idea of Visva-Bharati. I wish particularly to draw your attention to the use of the word Reconstruction rather than the word that has greater coinage today, Development. I feel an obligation to mention the name of Leonard Knight Elmhirst, the English agriculture scientist, who came to help Tagore in fulfilling his vision of rural reconstruction among the neighbouring villages of Visva-Bharati in rural Birbhum.

I conclude offering my deep tribute to Verrier Elwin. He may have been untrained but he naturally picked up the tools of the trade of anthropological reportage and recording – the meticulous sketches abounding in his books (Elwin 1950, 1960) bear testimony to almost a lost art from the teaching of anthropology today.

References

Behera, Deepak Kumar and Georg Pfeffer (eds.) 2015, *Contemporary Society: Tribal Studies: Tribal Children and their Childhood*, Vol. 10, New Delhi, Concept Publishing Co. Pvt. Ltd.

Bhattacharya, Kumkum and R.K. Bhattacharya 1997, 'Growing up in a Santal Village', Pfeffer Georg and Deepak Kumar Behera (eds.) *Contemporary Society: Tribal Studies, Structure and Process*, Vol. 1 pp 299-305, New Delhi, Concept Publishing Company.

Elmhirst, Leonard K. 2008 (1975), *The Poet and Plowman*, Kolkata, Visva-Bharati.

Elwin, Verrier, 1936, *Leaves from the Jungle: Life in a Gond Village*, London, John Murray.

- 1950, *Bondo Highlander*, London, Oxford University Press.
- 1960, *Philosophy for NEFA*, Shillong, Government of Assam.
- 1998, *The Tribal World of Verrier Elwin*, Delhi, Oxford University Press.

Guha, Ramachandra 1999, *Savaging the Civilized: Verrier Elwin, his Tribals and India*, New Delhi, Oxford University Press.

Hivale, Shamrao and Verrier Elwin 1935, *Songs of the Forest*, London, George Allen and Unwin Limited.

Marquez, Gabriel Garcia 1972, *One Hundred Years of Solitude*, Penguin.

Srivastava, Vinay June 1991, 'The Ethnographer and the People: Reflections on Field Work', *Economic and Political Weekly*.

Chapter - 5

Envisioning Elwin Through His Central Indian Experiences

Gautam Kumar Bera

More than four decades ago late Professor Surajit Chandra Sinha searched for the retrospect and prospect of an Indian tradition in the social/cultural anthropology of India through a serious question 'Is there an Indian tradition in the social/cultural anthropology in India' as reflected through a publication in the *Journal of the Indian Anthropological Society*. It was a methodological issue *par excellence*. His search centered on general reluctance among Indian scholars to seriously take note of the research publications of the pioneers of Indian anthropology, which ultimately laid a ground for the western scholars to continue it. Of late, there has been a tendency to get out of this academic exportation for the critical and constructive re-examination of the achievements of the founding fathers of anthropology taking cognizance of the development of anthropology in India beyond the frontiers of the nation. I have developed a serious concern for this endeavour and look forward for the development of this cause (Bera, 2008: 8-9; 2016: 37-38). It is expected that through such endeavours debates can be generated and minds can be churned in anticipation of a fruitful result of learning the historical development of the discipline of anthropology in this country.

Exactly fifty-three years ago, Verrier Elwin left for heavenly abode on February 22, 1964 in India, the land which he embraced as his home for lifetime. During his lifespan of sixty two years (1902 – 1964), he has left behind a huge corpus of anthropological data on Indian tribes for the posterity. At the same time these fifty plus years have evoked a question in anthropological minds that to what extent Elwin's anthropology is relevant in today's fast changing world of anthropology along with another question that is to what extent his data have been utilized for understanding the tribal question in the post-Elwinian era (Bera, 2013a; 2013b; 2014; 2016). However, I have a strong feeling that, of late, Elwin has been a victim of academic amnesia, at least among younger generations[1].

Conventionally within the fold of standard academic tradition, lectures are delivered to honour the personalities for whom the gathering is meant for and whose contributions are well known to the audience. All the speakers develop specific themes having some relation to the works of the personality in whose honour or memory the lectures are being delivered. Though Elwin does not need any introduction, yet I feel today that he may be reviewed in this forum by all the speakers in light of his anthropological journey in two geo-political entities, namely central India and north-east India, and bring out the contemporary relevance to relate them to the anthropology of contemporary India.

As great men all over the world are the stuff of legends, it is not surprising that so many legends continue to cling to the life and career of Verrier Elwin. His life was indeed cut to heroic proportions: the rejection for welfare reasons of a potentially successful and lucrative career in spiritualism – mystical rather than missionary – after securing first class degree in theology; his courage to confront English government officials despite being an English citizen; and many more including the mystery of working hard, living in an alien world till the end of his life. All these make him a heroic and legendary figure.

Most of his admirers – and their numbers are legion in India – are awed by the image of Elwin talking to political and administrative authorities in India or of Elwin on a government chair, leading his fellow colleagues against unbelievable odds. In a country marked by compromises, machinations and untimely withdrawals, Elwin's moment in anthropological history seems to mark a time of which Indian anthropologists can still be proud of.

The touchiness about Elwin can often go to ridiculous extremes. There is enough evidence to suggest that despite his heroism, romanticism and greatness, Elwin, as an anthropologist, was not very unlike other anthropologists of his time. Elwin was, probably, not very successful in government chair, as he (possibly) found himself completely out-maneuvered by government rules dictated by bureaucracy. Probably there were many occasions in his life when he was saddled with government resolutions and had the choice of acquiescing to government job or to resign. He chose the latter to return to active fieldwork.

There appears to be a contradiction between Elwin's achievements and the interpretations he evoked. Elwin, better known as anthropologist with romanticism, stirs people more than Elwin, the missionary with an anthropological mission. It is, therefore, necessary to consider the relevance of that anthropological acumen in an India looking ahead at the new millennium. However, there is no doubt about one thing: the hero worship of Elwin serves a social function.

Born on 29th August, 1902 in Dover, Kent (England) as the eldest son of Edmund Harry Elwin, an Anglican Bishop who died young of yellow fever, Harry Verrier Holman Elwin was educated at Merton College, Oxford, where he was Charles Oldham University Scholar and Matthew Arnold Prizeman. Securing first class degree in both English Literature and Theology, Harry became Vice-Principal of Wycliffe Hall, Oxford at the age of 24 only. In 1927, at the age of 25, he became the Chaplain at Merton College.

At Merton, he was doing well as a don with a promising career ahead when his spiritual search – mystical rather that missionary – led him to come to India to join the newly formed *Christa Seva Sangha*, an Anglican Order, in Poona (Maharashtra) with a serious possibility of becoming a monk. It was a small brotherhood of Christian intellectuals, both Englishmen and Indians, living together according to Indian customs. While living in India, he could hear the echoes of India's struggle for freedom and was attracted by the philosophy of the Father of the Nation, Mahatma Gandhi. Eventually he was not only attracted towards this great leader, but also he could develop a strong emotional feeling in Gandhi's mind that sometime in 1930 Gandhi proposed to him that he was taking him as his son. During a brief spell from 1928 to 1932 he was involved with the national movement as an associate of Gandhiji who wrote to him 'Son you have become of your own choice. I have accepted the responsible position. And son you shall remain to the end of time' (Elwin, 1964:56). His involvement with the national movement developed conflict between him and his church superiors or to the temporal authorities. During his immediate visit to England the Government officials refused to permit him to return to India. He was, however, allowed to visit India again after he signed an undertaking that he will abstain from any political activities in this country. His involvement with the national movement ended in 1932 and he confined himself to work among the Gond and not to take part in the civil disobedience and any other political movement (*ibid.*).

Returning to India was not so pleasant for young Verrier when he had least acquaintances in this country. Preferring to settle in a remote tribal village, he along with his Indian friend Shamrao Hivale opened a small school and equally small dispensary in Mandla district of Central Provinces. An Anglican Bishop of this region recommended him the place with additional information that of the last five Europeans to stay in this part of the country, four had died within a year. Though he wanted to live with the people at the grass root level, yet working among the tribal people was not his initial choice. While he was making up his mind to work among untouchables, Sardar Vallabhbhai Patel, a freedom fighter, dissuaded him on the plea that it was for Hindus to make reparation to the untouchables and there were many social workers and missionaries doing so. On the contrary, he was, however, advised by Patel to work among tribal people. Patel said, 'the untouchables are not your problem. They are the sin of the Hindus, and it is the Hindus who must make reparation to them' (Elwin, 1964: 58). This was, probably, a turning point in the life and career of young Elwin as is now felt while reviewing his works to pay him a tribute on his centenary, and also afterwards.

If one looks into the events pertaining to anthropological interest in the life of Verrier Elwin, he may confront, in some way or the other, his position in the world of anthropology and anthropologists in India. After working as a Research Associate in the Sir D. Tata School of Social Studies, Bombay in the late thirties (during his research days among the Baiga) his professional career in anthropology began in 1940 with the honorary appointment as Census Officer and Ethnographer in Bastar State. In 1942 he was awarded the Welcome Medal and he was credited with the honour that for the first time this medal was awarded to any person in India. He remained as one of the editors of *Man in India*, the first anthropological journal of the country, along with W. G. Archer and Ramesh Chandra Roy, the second son of Rai Bahadur Sarat Chandra Roy. In 1944 he was appointed the Sectional President for Anthropology and Archaeology of the Indian National Science Congress Association. He was appointed as the Anthropologist to the Government of India in 1945. In the successive year, i.e., in 1946, he was appointed as the Deputy Director of the Anthropological Survey of India, called Department of Anthropology, Government of India then, which he continued till 1949. This was, eventually, the first ever appointment of a Deputy Director made in the Anthropological Survey of India. In fact, in 1945, Elwin suggested the British Government to appoint an Anthropological Advisor in India to advise on tribal affairs. But the British officials who were suspicious of Elwin's views on tribes and his politics dismissed the idea of having an 'Anthropological Dictator' and thought that Biraja Sankar Guha was too good a Hindu to be made the

Director. The Royal Anthropological Institute of London awarded him the Rivers Medal in 1948. In 1951 he was awarded the Annandale Medal by the Asiatic Society of Bengal and was also elected a Fellow there. The Government of India appointed him as the Advisor for Tribal Affairs to North East Frontier Agency (NEFA) in 1953. A turning point was marked in his life in 1954 when he became an Indian citizen. For his outstanding contribution towards tribal studies in India he was conferred upon the Degree of the Doctor of Science (D. Sc.) by the Oxford University. In 1960 he was awarded the Campbell Gold Medal by the Asiatic Society of Bombay. In the same year he was appointed as the Member of the Scheduled Castes and Scheduled Tribes Commission to look after the welfare of these people. The Government of India, in 1961, honoured him with *Padma Bhushan*, one of the highest civilian awards conferred upon to any person by the Government of India. In the early sixties he was appointed the Regional Editor of the journal *Folklore*, which he continued for some time, probably till his death. On the 22nd of February 1964, he died in a Nursing Home in New Delhi, two hours after he was hospitalized. On the following day, i.e., on 23rd February 1964, he was cremated in Shillong (Meghalaya, India) following Buddhist traditions along with a little statue of Gautam Buddha, which he always carried in his pocket.

The chronology of events suggest that after devoting almost all his time to the study and service to the tribals, Elwin received the formal appointment as Honorary Ethnographer, Bastar State in Central India in 1940. During this time he was closely associated with Rai Bahadur Sarat Chandra Roy, the Father of Indian Ethnology, and rendered editorial assistance to his journal *Man in India* (first anthropological journal of the country founded in 1921 by Sarat Chandra Roy). It was the time when he developed acquaintances with Roy's family and W. G. Archer, an eminent British anthropologist. The ailing Roy was much benefitted by Elwin's assistance in editorial work, which could virtually help him to publish the same easily. After Roy's death in April 1942, Elwin was appointed one of the editors of *Man in India*, in May 1942, along with W. G. Archer and Ramesh Chandra Roy, which he continued till 1949. He had a brief stay in the Anthropological Survey of India for about four years, which he relinquished in 1949 to return to active fieldwork. In 1953, at the behest of Pandit Jawaharlal Nehru, the then Prime Minister of India, he accepted the appointment as Advisor for Tribal Affairs in NEFA, where he could find the practicability of the method of application of tribal development administration. Perhaps this was the most satisfying period of his work with the tribal people. While heading a committee, as its Chairman, to evaluate the working of the Multipurpose Tribal Blocks, he submitted a valuable report, which had wide influence. His book *A Philosophy for NEFA* (1957) opened up new vistas in the tribal policy and the tribal development administration of the government of the Union of India. His appointment as a Member of the Scheduled Castes and Scheduled Tribes Commission was another dawn in his life, which could virtually portray the spectrum of tribal India from a perspective not covered so far (*c.f.* 1963). His settlement in a remote village could not enhance a geographical distance between him and rest of the world.

The events suggest that Harry Verrier Holman Elwin spent an unusually varied and productive life. A part of it is reflected through his autobiography (1964), which is the statement of his life, a self-appraisal of his life. Incidentally as his autobiography was published just before his demise, it stands as the monolithic structure drawing a final inference of his life and works.

Anthropological researches remained a personal element for notable anthropologists of the first generation till the spread of formal teaching of the discipline in India and other cohesive efforts by some academic institutions. It was then a special form mainly popularized by the works of Rai Bahadur Sarat Chandra Roy and Dewan Bahadur L. K. A. Ananthakrishna Iyer until a time when 'romantic movement' affected the discipline of anthropology almost as much as it affected poetry. With Elwin the personal element did not fade from anthropology; on the contrary, it became more important, and it was often bathed in an atmosphere of romantic charm. Nature never repeats herself precisely in the making of two personalities; and each personality has a charm and interest of its own. Any anthropologist who gives us a sincere revelation of a part of himself hopes for an audience. But there are not likely to be more than one or two anthropologists of outstanding genius in one generation (Bera, 1993:91; 2001:89). It is now already eight decades since the earliest of the writings on anthropology were published by Verrier Elwin where one could find a flair for romanticism and a rhythm of poetry, which encouraged a host of younger scholars in anthropology to work, or at least, to emulate his qualities: yet so far no one has succeeded in quite the same manner (Bera, 2002:81; 2008).

Probably earlier notable anthropologists never had a formal training in anthropology. It was true to Rai Bahadur Sarat Chandra Roy and also to Dewan Bahadur L. K. A. Ananthakrishna Iyer. It was more emphatically true for Verrier Elwin who came to anthropology after starting on another career and after leaving another career. It was a matter of sheer chance, sheer consequences of life happenings that he had to choose to settle in a remote tribal village in the heartland of the country called India. At this point of life he renounced his membership in the Church of England both as a priest and as a communicant and started living on his own at a subsistent village level, putting most of the donations that came to him for the cause and welfare of the tribal people. Here he envisaged that the tribal people are the real people, and not the savages as is generally conceived of in the western world. Their cultures are really worthy of respect. This impetus opened the floodgates of his ethnological writings.

Elwin himself stated that he had written twenty-six anthropological books, of which fourteen are monographs of Indian tribes, seven general books, two novels, two anthropological works (jointly with Shamrao Hivale) and his last document of life. Obviously he still stands as one of the most prolific anthropological writers of times, ranging over a century, just because the largest corpus of data on ethnography, which he could produce was operated single-handedly even at such a period of time when technological advancement was quite slow paced in comparison to the present day world.

Through his style of writing one can envisage the profound sense of romanticism as is embedded in his work. He said 'the essence and art of anthropology is love. Without it, nothing is fertile, nothing is true' (1964: 142). Anthropologists if held by the people observed rather than by an observer better accept his poetic and romantic views. Probably this was the reason why despite having such quantum of contributing works he has been infrequently quoted in the general anthropological literatures.

Because of his long and close association with the tribal people, Elwin's empathy with the tribal culture developed so intense that during his working days in central India he witnessed the rampant exploitation of the tribesmen by the *banias* and the other non tribal groups, which made him to desperately propose the idea of keeping the tribesmen 'isolated' and protected from the outside world. His concept for the prohibition of tribal life and culture was referred to as 'National Park' theory. Attesting the view Barnouw (1978:323) refers to that 'Verrier Elwin strongly opposed contacts between aboriginal hill tribes in India and the outside world. It was his belief that the hill tribes had a vigorous, creative way of life that would be spoiled by the growing influence of village India. Elwin's campaign to isolate the hill tribes was attacked by Indian nationalists who wanted to develop a unified, modern nation'.

Initially he might have started with romantic obsession. His advocacy for setting up of a 'National Park' under the direct control of a Tribes

Commissioner was meant to ensure protection for the tribes against exploitation and for freedom from fear, want and interference. The idea of exploitation of tribals by moneylenders, corrupt and rapacious officials and oppressive landlords could not be denied. The idea of a 'National Park' should not be conceived of as an 'Anthropological Zoo'. Probably later he thought of preserving tribal culture in the general national interest with the concept of unity of the hills and the plains as a means of maintaining tribal cultural identity in the wider context of national unity, territorial integrity and socialistic goals. Probably this static approach led him closer to the nationalist school.

In Elwin's language it was a suggestion that the administration for the tribals should be so adjusted as to allow them to lead a life without interference from outside agencies. He said, "I am not one of those who advocate a policy of absolute isolation, but I do urge a policy of isolation from debasing and impoverishing contact. The aboriginal cannot remain as he is – but is it necessary for him to pass through a long period of degradation before he emerges as the civilized man of the future? Could we not keep him in his innocence and happiness for a while till 'civilization' is more worthy to instruct him and until a scientific age has learnt how to bring development and change without causing despair" (Elwin, 1942).

A little later he further advocates for the aboriginals "a policy of temporary isolation and protection, and for their civilized neighbours a policy of immediate reform...The essential thing is not to 'uplift' them into a social and economic sphere to which they cannot adopt themselves, but to restore to them the liberties of their own countryside ... But whatever is done, and I would be the last to lay down a general programme, it must be done with caution and above all with love and reverence. The aboriginals are the real *swadeshi* products of India, in whose presence everyone is foreign. These are the ancient people with moral claims and rights thousands of years old. They were here first; they should come first in our regard" (Elwin, 1943).

During this period of time in consonance with his views on tribal isolation his ideas regarding religious conversion became strongly antagonizing and he advocated for the prohibition of proselytization because he was alarmed to see 'the rapid pace of conversion of tribes and the danger of the conversion within a few years of the entire aboriginal population in to a querulous, antinational, aggressive minority community, with none of the old virtues and few of the new, which will be a thorn in the side of the future Government of India' (Elwin, 1944). He felt that 'change of religion is actually harmful to the aborigines. It destroys tribal unity, strips the people of age-long moral sanctions, separates them from the mass of their fellow countrymen and in many cases leads to decadence that is as pathetic as it is deplorable, the methods employed are questionable. There is economic exploitation, exploitation of ignorance and social exploitation. Therefore, missionaries should be withdrawn from tribal areas' (*ibid.*).

Elwin denied of being an isolationist but the nationalists reacted. The isolationist school of policy makers included anthropologists and British members of the Indian Civil Service of whom J. H. Hutton was an arch exponent. While writing the Foreword for Elwin's book *The Baiga*, J. H. Hutton (Cambridge, July 25th, 1939) advocates that "interesting, however, as the sociology and psychology of the Baiga are, the most important part of Elwin's work is probably to be found in that part of his book which deals with the future. For the saving of the Baiga he advocates the establishment of a sort of National Park. His proposals are reasonably concrete and have definite references to existing conditions. If made by an anthropologist pure and simple they would immediately be suspected or at any rate accused of being a selfish if not satanic scheme for the establishment of an anthropological zoo, but no one who knows Elwin and his work could accuse him of that. For years he has lived among the Baiga and the Gond as nearly as may be under the conditions under which they live, working for their betterment through his school, his dispensary, his leper asylum. Readers of his *Leaves from the jungle* will know just a few of the hardships, the dangers and the very narrow escapes from death by sickness and even by poison which he has suffered in the course of such work and in the full knowledge of the risks he runs. Readers of this book will as easily appreciate his unqualified affection for his Baigas as his intimate knowledge of their life. Neither could for a moment accuse the friend whom the Baiga know as 'Big Brother' of advocating their segregation for exhibition purposes or as specimens for scientific inquiry. His plea for their protection, therefore, and in particular for their establishment in a reserved forest area, carries no less weight than his pleas for their protection from the callous but too familiar capacity of the subordinate officials of the forest, police, excise and revenue departments, and for their administration by more suitable codes than those of the Indian law courts. It carries no less weight than his protest against the equally familiar but if possible even more infuriating practice by which any subordinate 'who has proved himself a blackguard or incompetent elsewhere' is posted to some inaccessible tribal area (where his opportunities for evil though far greater are less lucrative) as a punishment for his misdeeds or as a means of obliterating him, and them, from an inconvenient publicity. Strongest of all perhaps is his plea for the Baigas' enjoyment of reasonable rights in the forests that have been their home from time immemorial and were their property till British administration deprived them of it. The latter have no longer the power to make amends. That power lies in the hands of the Baigas' Indian compatriots, but whether they have the will to use it remains to be proven" (Hutton, 1939: xxiv-xxv).

Philanthropists in particular, strongly opposed it, and alleged that instead of promoting 'assimilation' Elwin advocated for 'isolation' of tribesmen from the mainstream of Indian life and culture. As a vehement cintic of National Park, Ghurye (1943) dismissed Elwin as a 'no changer' and 'revivalist' seeing the 'aborigines reinstated in their old tribal ways, irrespective of any other consideration'. The polemic extended even to Ghurye's student M. N. Srinivas, who considered Elwin's idea as 'conveniently vague expression' (Srinivas, 1944). However, Srinivas probably later realized that Ghurye was jealous of Elwin's popularity and had a deep animus against Elwin, who (Ghurye) even has expressed elsewhere that 'Do you see his face? He has the mouth of a sexual pervert' (Guha, 1996: 2385; 2014).

Being stirred in the controversy Guha (*ibid.*) is provoked to write "were this a scholarly debate conducted in (say) 1920 in the pages of a journal of anthropology, Elwin might well have shrugged it off as a dispute between Oxford and Cambridge, the Protectionist and the Interventionist, the Aesthete and the Puritan, the Fieldworker and the Library Worm. But this was India in 1943, a nation on the eve of independence, struggling to come to terms with the problems of its vast and diverse population. This was a time of rising patriotism, but also of a growing confusion and division within the ranks of a once united national movement. The claims of the Congress to represent all of India were being strongly challenged by the Muslim League, which accused it of being a party of the Hindus, and a little less successfully by untouchables and socialists, who charged it with representing the interests of upper castes and capitalists. The thesis of tribal autonomy and distinctiveness put forward by Elwin appeared, in the circumstances, to be yet another blow to the unity of a nation in the making. Faced with the prospect of Pakistan and growing tension with Hindu society, the national movement could ill afford the merest thought, let alone the creation, of an 'Aboriginalisthan'. Like Mohammad Ali Jinnah of the Muslims and B. R. Ambedkar of the untouchables, Elwin was being cast as a 'betrayer' of the cause of a greater united India".

This is where Elwin stands amidst a turbulent controversy whirling between his anthropological standpoint and his 'isolationist' viewpoint. In fact he has actually carried forward the ideas previously laid by S. C. Roy (the Birhor and the Korwa of Chotanagpur), J. H. Hutton (the Great Andamanese) and by J. P. Mills (the Naga). While Roy speaks of 'a loss of interest in life', Hutton says 'physical apathy and physical decline', and Mills attests 'the awful monotony of village life' of 'unspeakable drabness', the drabness and deadness that will destroy the tribesmen of India (Elwin, 1939: 512).

Elwin considered the application of anthropology as the major influencing aspect in the field of tribal welfare. He relentlessly worked for making them known to the leaders of the country and for making them known as worthy of respect and of special welfare attention. Both as a prolific writer on tribal affairs and as a member of high level government committees he helped in moulding government policies into a far more useful instrument for tribal welfare.

With a note of admiration towards Elwin's mission Guha (1996: 2376) attests that "a self-taught and self-trained anthropologist, Elwin ranged widely over the Indian heartland, studying and writing about tribes in the British ruled territories of Orissa, Bihar and the Central Provinces, as well as the large tribal chiefdom of Bastar. His travels bore fruit in a series of ethnographies and folklore collections for 'academic' consumption, and in numerous policy pamphlets, reports, and newspaper articles for a more general audience (he also published two novels). Through all of his work runs a contrast between the 'pure' and the 'decayed' aboriginal, the latter corrupted by contact with civilization. Elwin himself does not offer, in any one place, a succinct definition of the first type, whom he both admired and identified with. In constructing a picture of Elwin's 'pure' aboriginal, I have relied almost exclusively on his writings in the years leading up to Indian independence (roughly, 1939 to 1947). This was a time when he came to regard himself as a spokesman not merely of the Gonds of Mandla, but of the 20 million tribals of central India".

The geographical entity which Elwin loosely calls 'middle India' encompasses a vast stretch of Central Provinces (now states of Madhya Pradesh and Chattishgarh and parts of Maharashtra including Nagpur), and the states to the south and east which have now become parts of the state of Orissa specially Koraput, Malkangiri and Ganjam districts and in a sketchy, comparative sort of way parts of present Jharkhand state, formerly of Bihar. In the early thirties when Sardar Vallabhbhai Patel and Jamnalal Bajaj persuaded him to work among the tribals, he settled in a remote tribal village in Mandla district along with his Indian friend Shamrao Hivale. Working among the Gond and the Baiga was his initial choice as is reflected from his writings. He, however, lived among the Gond, Pardhan, Agaria, Korku and the Baiga since 1931 and had grown to know them fairly well. Later in early forties he toured extensively in the present day state of Orissa making acquaintances with the Juang, Bhuiya, Kuttia Kond and the Bondo, and the present day state of Jharkhand knowing fairly well the Munda, Asur, Oraon (Elwin spelt them as Uraon) and the Santal. In spite of spending about ten months in a year over these two decades, he was modest enough to declare that he has only touched the fringe of this enormous area. This is how he began to write about the tribal people of India.

Probably his first full length monograph was on the Baiga where Hutton (1939: xxi) writes in the Foreword that 'anthropology has waited a hundred years for a full account of the Baiga, but Elwin has paid the debt as fully as any single author could who had to work on a tribe after its tribal life and organization had largely gone'. He further notes 'an account of the Baiga has long been delayed, but in proportion to that delay is the one we have here detailed and thorough. One can only hope that the no less lengthy delay in measures for protecting them may find an equally complete and thorough determination' (*ibid*., xxv).

Elwin claims that the Baiga are one of the few remaining tribes in Central India who have not been greatly affected by civilization clinging to the most secluded solitudes raising themselves above the condition of the mere hunting savage and whose material cultural life has 'almost disappeared before the highly organized and efficient trades-unionism of the Hindu caste system' (Elwin, 1939: xxvii). As a result they have entered into a network of relations with the neighbouring communities like the Mehera and Panka for weaving clothes; Chamar for shoes; Kumbhar for pots; Agaria for arrow-heads and axes; Bania for ornaments; Badnin for tattooing; and the Basor for baskets. It is surprising to note that the Baiga had been known over centuries for their basketry skill, which they have totally abandoned, and now they depend on the Basor for this.

For almost six years or so Elwin lived in the Baiga land, speaking with his Baiga friends in Baigani, a mixture of Dravidian Gondi with Indo-Aryan Hindi and Marathi, formed as a result of linguistic borrowing. A distinction is commonly drawn between cases where one language is holding its own despite the influence of powerful neighbours (*language maintenance*) and cases where a language has yielded to this influence, and speakers have assimilated to the dominant culture (*language shift*). But perhaps the most striking of these survivals of ancient culture among the Baiga is the social organization, which allows a grandparent to marry a grandchild. They have the ideal type of classificatory kinship system and marriage is possible not only with classificatory grandchildren but also with actual one. A parallel has been drawn here with four-class system of Australia, which allows marriage between grandparent and grandchild as socially approved institution. The Baiga marriage system appears to be in a state of disruption or at least in transition. They have localized social units (*jat*), which are to some extent endogamous groups, divided into exogamous territorial divisions (*garh*) and also into clans (*goti*) that are theoretically exogamous but practically not so. The units of exogamous clan have been a matter of recent borrowing particularly from the Gond, which survive on vegetables as a totemic object. Borrowing of the concept of untouchability on the basis of purity and pollution has infiltrated among the Baiga as also among other neighbouring tribal groups. Percolation of this trait of purity and pollution on the basis of untouchability among the Baiga has created a network of commensal relationships with other communities.

The part that aroused much controversy making it a national debate probably deals with the 'future' of the Baiga. It was Elwin's proposal for the establishment of national park that has been discussed earlier. Elwin (1939: 515) argued here that "many people in India suffer from the curious and rather puerile belief that the anthropologist wishes to keep primitive people 'as they were' as materials for his research. But this is not so: the scientist is not interested in any particular grade of civilization: he is concerned with things as they are: the semi-civilized Gond is just as interesting and important as the wilder Baiga. But the anthropologist who has come to know and love the people he has studied will naturally desire the best for them, and his views on that may well clash with those of the politician who merely desires to exploit them in the interests of his own party". One can argue here that the anthropologist will not be unfaithful to science in general and his discipline in particular and will think of the tribe's progress without impairing the quality of tribal life, without destroying the tribal culture and by restoring and maintaining tribal freedom.

After the work on the Baiga, he travelled across the Agaria land, a charcoal iron-smelting community catering to the needs of the people who use iron for survival strategy either for subsistence economy or for developed economy. It was a sympathetic account of a tribe impaired by high taxes and the infiltration of modern steel that commends to Indian politicians the comparison shown to forest tribes by the great Emperor Ashoka. Shyama

Charan Dube who came to study Indian tribes during 1940s observes that by that time, Elwin had become the 'most important single influence' from whom urban Indians came to know of their tribal countrymen: their culture, their way of life, their poverty and their vulnerability (Dube, 1964). Guha (1996: 2376) attests that 'his work for the tribes was widely known and widely discussed, fervently praised as well vehemently attacked. In one of those paradoxes in which the history of anthropology abounds, it fell to this one-time Oxford don to formulate the tribal question in its most striking and contentious fashion'.

His another notable work was among the Bondo who still cling to palaeo-technic means of subsistence economy living in a primordial state of existence even at the threshold of the new millennium. The Bondo have probably, not changed over this half a century since the days of Elwin till date. The Bondo have totemistic concepts relating to their moieties, cobra and tiger, who do not kill their totems. The Bondo say, 'when we go out hunting, we feel very embarrassed if we meet a tiger; we just don't know what to do and our weapons fall of their own accord from our hands. The tiger also feels awkward and goes away'. Elwin, while recording this statement, added, 'but I suspect a certain apprehension on the part of the Bondo that, while he himself may be strictly orthodox, the tiger may not be equally observant of the rules' (Elwin, 1950: 29).

Elwin's 'middle India' provided him love for nature, and to his aboriginals the significance of forest was as much economic as cultural; it was practical as well as symbolic. Bera (1996:223) writes about central Indian tribes elsewhere that their cognition of the forest is immense. They consider it as the greatest gift the supernatural has given to them. They speak of it with almost poetic enthusiasm. They often contrast the forest with the village. In the heat of the day, when the dusty village is unpleasantly hot, they like to escape in to the cool, dark and deep woods, far from the madding crowd, far from the dust and din of the village. Amidst such environment lie Elwin's ethnographies that create a world, which is as varied as human life. This is where Elwin's romanticism enters into real life of the aboriginals.

The exponent of field work tradition in anthropology, Malinowski, says 'in anthropology the essential facts of life must be stated simply and fully, though in scientific language, and such a plain statement cannot really offend the most delicately minded nor the prejudiced reader; nor can it be of any use to the seeker after pornography; least of all can it entice the unique interest of the young. For pruriency consists in oblique daydreaming and not in simple and direct statement. The reader will find that the natives treat sex in the long run not only as a source of pleasure, but, indeed, as a thing serious and even sacred. Nor do their customs and ideas eliminate from sex its power to transform crude material fact into wonderful spiritual experience, to throw the romantic glamour of love over the technicalities of love-making' (Malinowski, 1932: xiv).

The Malinowskian ideal fits well among the Muria, who regard sex as something much higher than eating and drinking and their technique of lovemaking has developed into an ideal level through their traditional institution called *ghotul*. Elwin visited altogether 347 *ghotuls* and in some of which he made extended stays witnessing all the ceremonies, festivals and dances. His two thousand case histories throw light on their entire institution of marriage, and on the factors that influence a case of divorce.

The Muria are farming people who live in the hills of central India. Tracing its origin to *Lingo Pen*, a famous cult-hero of the Gond, the Muria maintain a social institution call *ghotul*, where all unmarried boys and girls are enrolled as members. The institution has a wonderful organizational pattern where after initiation members are given a special title that carries with it a graded rank and social duties. Leaders belong to both the sexes; the boys' leader called the *Sirdar* and the girls' leader called the *Belosa*, who hold the reins of discipline. Male members are known as *chelik* and the female members are called *motiari*, both of whom perform important duties at all social occasions; the former one acting as acolytes at festivals, and the latter one as bride's maids at weddings. Both dance in front of the clan-god and they also form a choir at the funeral of important people. The *ghotul* is considered to be a religious sanctuary dedicated to a god.

Two types of *ghotul* are found among the Muria. In one, which is presumed to be of older type, a boy who joins the group is given a *ghotul* wife. A kind of mock marriage ceremony is performed in imitation of an adult wedding. The second type of *ghotul* is the one that resembles group marriage where no mock weddings are celebrated and where no spouses are assigned. But in both cases, however, there is, of course, a simple, sensuous and passionate sex-life. Roy (1915) who long ago studied the Oraon dormitory considered it 'an effective economic organization for purposes of food quest, a useful seminary for training young men in their social and other duties, and an institution for magico-religious observances calculated to secure success in hunting and to augment the procreative power of the young men'.

Today an anthropologist of structuralist persuasion finds pleasure in discovering the symbolism connected with human culture and in deciphering the ideational systems present in the social organization. Elwin with his Malinowskian bent of mind looked into the functional character of myth and for the Baiga he says 'myth does far more than explain the Baiga's institutions; it is their motive power and their authorization' (Elwin, 1939: 305).

Elwin belonged to an era when French School of structuralism had not emerged. Though himself a British, Elwin did not represent the British School of Social Anthropology at all. His anthropology allowed him to live among the people whom he called 'aborigines'. Hence, his works, probably, never took into consideration the developments that were taking a shape in the far west. He refers to his works on myths as a sort of Aboriginal *Purana* where fantastic stories, unreal and unusual names, and far-fetched analogies abound. His romanticism guided him to reveal without embarrassment or self-consciousness theories of the origin of life and the sexual function.

Elwin had a Malinowskian bent of mind as regards his fieldwork tradition in anthropology is concerned. The latter was one of the first to deride the view that myths were an attempt to explain or make intelligible abstract ideas. Much earlier Frazer had emphasized the connection between myth and magic, who said 'we shall probably not err in assuming that many myths, which we now know only as myths, had once their counterpart in magic; in other words, that they used to be acted as a means of producing in fact the events which they describe in figurative language. Ceremonies often die out while myths survive, and thus we are left to infer the dead ceremony from the living myth' (Frazer, 1911-15: 374).

Elwin, however, felt that ideas about the importance and function of mythology have been considerably revised in the last few decades. He laid stress on function, to some extent in the Malinowskian tradition, and felt free to say that no one now seriously believes that a myth is a piece of bad history written in symbolic language, neither it is a speculative symbolization of natural phenomena (Elwin, 1949). He held the thought of S. C. Roy and manifested that myths are merely a form of recreation.

It will be no denying to attest here that Elwin, in reality, educated the Indian elites about the 'aboriginals' and kindled a feeling to improve their condition in the face of struggle and disaster that were raging the Indian nation with ideology and idealism of the country's freedom struggle. His concept of integration urged the maintenance of cultural identity of the tribals in the wider context of national unity, territorial integrity and socialistic goals. Creating an impact on the nationalist school he said, 'the special care and protection given to the tribesmen must not cast shadow on the unity of India. They must be educated to feel that they are full citizens of the Republic, with real rights and still more urgent duties' (Singh, 1985:193).

Obsessed with his initial feelings of earlier days, full of romanticism, he maintains the view even in the later days of his life and continues to say, 'the tribal people of India offer us a very special challenge. Their simplicity, which is most lovable; their art, which often gives them the dignity of princes but is so easily destroyed; their courtesy and hospitality, discipline and self-reliance; their ability to work hard and co-operatively; their occasional bewilderment before the advance of an unfamiliar world, and yet their welcome and friendliness to that world; these things win the heart and call for the very best in those who try to serve them. Nothing can be too good for them, but with what care that good has to be shared' (Elwin, 1960: 288).

In contrast to his impact on tribal policy in India, Elwin made another noteworthy contribution, which had a far-reaching implication in the study of Indian civilization and society especially when one looks towards it from the hierarchic and stratificatory points of view. Holding the shields of defence for the tribal people he vehemently opposed the Hindu puritans who try to reform the tribal society in their ascetic mode. Elwin vigorously denied that this brand of Puritanism was, as they claim, the essence of the true spirit of India. On the contrary, he argued that the life affirming, sense-enjoying qualities of most tribal folk were closer to the true India (Elwin, 1964).

Since a narrative authority becomes a crucial issue in anthropological writings, it cannot be analyzed in isolation from the theoretical-critical or epistemological debates. This is where Verrier Elwin, an ethnographer, methodologically speaking a field-worker-theorist, a participant-observer, an anthropologist of aboriginal people stands. His works in central India had a Malinowskian influence except the fact that the only difference between Elwin's narrative and Malinowski's work was the subjective touch. Malinowski, in many instances, expressed generalized views rather than particular; on the contrary Elwin portrayed illuminating account through character and example.

Above all, Elwin can be credited with the distinction that unlike other 'primitivists' or 'aboriginalists' he actually lived among the people whom he referred always to in his writings. Anthropologists, in practice, return to their homeland after the completion of their work, which otherwise, Elwin did not ever practise and lived among them, loved them, and defended them. While self-portraying he says, 'I have lived, by choice, in remote and primitive villages. I have married into tribal society and found felicity there' (Elwin, 1964: vii). He actually recognized both the tradition he came from as well as his departure from it (Guha, 1996: 2378).

Elwin passed through three major debates in his life. The debate with A. V. Thakkar, popularly known as Thakkar Bapa, encircled around one style of social work with another; the 'National Park' debate with Govind Sadashiv Ghurye manifested one style of anthropology against another; and lastly himself a Christian priest in the past, Elwin confronted Dutch Catholics who pursued their own faith religiously making it an Elwin-Missionary debate. As an attack on the Catholics he wrote, 'the priests in Mandla are the Chindits of the Christian Army. Compared to them, most other missionaries get to work with Italian infantrymen. These fathers are from Holland. Fortified by the *philosophia perennis*, inspired not only by a divine love of souls but also by the remarkable Dutch instinct for colonial expansion, they are busy turning Mandla into a Dutch colony ... Within 10 years Mandla – the ancient home of the *Rishis*, former kingdom of the Gonds, whose fields are blessed by the sacred Narmada – will be virtually a Dutch colony with a hundred thousand Catholic converts'.[5]

As an anthropologist Elwin was modest enough to respond to his critics, particularly Ghurye, by way of an amicable settlement for and against controversial issues time and again, which, otherwise, Ghurye did not accede to and continued the issue even much after Elwin's death partially because of his British Christian origin and partially for his proximity towards Jawaharlal Nehru. However, the issue of integrating the tribes with the mainstream still raises debate as the two ideological traditions put forth by Elwin and Ghurye have not waned.

Despite involving himself in the formulation of tribal policy for a national cause during the latter part of his anthropological career, Elwin could not, probably, create much dent except for the matter of influencing (if not formulating!) Nehru for *Panch Sheel*. The tribal question has remained unanswered to a great extent till date and probably no anthropologist, since the demise of Elwin, has been seen to exert pressure for a common tribal cause. Of late, as Guha (1996: 2387-88) attests, 'in a political (and intellectual) climate that is radically altered, one might think that the horse is not so dead after all. When the claims of unitary nationalism are being assailed from all sides, when sectarian identities of *dalits*, backward castes and Hindus are being aggressively crafted, the tribal question is once again emerging in its most starkly polarized form. For the encounter between tribals and the outside world is yet conducted on grossly unequal terms: the loss of land and forests being joined by the loss of the *adivasi's* living space, as tribals come to form a very large proportion of the millions displaced by steel mills, coal mines, and dams. In cultural terms, movements that assert tribal autonomy and distinctiveness (as in the reinvigorated Jharkhand movement) have been met by counter-movements, helped along by the *Sangh Parivar*, which hope to more fully assimilate tribals into the Hindu way of life'.

Elwin remains immortal even through his debates. The Bhuria Committee recommends that – "tribal communities should be respected as in command of the economic resources, with *gramsabhas* placed in charge of land, forests, and minerals, with larger tribal regions given 'sub-state' status, and with traditional tribal conventions and laws (to) continue to hold validity".[6]

Taken as a whole, Elwin's anthropology, as a part of Indian anthropology, could create a dent in the minds of the men comprising both anthropologists and non-anthropologists, when both British and American anthropologists dominated the Indian anthropological soil over decades. While an anthropologist fresh from of fieldwork in an Indian village might not wholly agree that all of Elwin's experiences are typical, it is the most important kind of statement for those Indians who think and write about what is typical of Indians; that is about their character as a nation. The cultural heritage of Indian anthropology could witness Elwin's monumental work as a historical experience in terms of the dimensions of time and space. There is enough room of evidence to suggest that despite his romanticism in anthropology Elwin was not very unlike other anthropologists of his era. A part of these, if not the whole, makes Harry Verrier Holman Elwin a hero of his time, an erudite scholar of his era, a romantic anthropologist with poetic vision, and a missionary with an anthropological mission, not witnessed ever before, who created a passage through *aboriginal* India.

Now let me come to the final stage. While conceiving of such an idea of a seminar on Elwin my greatest hope is that it will introduce non-anthropologists to anthropology and Verrier Elwin. I also feel that the endeavour should lead to an understanding that the anthropological world and culture move in a connected as well as in a parallel manner. But, more importantly, there is a Western view, especially colonial view that Indian anthropology ended sometime with Elwin, soon after his demise. Yes, luminaries of the past, like the works of Dewan Bahadur L. K. Ananthakrishna

Iyer, Rai Bahadur Sarat Chandra Roy, Govind Sadashiv Ghurye, Nirmal Kumar Bose, Dhirendra Nath Majumdar, Iravati Karve, Stephen Fuchs, Shyama Charan Dube, Mysore Narasimhachar Srinivas, Surajit Chandra Sinha, Lalita Prasad Vidyarthi, Baidyanath Saraswati and others are breath taking, but Indian anthropology continues to evolve from this rich heritage and is vibrant today.

While looking into such analogy, I have certain things in my mind to defend it. Early in his career, Elwin was faced with the conundrum that all ethnographers must try and resolve at some point: 'How can I be modern and unique and true to myself'? In this context, it was being Indian. What makes Elwin a great ethnographer, beyond merely an accomplished poet, was his resolution to this puzzle. Elwin found his voice in central India and the 'flat technique' that was in opposition to the Western lifestyle he was trained in at Oxford. The medium was a tropical country instead of western climate, the subjects were indigenous population and rural rather than the wealthy Western patrons and the technique was Indian in its representation, in contrast to the Western realism. Elwin borrowed but never mimicked. His line and perspective had the sophistication to transform indigenous tribal life into high life. Beyond the academic beauty is the fact that Elwin's search for cultural independence was taking place simultaneously with the fight for political freedom. It was the search for the modern Indian identity. And, it was this idea that increasingly attracted me over and above the 'love at first sight' based on the lyrical beauty of his writings (Paul 2017, based on an interview of the present author). So, the romanticism continues to be remembered; after fifty three years of his demise.

***

Notes

1. With due apology and off the record I mention here that I developed this feeling through an exercise of several library visits where I found that almost over the two and a half decade the books authored by Elwin were neither issued nor referred to by scholars of this generation, what to talk about the archival data anymore.
2. Colonel Rashid Yusuf Ali, who was posted in NEFA when Elwin visited the area, also expressed similar opinion to the present author, in August-September, 2002, at Shillong.
3. Mother tongue of the Baiga, classified under Chattisgarhi (Hindi) in 1961 Census on the basis of Linguistic Survey of India.
4. In February 2004, the present author could meet a gentleman, Sri Sukhendu Roy Chaudhuri, aged 102 then, an acquaintance of Elwin, when he (author along with colleagues S. S. Datta Chaudhuri and Sri Anup Kumar Giri) was working

among the Bondo in Mudalipara and could gather many personal information of the then time and also many information of the present day Bondo.

5. The Hindustan Times (New Delhi), June 14, 1944.
6. Report of the High Level Committee to make Recommendations on the Salient Features of the Law for Extending Provisions of the Constitutional (73rd) Amendment Act 1993, to Scheduled Areas. New Delhi, 1995.

References

Barnouw, Victor, 1978. *An Introduction to Anthropology: Ethnology*. 3rd Edition. Illinois. The Dorsey Press.

Bera, Gautam Kumar, 1993. 'Morgan and Roy: Appraisal of Thought and Works'. *JIAS*. 28(1): 91-95.

Bera, Gautam Kumar, 1996. 'The Symbols of Forest: Structure and Cognition in Maria Cultural Tradition'. In K. K. Chakraborty eds. *Tribal Identity in India: Extinction or Adaptation*. Bhopal. IGRMS. 216-228.

Bera, Gautam Kumar, 2001. 'Nirmal Kumar Bose: The Doyen of Indian Anthropology'. *The Oriental Anthropologist*. 1(2): 88-112.

Bera, Gautam Kumar, 2002. 'Verrier Elwin : An Anthropologist with Romanticism'. *The Oriental Anthropologist*. 2 (1): 81-96.

Bera. Gautam Kumar. 2007. 'An Appraisal of Tribal Development: The Elwin Era and Afterwards'. In A. N. Sharma eds. *Role of Anthropology in Human Welfare*. New Delhi: Sarup and Sons. pp. 67–85.

Bera. Gautam Kumar. 2008. *Passage Through Aboriginal India: Anthropological Profile of Verrier Elwin*. Allahabad: The Oriental Institute of Cultural and Social Research.

Bera. Gautam Kumar. 2013a. 'One Hundred Years of Anthropology in India'. [Rabindranath Tagore Sesquicentennial Lecture delivered on 11th November, 2011 in the National Seminar on Anthropological Researches in India: Retrospect and Prospect]. In Gautam Kumar Bera and K. Jose SVD eds. *Anthropological Researches in India: Retrospect and Prospect*. New Delhi: Abhijeet Publications. pp. 45-69.

Bera. Gautam Kumar. 2013b. 'A Reappraisal of Elwin's Anthropology in Aboriginal India'. (Verrier Elwin Memorial Lecture delivered at Indira Gandhi National Tribal University, Amarkantak, Madhya Pradesh on 29th August, 2013).

Bera. Gautam Kumar. 2014. 'An Appraisal of Elwin's Anthropology in Aboriginal India'. *Man and Life*. 40(1-2): 69-90.

Bera. Gautam Kumar. 2016. 'Elwinian Vision of Tribal Policy *vis-à-vis* Scheduled Areas: Promised Future or Lost Horizon'. In Gautam Kumar Bera et. al. eds. *Romanticism Remembered: Verrier Elwin after Fifty years*. New Delhi: B. R. Publications. pp. 36-60.

Dube, S. C., 1964. 'Book Review' (The *Tribal World of Verrier Elwin). The Eastern Anthropologist*. 12(2): 134-136.

Elwin, Verrier, 1939. *The Baiga*. London. John Murray.

Elwin, Verrier, 1942. 'Loss of Nerve'. *The Statesman*. Sunday. April 5.

Elwin, Verrier, 1944. *The Foreign Missionary Danger*. Ranchi. All India Dayanand Mission.

Elwin, Verrier, 1949. *Myths of Middle India*. Madras. Oxford University Press.

Elwin, Verrier, 1949. *The Bondo Highlander*. Bombay. Oxford University Press.

Elwin, Verrier, 1957. *A Philosophy for NEFA*. (Foreword by Jawaharlal Nehru). Shillong. North East Frontier Agency. (Second Edition 1959, Reprint Edition 1960).

Elwin, Verrier, 1963. *A New Deal for Tribal India*. (Ed.). Delhi. Manager of Publications. Government of India.

Elwin, Verrier, 1964. *The Tribal World of Verrier Elwin: An Autobiography*. Bombay. Oxford University Press.

Frazer, J. G., 1911 to 1915. *The Golden Bough*. ix. London.

Ghurye, G. S., 1943. *The Aboriginals - so called - and their future*. Poona. Gokhale Institute of Politics and Economics.

Guha, Ramchandra, 1996. 'Savaging the Civilized: Verrier Elwin and the tribal question in late colonial India'. *EPW*. Special Number. September. 2375-2389.

Guha, Ramachandra. 2014. *Savaging the Civilized: Verrier Elwin, His Tribals and India*. Gurgaon: Allen Lane an imprint of Penguin Books.

Hutton, J. H., 1939. 'Foreword'. *The Baiga*. London. John Murray.

Malinowski, B., 1932. *The Sexual Life of Savages*. London.

Roy, S. C., 1915. *The Oraons*. Ranchi.

Singh, K. S., 1985. *Tribal Society in India: An Anthropo-historical Perspective*. New Delhi. Manohar.

Paul, Sumana. 'A Passage Through Verrier Elwin (1902 – 1964)'. *The Shillong Times*. ....September, 2017.

Permanent address of the author: Gautam Kumar Bera, 'Upanishadam', 147/1 Jaigirghat Road, Thakurpukur, Kolkata – 700 063.

Chapter - 6

Elwin's Philosophy and Its Contemporary Relevance

Kanchan Mukhopadhyay

I

When we look back at the controversy over 'tribal policy' in India in years immediately after independence, in which Verrier Elwin was often bestowed with a key role, we see the debate often revolved around two approaches; that of 'integration' and of 'isolation'. At one point of time Elwin was accused of being an advocate of isolationism, some of his statements were at the centre of the storm. Elwin had to clarify his statements on several occasions and say he did not support any isolationist viewpoint; he had to write pages to refute the allegation (Elwin 1960: 25-28). He was well aware of reasons responsible for genesis of such a viewpoint and has critiqued that too. While commenting on the British policy of 'leaving the tribals alone', he identified the major factors responsible for such a strategy. Elwin noted, task of administering the wild border areas was not rewarding enough for the colonial government, so they preferred to stay away and leave those areas un-administered or only partially administered. In addition, the government was desirous of isolating the tribes from political influence of the nationalists. While the Christian missionaries or the exploiting moneylenders had free access to the excluded tribal areas, persons involved in any kind of anti-British political activities were rarely allowed to visit those areas. This approach of selective political isolation was not imagined by Elwin, it was stated by the government in House of Commons in 1936. Finally, some officers of the colonial government truly believed the tribal people were 'better and happier as they were'. Such an isolationist view was not invented by officers serving the government in India, several

American and European intellectuals of that time held such a view and called it 'primitivism' (Elwin 1958: 36-40).

The intellectual tradition of primitivism shows a close resemblance with seventeenth century romanticism. While cultural primitivism discovered all fundamental values of life among the primitive societies in superior form than civilized people, it was chronological primitivism that realized pre-civilized periods of human life were happiest and best. Such a view was common among the early colonialists while later day imperialists and missionaries imagined and described the 'primitive' people in very gloomy terms. Developing and supporting such a viewpoint was essential for the colonial forces to justify their activities in the colonies.

In *A Philosophy for NEFA* Elwin did not take an impartial standpoint, he announced his opposition to primitivism and described it as 'confused and inspired by largely sentimental motives'. He, on the other hand, declared his preference for 'scientific anthropology'. In his argument Elwin somehow avoided discussing the political dimensions of ideas related to 'primitive societies', whether to glorify or to vilify such 'imagined' categories. Years later Kuper described the idea of primitivism as a myth persisting even in contemporary times to serve different political purposes. It has been used by apparently opposing political forces like imperialists and nationalists, anarchists and Marxists. The myth has provided legitimacy to political discourses on formation of societies on the basis of either blood or soil; that the political philosophies have used to explain ideas of race and citizenship (1988: 239-240).

II

Elwin was appointed Adviser for Tribal Affairs in North East Frontier Agency (NEFA) in early 1950s.After working in that position for about three years he wrote the book *A Philosophy for NEFA*. In preface to the second edition Elwin explained why writing the book became necessary and what purpose it has served in the period between publication of the first and the second editions. He thought administrators should be clear in their minds about what they are trying to do in NEFA. Unless they are driven by a philosophy, the administrative activities might do more harm than good. By the time the second edition was published in 1958 Elwin was convinced that the philosophy, about whose efficacy he himself was doubtful initially, can in fact help to preserve and enrich 'the rich and varied tapestry of NEFA' (Elwin 1958: IX).

The publication puts forward two objectives. Proper administration of a socially and culturally heterogeneous area like NEFA must ensure that the existing heterogeneity is preserved and enriched. In tune with what Jawaharlal Nehru wrote in foreword to the first edition of the book, Elwin expected that the philosophy and the 'model of tribal administration' would be useful in other areas of India having tribal and hill-dwelling people. It was argued by Elwin that 'scientific anthropology' can provide with tools required to achieve those objectives. After explaining the contemporary theoretical premises of the discipline of anthropology in rather lucid language for benefit of non-technical persons among the readers, he proceeds to explicate what the 'recently grown' subject called applied anthropology is. He informed the readers how professional anthropologists were working with governments all over the world and stressed upon the importance of tribal systems of jurisprudence or their social and religious institutions. He has also explained in many words how anthropologists have helped to understand the processes of social change that were expressed through 'extraordinary' movements (Elwin 1958: 42-43).

Elwin's repeated emphasis upon 'new anthropology' in *A Philosophy for NEFA* needs to be noted and the context has to be comprehended. The context has several dimensions, which are spatial as well as temporal. When he claims 'new anthropology' is "based on observation and recorded fact" and it has "helped the world to take a more balanced view of the entire problem", he endorses objectivity over subjectivity and dissociates the discipline from 'emotional' and 'confused' approaches adopted in the past.

The term 'new anthropology' also needs to be understood against the national and global political context of that time; a nation just unfettered from imperial governance in the post-war world was charting its course to move into the future. It was a time when dissociation from ideas and efforts of the past and finding new approaches were integral to the task of reshaping agencies engaged in serving the people. Globally it was a time of remorse, hopelessness and confusion; a large part of the world was literally in rubbles and civilizations at peril.

Elwin's Philosophy raised those issues, took note of the unprecedented circumstances that gave rise to problems that were extremely difficult to solve. Weapons of mass destruction, totalitarian governance over a large part of the planet, and immensely powerful bureaucracy even in the democratic world complicated the difficulties and compelled the citizens to reconsider their outlook towards civilization and progress. This, Elwin admitted, was the context where fundamental problems of the tribal people were to be considered. He questioned the fairness of the idea of making them part of a life unconditionally in qualities of which serious doubts had been raised.

Though not spelt out explicitly, it can be guessed Elwin had another issue at the back of his mind when he emphasised the importance of 'new anthropology'. *A Philosophy for NEFA* was published after more than a decade of end of the Second War. By that time it was known that some people claiming expertise in anthropology and eugenics helped racial campaigns of fascist political forces and aided holocaust directly or indirectly. The brand of 'new anthropology' was used to assert dissociation not only from a colonial policy of exclusion and isolation, but also from racism and ethnocentrism of all forms.

III

There, however, were reasons to feel optimist as India was finally a sovereign republic and there was freedom to build a welfare state. Elwin doubted his own doubts and wrote that those doubts were perhaps inappropriate. Though there are 'the bombs, the secret police, the tortures in hidden prison cells, the taxation, the corruptions', those are not everything the 'modern world' is about.

Long before India became independent the tribal policy of independent India was taking shape albeit slowly and tentatively, but not without a direction. In an article written in 1928 Nehru appreciated certain declarations made by Congress of Soviets. Those declarations accepted equality and sovereignty of the people of that country, their right of self-determination, even to the extent of separation, abolition of all kinds of national, racial and religious privileges, and especially the right of free development of minorities and ethnic groups (Nehru 1972: 424-427).

In 1946 when Nehru was informed that some people of the Naga and Lushai Hills districts of Assam were not keen to join Independent Federal India, he told them such small territories with an impoverished population cannot stand on their own. To assure the people that state will take care of their concerns he spelt out an outline of 'tribal policy' that India would adopt once it gains independence. Under that policy tribal areas would be given maximum possible freedom and autonomy to ensure they can live their lives 'according to their own customs and desires'. Incorporation of excluded areas with other areas was on agenda. Another important statement he made was, after independence there would be special departments at centre and in provinces for protection and advancement of tribal areas. Nehru expressed his dislike of the possibility that the tribal areas might be swamped by people from other parts of the country.

It is evident from selection of words that the outline of tribal policy was more concerned about land than inhabitants of those areas. In his speech at the 1952 'Scheduled Tribes Conference' Nehru identified psychological integration and consolidation of the tribes with rest of the citizens as the core issue. To achieve that goal the method he preferred was 'one of learning from them and having learnt, to try to help and co-operate.'

Rustomji, who like Elwin was closely associated with tribal affairs in North Eastern parts of the country, noted that Nehru did not wish to be remembered as somebody who transformed the tribals, but as a person who understood them as "parents do their children, without any ulterior motive". This quality he found in Verrier Elwin too (Rustomji 1989: 28-29).

IV

It is true that political situation in some parts of the world was not favourable for conservation of cultural diversity and maintenance of political autonomy among small communities in years during and after the Second World War. It is also true, even favourable standpoint of some key policy makers including the then Prime Minster of independent India could not ensure the tribal people complete freedom to maintain their cultural identity or political autonomy. Certain developments in India that were not favouring the above-mentioned standpoint have not been explicitly mentioned by Elwin possibly for his positional encumbrance.

The rift that was created between the tribal and non-tribal populations of India by colonial governance was required to be addressed. Instead of going for judicious psychological integration, a section of Indian citizens, including some articulate ones, were keen to see the tribals are rapidly assimilated in the mass of 'majority' (Fuirer Haimendorf 1982). Assimilating activities were noticed at the ground level; an official note written in early 1950s states most of the lower level officials and some higher-level officials were trying to 'Assamize' NEFA; there was a dominance of Assamese officials in that area (Mukhopadhyay 1989: 19).

The assimilationists expressed their disagreement with the suggested model of judicious psychological integration quite vociferously, particularly after the Sino-Indian border conflict in 1962. It was noted by some of them that the tribal policy for NEFA, especially the decision to maintain Inner Line to restrict entry of visitors from other parts of the country was held responsible for all maladies. The critics felt the Inner Line prevented integration of residents of NEFA with rest of India by keeping them in archaic social conditions, and the Line caused inadequate vigilance over international border. Das Shastri had worked closely with Elwin during his

Shillong days; he observed that the critics failed to note there was no dearth of personnel in NEFA working for modern development and the people of NEFA were never stopped to mix freely with people from other parts of India (Mukhopadhyay 1989: 21-22).

The border conflict was not a sudden event, India had ample time to prepare for it. In November 1950 Prime Minster Nehru, who at that time was also looking after External Affairs, made a significant statement in Parliament. Being asked to comment on maps issued by China that show NEFA as part of Tibet, he said Indian maps show MacMahon Line is the boundary of the country. So "we stand by that boundary, and we will not allow anybody to come across that boundary" (Maxwell 1970: 75).

Large scale border conflict with China took place in 1962; it is difficult to believe sufficient arrangement for defending the boundary could not be made in all those years simply because Inner Line regulations were in effect restricting civilian population from other parts of the country into NEFA. N K Rustomji, who was Adviser to Governor of Assam for tribal areas from 1948 to 1954 and then again from 1959 recounted that his second term as Adviser "was the period preparatory to the Chinese invasion of the North-East in 1962, and our main pre-occupation was liaising with the army and the Border Road Oraganisation in preparation for the threatened attack."

That the Chinese forces could penetrate the territory of NEFA so deep was more traumatic for the inhabitants of that region than for people from elsewhere in India, felt Rustomji. He has disagreed with the view that the tribal policy showed too much respect for tribal culture and institutions and rejected the suggestion that thinly populated hill areas could be populated by certain communities of India having martial traditions.

"It is my conviction," wrote Rustomji, "…that it was mainly on account of our not having infringed upon the tribals' rights in their land and forest that they remained loyal to the country, despite the fact that we had failed in protecting them during their time of need" (Rustomji 1989: 29-30).

V

Certain basic information on antecedents of the territory that came to be known as NEFA and subsequently as Arunachal Pradesh and about the inhabitants of that area can help to contextualise the 'tribal policy' championed by Elwin.

The territory acted as a buffer between two great civilisations, India and China for ages – none of the countries ever administered the land or its people directly. The British took interest in the area in mid-nineteenth century and sent troops into territory to occupy it. The territory was being held by Tibet at that time and purpose of the British expedition was to impose a treaty on the Tibetan government of the day. When the Qing rulers of China brought Tibet under their administration in 1910-12 by force, the British responded by bringing the territory that was to be known as NEFA under their administration. Immediately after fall of the Qing dynasty in 1913 Tibet declared itself independent; within a year the British and the Tibetan authorities agreed upon the boundary between India and Tibet, which was the MacMahon Line. As Tibet was not being administered by China at that point of time, the Chinese were kept out of this negotiation. The map, however, was too sketchy and the line was never marked on ground by either of the parties. Till 1950s it was not clearly known whether Tawang is part of Tibet or of India (Lamb 1966).

In fact, by end of 1949 the situation in NEFA was not different from the time when the British left. The Indian post nearest to MacMahon Line was at Walong, it was close to the eastern end of the Line. Northernmost Indian post in Tawang tract was at Dirang Dzong, more than eighty miles from Tawang, which was under Tibetan administration till that time. Twenty additional posts were set up within next one year and in February 1951 one Indian official accompanied by an escort and several hundred porters reached Tawang to establish Indian claim over the entire tract. In spite of protest from Tibetan authorities in Lhasa representatives of Tibetan administration were pushed out of Tawang (Maxwell 1970: 73).

Though the situation was politically volatile, the Tibetan authorities did not consider use of force but stuck to diplomatic dialogue with Indian government. Some of the local people, however, were thinking differently. In early 1950s a large contingent of Assam Rifles personnel moved up the Subansiri river. There they were warmly welcomed by one of the local communities who offered them food and shelter. Later the contingent was massacred, seventy-three persons including soldiers and civilians were killed. After the incidence the government "...dispatched a punitive expedition but seems, under Nehru's orders, ...have been content with an overwhelming show of force and did not burn villages and take prisoners as the British would certainly have done" (Maxwell 1970: 74).

Appropriateness of the 'tribal policy' and its philosophical roots cannot be assessed without understanding the volatility of the situation prevalent there at that time. It is not very difficult to guess what the consequences could be if the local communities of NEFA were forced to adopt lifeways that some of the 'other' people were expecting them to do.

VI

After the 1962 border conflict India's national pride was bruised severely and a section of the political community of the country were looking for scapegoats that could be held responsible and if possible, sacrificed. Some of them found a rather soft target in tribal policy for NEFA and condemned it mercilessly. The attack was strong enough to derail the policy that was based on a philosophy of respect for diversity, of freedom to remain different and of negating the superiority of those in power. Certain subsequent developments made it clear, so much of diversity as was found in that area was too much for certain state and non-state agencies to handle. Emergence of Donyi Polo cult in NEFA, now known as Arunachal Pradesh, is one example of how multiplicity was dealt with.

It has been noted that the tribal communities of Arunachal Pradesh had remarkable cultural heterogeneity among them, especially in their religious beliefs and practices. Plurality of their deities, spirits, religious specialists, festivities, and oral traditions was remarkable. Since late 1960s some reformist religious faith known as Donyi-Polo, Intya and Rangfra made their appearance. Those belief systems took shape of movements that were looking for common denominators in diverse faiths and trying to bring different communities closer. Donyi-Polo appealed the Tani group of tribes, namely Adi, Nyishi, Apatani, Tagin, and the Galo, to embrace the common faith. To justify the process of homogenisation of apparently heterogenous cultural elements, it has been claimed that institutionalization of indigenous tribal faiths became necessary when they encountered new faiths and practices like Christianity.

The process of institutionalization of tribal religions has found to be multifaceted. Images of gods and goddesses were invented, temples were constructed and religious chants and oral traditions were codified "in a manner very similar to that of Hinduism." Such development could be possible because a discriminatory policy was put in place. On one hand the NEFA administration did not allow Christian missionaries to build churches or to carry out proselytizing activities within the limits of the Agency, on the other hand Hindu organizations were patronized by the state to carry out activities in areas of education and health. In addition, the military and civilian personnel working in the state, majority of them were Hindu, have set up their religious places and celebrate their religious festivals. Exposure to such practices has found some place in thoughts of the local communities, especially those residing in urban or semi-urban areas (Chaudhuri 2013: 260-1, 273-4).

Another noteworthy situation, somewhat similar to the developments in Arunachal Pradesh, can be found in the state of Mizoram. That area, which once was Lushai Hills district of Assam, was inhabited by several ethnic groups and known for extensive cultural heterogeneity. In course of a protracted struggle for secession and then for statehood a new identity of Mizo (literally hill people) emerged; construction of this new identity glossed over multiple identities. The process of Mizoization that brought disparate groups of Lushai Hills together has been found to be complementary to the process of Indianization (Patnaik 2016). Complementarity of the two processes was noticed and the efforts of constructing common identity markers was sometimes sponsored by the state.

The developments in Arunachal Pradesh have possibly 'gone far beyond Elwin's apprehensions', noted Chaudhuri (2013: 275). Subtly but steadily the path of development has moved away from Elwin's philosophy that sought a departure from ideological traditions of totalitarianism and of homogenization, that preferred the communities to stay close to less complicated but diverse cultural forms and societal relations that was still found in them. Basic tenets of the philosophy need to be reviewed and reconsidered because that could and still can restore faith of the people in civilization and in progress.

References

Chaudhuri, Sarit Kumar 2013 The Institutionalization of Tribal Religion: Recasting the Donyi-Polo Movement in Arunachal Pradesh *Asian Ethnology* Volume 72, Number 2, 259-277.

Elwin, Verrier 1958 *A Philosophy for NEFA*, Shillong, North-East Frontier Agency.

Elwin, Verrier 1960 Beating a Dead Horse *Seminar*, Vol. 14, 25-28.

Haimendorf, C. V. Furer 1982 *Tribes of India: The Struggle for Survival*, New Delhi

Kuper, Adam 1988 *The Invention of Primitive Society: Transformation of an Illusion*. London and New York, Routledge.

Lamb, Alastair, 1966 *The McMahon line: a study in the relations between India, China and Tibet, 1904 to 1914*, London, Routledge & K. Paul.

Maxwell, Neville, 1970 *India's China War*, Bombay, Jaico Publishing House.

Mukhopadhyay, Kanchan 1989 The Tribal Policy of Jawaharlal Nehru In *Jawaharlal Nehru, Tribes and Tribal Policy*, Edited by K. S. Singh, Calcutta, Anthropological Survey of India, 12-26.

Nehru, Jawaharlal 1972 'The Problem of Minorities' In Selected Works of Jawaharlal Nehru, Series One, Vol. 2, New Delhi: 424-427.

Patnaik, Jagadish K. 2016 Mizo Identity and Indianisation: A Case of Conflict Transformation in Mizoram, in *Indian Journal of Public Administration*, Vol. 62, Issue 3: 623-635.

Rustomji, N. K. 1989 Jawaharlal Nehru and the Tribes: Romance and Compassion In *Jawaharlal Nehru, Tribes and Tribal Policy*, Edited by K. S. Singh, Calcutta, Anthropological Survey of India, 27-32.

Chapter - 7

Verrier Elwin and Anthropological Survey of India

Jayanta Sarkar

About 74 years from now (December 2017), Jagdalpur, where we have assembled to look back at the contributions of Verrier Elwin, had witnessed a meeting of two great scholars of anthropology. One of them was Verrier Elwin, the other was none other than Biraja Sankar Guha, who at a later date became the founder Director of the Anthropological Survey of India, the premier institution of anthropological research in our country.

There is no dearth of scholarly writings on the academic contributions of Elwin. However, very little is known about his interest in expanding anthropological research among the tribes of India by other trained anthropologists attached to a government institution.

The meeting under reference and some of his follow up actions were no less significant towards expanding anthropological research in our country.

The referred meeting of Elwin and Guha; the two illustrious personalities culminated in writing a recommendation to the Governor of Central Provinces, Sir Francis Wylie suggesting appointment of a scientific advisor on the aboriginal problems. The recommendation letter was written by Verrier Elwin.

At the time of writing this recommendation letter in 1944, Elwin had already made his presence felt not only among the academician, but also to those who were at the helm of administration, through his two excellent ethnographies; one each on the Baigas and the Agaraias of the then Madhya Pradesh. Besides this, his close association with Mahatma Gandhi during 1928-1932, his active involvement in welfare measures, particularly among the Baiga tribe placed him in a respectable position with regard to the tribal affairs, which was difficult to ignore by the authorities in administration. This a part then being a British scholar, working among the tribes of India Elwinmost likely had some influence in the British administration.

During those years Biraja Sankar Guhawas working as an Anthropologist in the Anthropology section in the Zoological Survey of India. He had been deeply involved in negotiating with the Government of India for establishing a separate research organization curving out from the Zoological Survey of India that would devote entirely to the study of weaker sections of India, particularly tribes (Bhattacharjee and Sarkar 1996:1-2).

Perhaps the special qualities in Elwin brought Guha to Jagdalpur to have a meeting and obtain support from Elwin in his endeavour.

A portion of the letter dated 8th November, 1944 bears strong recommendations for appointing B.S. Guha as scientific advisor on aboriginal problems. Elwin in his letter of recommendations emphasized upon the outstanding qualities, both academic and administrative of Guha. He wrote 'B.S.Guha is indisputably the most eminent of our anthropologists and has the advantage of being both a biologist and sociologist'. Elwin further emphasized on Guha's academic experiences of 20 years in the Zoological Survey of India and his work with Hutton, the Commissioner of Census in 1932 that made Guha familiar with the tribes in every part of India.

Justifying Guha's position Elwin also wrote

'Most useful of all, he (Guha) has had experience of how the Americans handle their problem, for he was engaged by the Smithisonian Institution in the Indian reservations of Colorado and New Mexico. He is a Hindu, but not too much one, and his scientific identity as well as his administrative ability is beyond question'.

Why Elwin had projected Guha as a 'Hindu not too much one' can only be understood, if we look back at the fate of his earlier recommendations to the authorities on the same issue.

In early 1940s Elwin had written a letter to the Governor of Bengal 'suggesting the establishment of the Anthropological Survey of India and recommending B.S. Guha for appointment as Director.

The Governor turned down the proposal and dismissed the claim of Guha as he was considered too good a 'Hindu' (Singh 1991:1). It seems, it is in this context Elwin had described Guha as 'Hindu not too much one' as a clarification.

In a latter year Elwin once again took up the issue. In an editorial to '*Man in India*' (Volume 25 No.1, 1945) he viewed:

'In the judgment of Man in India the time has come for the Government of India to establish a separate Anthropological Survey of India as part of its scheme for post-war reconstruction. The most grandiose plans for scientific research are being considered. Every aspect of man's material environment is to be investigated: only Man himself is being ignored. Yet the lesson of history is emphatic; an exclusive emphasis on the physical sciences and neglect of social, psychological and moral side of human life ends only in destruction. In India, both for the credit of science and for the wellbeing of the population – especially of the tribal population – the establishment of the Anthropological Survey is an urgent necessity.'

Finally, the original proposal for creation of a separate department of 'Ethnological Survey of India; initiated by Nelson Anandale in 1916, pursued by Lt. Col. R.B. Seymour Sewell in 1927, both as Director of the Zoological Survey of India materialized. Guha carried forward this proposal untiringly in which Verrier Elwin also extended his full support. A new department Anthropological Survey of India came into existence as an independent government institution in December 1945 with B.S. Guha as its Officer on Special Duty and then as its first Director from August 01, 1946 (Bhattacharjee and Sarkar 1996:2).

Against this historical backdrop of Elwin's interest in creating an institution like Anthropological Survey of India let me look at his role in the Survey when he actually became associated with this newly created institution.

Elwin in Anthropological Survey of India

Two months after Guha took over charge of the Director, Elwin joined this newly created institute as its Deputy Director on 17th October 1946 for which he constantly advocated and functioned in the same capacity till 1949.

He, however, was not happy in the Survey that he expressed in his autobiography. He wrote "I was not happy in the atmosphere of the Department". Further he stated "lived in Banaras over ayear and had I not been able to go out frequently on tour in the tribal hills, I doubt if I could have stood it. The atmosphere was academic in the worst sense, there were quarrels and jealousies; very little work was done; Banaras Cantonment where we lived was devastatingly tedious—and it was a great relief when the Survey was shifted to Calcutta". Even in Calcutta office he was not happy in the atmosphere of the Department (Elwin 1964:202). In fact he even felt his days in the Anthropological Survey of India as 'most wasted and uncreative' (Guha 1991:191).

Elwin has clarified reason of his unhappiness while in Banaras office. He, however, remained silent about the reasons why the days with the Anthropological Survey of India was 'most wasted and uncreative period', except indicating the non-congenial atmosphere in the Department.

It may be presumed that the kind of anthropology Elwin loved to pursue was incompatible in a government set up. As we know Elwin came to the discipline of Anthropology by choice and not by any formal training. In fact, he himself stated that:

"When we went to Karanjia (a Baiga village in Madhya Pradesh), I had never so far as I remembered- opened book on anthropology: our interest was entirely humanitarian" In 1936 we moved from Karanjia to another village. There was no Chapal in our new settlement. We became interested in anthropology, or rather in what Haddon once called philanthropology (Rustamji 1989: 12 & 17).

Elwin clarified the kind of anthropology he loved. In his words

"The essence and art of anthropology is love. Without it nothing is fertile, nothing is true.

For me anthropology did not mean 'fieldwork'; it meant my whole life. My method was to settle down among the people, live with them, share their life as far as one outsider could, and generally do several books together. ...I did not depend merely on asking questions, but knowledge of people gradually sank in until it was part of me" (Elwin 1964: 142).

In another context he had underlined the necessity of having a true humanist background for the anthropologist. He writes:

"Anthropology is a very big subject, the science of man, man as a whole. We need different kinds of people to study it. We need the scholar trained in pre-history, archaeology, the exact measurement of physical characters, biology, statistics. But we also need some who come from a humanist background and I think it is unfortunate that now a days what I may call the *technical anthropologists* (emphasis mine) look down on the *humanist anthropologists* (emphasis mine) though I must admit that the latter fully return the compliment" (Elwin 1964:141).

Needless to say the kind of anthropology (as outlined above) was difficult to continue in a government set up that had set objectives to achieve within a stipulated period on the basis of grass-root level information generated through application of globally accepted methods and techniques.

Anthropology to a formally trained anthropologist in the Anthropological Survey of India is the science of man that entails understanding human being through holistic approach. A 'technical anthropologist' as termed by Elwin, in course of training learns looking at the human societies in a dispassionate manner setting aside love, affection, sympathy and similar emotions. Such approach leads the anthropologist to unveil the actual truth or near truth of the subject of investigation without any bias.

Before joining the Anthropological Survey of India, Elwin through his excellent descriptive ethnographic accounts on the Baiga and the Agaria tribes of central India and equally exhaustive writing on "*Maria Murder and Suicide*" became known to the world over as philanthropologist, as a great lover of tribes of India. None of these studies were conducted as a part of any government agency.

In fact, he had no idea of working in any government organization that has set pattern of functions. Naturally he was not comfortable in the office of the Survey, then at Banaras. Disliking continued even after the shift of the Survey to Calcutta in 1947 for the same reason.

This is clear from his statement regarding his office days in Calcutta. He wrote "This was the first and only time in my life when I have gone physically from a house to an office" (Elwin 1964:202).

In spite of his disliking conducting 'fieldwork' like other anthropologists, during his tenure in the Anthropological Survey he had been among the Bondo tribe of Koraput district in Orissa along with a research assistant, Asutosh Bhattacharjee, who in latter days emerged as an eminent folklorist of our country. It was Elwin's fourth visit to the Bondo tribe, his first visit to this area dated back to 1943. The area being not easily accessible, approach of the team was not comfortable.

Bhattacharjeeas an assistant researcher had a lot to learn on the field techniques from a scholar of Elwin's stature.

In his Bengali book "*Dandakaranyer Andhakare*" (1974) based on his visit to the Bondo tribe of Orissa, as assistant of Elwin, Bhattacharjee has highly appreciated his senior for his hard work and accommodative nature in very difficult field situations. But, some of his observations on the way Elwin handled the field situations portrait a different dimension of his personality.

Let me cite two examples from Bhattacharjee's writings that to me, mismatch with the then widely accepted image of a philanthropologist and a great 'humanist anthropologist' who had deep love and sympathy for the tribes of India.

While proceeding to Koraput the team had the plan to have night halt at the guest house of Missionary School at 'Salar'. But Elwin was not sure about his acceptability to the Christian Missionaries as he had already dissociated himself from the Christian Mission. Therefore, he advised Bhattacharjee to suppress their actual official identities, Deputy Director and Research Assistant to the authorities of the Guest House. Instead, he preferred to identify himself as 'Director' and Bhattacharjee as 'Deputy Director' of the Anthropological Survey of India. As a matter of fact Elwin has expressed such an opinion in his autobiography. He remarked:

"In India of that time, unless you were an official, rich or had unimpeachable or intimidating introductions, no one take very much note of you. This was evident when we continued our journey for further fourteen miles to Jeypur where a sumptuous guest house was maintained by the Maharaja" (Elwin 1964:181-182).

It is true that in certain field situations an anthropologist has to behave in a way that does not always appear 'ethical' to the profession of anthropology. But then, such a seemingly 'unethical' act by a very eminent personality is likely to convey a wrong message to the junior scholars in the discipline. This also does not fit with his almost a 'cult' personality so far his ideal relation with the tribes of India is concerned.

Bhattacharjee in a different context mentioned that Elwin used to describe Baiga women as "Ugliest women of the world" (1974:108). The same expression in a slightly modified way appears in Elwin's autobiography where he remarked "At first sight a visitor may exclaim that Bondo women are the ugliest he has ever seen" (Elwin 1964: 184).

An instance occurred in the village Bandpada during the same field visit unveil two sides of Elwin's personality. We know him from his previous ethnographies as excellent observer of every aspects of the tribes with whom he used to live for months together. This is a very important quality that every trained anthropologist is expected to have.

While in the Bondo villages, Elwin was eager to closely observe rituals related to the death ceremony of a Bondo child through direct observation in the spot of death and cremation. In his previous three visits, not as a member of the Anthropological Survey of India, he could not observe such an incident. Recording of all rituals related to a death of a child was essential for his book "*The Bondo Highlanders*" (Bhattacharjee 1974:116). Elwin's fourth visit, as apparent from Bhattacharjee's description, was primarily made for detail recording of rituals of a child death. Therefore, Elwin stayed back with his team in the village Bandpada till the death of a child occurred after eight days of completion of other works. This underlines beyond any question about Elwin's integrity towards gathering anthropological information only on the basis of direct observations and not through asking questions or interviewing villagers.

The incident has another part to note.

According to Bhattacharjee after waiting for eight days when Elwin received the message of death of a child, he could not suppress his delight and happiness. He literally jumped leaving his work and rush almost running and told Bhattacharjee 'You may now thank your god, the incident has ultimately happened for which we have been hoping so far. A child has expired in the locality down below this place' (Bhattacharjee 1974: 116). Bhattacharjee was surprised observing his respected senior's delighted expression that was unexpected of a 'humanist anthropologist' of Elwin's stature.

Occurrence of similar instances is not unlikely in case of some other eminent anthropologists. However, how many of them carry an image of 'humanist anthropologists' would remain a subject of debate.

The incident indicates beyond any doubt that for the sake of perfection this great scholar of anthropology, at times had to act in such a way that does not conform to the qualities of an ideal 'humanist anthropologist' like Verrier Elwin.

Elwin left the Anthropological Survey of India in April 1949 as a unhappy scholar just 16 months after his fourth visit to the Bondo tribes, leaving behind not so high impression amongst his colleagues as a 'humanist anthropologist'.

References

BhattacharjeeAsutosh 1976 *DandakaranyerAndhakare* (Bengali), Calcutta, Biswas Publishing House,

Bhattacharya, R. K. & Jayanta Sarkar 1996 *Anthropology of B.S.Guha,*, Calcutta, Anthropological Survey of India

Elwin, Verrier	1964	*Tribal World of Verrier Elwin: An Autobiography,* Oxford University Press, New York and Bombay
Guha, Ramachandra	1999 (2nd impression)	*Savaging the Civilized-Verrier Elwin and the Tribal Question on the Late Colonial India*, New Delhi, Oxford University Press
Rustamji, Nari	1989	*Verrier Elwin: Philanthropologist: Selected Writings*, Shillong, Oxford University Press & North Eastern Hill University
Singh, K.S.	1991	*Introduction, The History of Anthropological Survey of India,* Calcutta, Seagull Books
Singh K. S.	N. D.	*A Perspective on the ASI,* www.india seminar.com/2000/495/ 495K

Chapter - 8

जनजातियों के प्रति वेरियर एल्विन का लगाव

गंगाराम कश्यप

''बस्तर में बसने वालों को बस्तरिया कहा गया जो बस्तर राज के अनुसार व्यवस्था से जुड़े होते थे, इन्हें बस्तीदार का प्रमुख यहां आदिम संस्कृति विरासत के धनी आदिवासी ''जनजाति यहां मूलवासी है, वेरियर एल्विन उन्हीं की विरासत को जो अजूबा था उसे सभी के सम्मुख लायें।

औपनिवेशक ब्रिटिश राजसत्ता के प्रति नास्टेलिजिया रखने वाले के ब्रिटिश नागरिक और विदेशी साम्राज्य वाद से नफरत नाम है। एक अंग्रेज और ईसाई धर्म प्रचारक होकर भी गांधी और उनके राष्ट्रीय आन्दोलन में निष्ठा रखने के कारण जहां तत्कालीन ब्रिटिश राजसत्ता एल्विन को खतरे की घंटी मानकर भारत से बाहर रखने की पक्षधर थी, वहीं आगे चलकर भारतीय स्वाधीनता आन्दोलन से किनारा करके भारत की आदिम जनजातियों के अध्ययन और उनके हितों के प्रति स्वयं को पूर्णतः समर्पित कर देने वाला एल्विन हिन्दुवादी कांग्रेसियों को भी खटकने लगता है। राष्ट्र की मुख्यधारा में आदिम जनजातियों को लाने के नाम पर कांग्रेस ही हिन्दुवादी मान्यताओं और नीतियों का विरोध करने वाला भला क्योंकर राष्ट्रवादियों का सहाय हो सकता था। एक बिशप पिता का पुत्र एल्विन ईसाई धर्मशास्त्रों का गहन अध्येता होने के साथ–साथ अपने जीवन के आरंभ में ईसाइयत के प्रचार के प्रति समर्पित रहा हो, लेकिन आगे चलकर आदिम–जनजातियों के प्राकृतिक धर्म की हिमायत में आदिवासियों के ईसाईकरण के प्रति विरोध पर उतर जाना उसे ईसाई चर्च के लिए भी गले की हड्ड़ी बना देता है। जहां भारत के आदिम आदिवासी समुदायों के लिए एल्विन अंबेडकर सरीखी हैसियत रखता है, वहीं राष्ट्रवाद के हिमायती उसके स्वायत आदिवासी दर्शन और दिशा निर्देशों को राष्ट्र की एकता और अखंडता के लिए खतरा बताते आये है। मध्य भारत और पूर्वोत्तर की आदिम जनजातियों पर पूरी संवेदनशीलता और आदिवासी दृष्टिकोण से 45 के आसपास पुस्तकें और सैकड़ों लेख लिखने वाला वाला यह नेतृत्व शास्त्री ऑक्सफोर्ड़ विश्वविद्यालय का प्रथम श्रेणी का विद्धान था, लेकिन धुर्ये जैसे हिन्दुवादी नेतृत्वशास्त्री एल्विन के लेखन में वैज्ञानिक तटस्थता और विश्लेषण की गहराई नहीं पाते।

वैरियर एल्विन वह अंग्रेज साहब था जो ब्रिटिश साम्राज्य वाद द्वारा किये गये शोषण की प्रतिक्रिया में भारतीय आदिम आदिवासियों की सभ्यता, संस्कृति, और श्रेष्ठता के साथ–साथ उनकी समस्याओं को राज के समक्ष लाकर अपने स्तर पर एक प्रकार से उऋण होना चाहता है, ब्रिटिश साम्राज्यवाद के पापों का प्रायश्चित करना चाहता था। तमाम विवादों और किन्तु–परन्तु के बावजूद आदिवासी बस्तर अंचल के प्रति उनकी निष्ठा संदेह से परे थी। यही कारण है कि स्वतंत्रतोत्तर

भारत के प्रथम प्रधानमंत्री जवाहलाल नेहरू ने एल्विन को आदिवासियों बहुल पूर्वोत्तर विशेषतः नेफा के आदिवासी विषयों का सलाह कार नियुक्त करके उनके निर्देशन पर चलकर अपनी सरकार की आदिवासी विषयक नीतियां बनाई।

आदिम आदिवासियों की परंपरागत पहचान और व्यक्तित्व का संरक्षण करते हुये इन्हें आधुनिक सभ्यता की मानवीय उपलब्धियों के साथ कैसे संबंध करें? इसी सवाल का जबाव है–एल्विन का वृहद लेखन। एल्विन आदिम, आदिवासियों को पिछड़ा और असभ्य मानने के बिल्कुल खिलाफ थे। उनका स्पष्ट मानना था कि आदिवासि समाज और सभ्यता तथा कथित सभ्य कहीं जाने वाली आधुनिक जातियों से कहीं ज्यादा श्रेष्ठ है।

वैरियर एल्विन का पूरा नाम था हैरी वैरियर हालमन एल्विन किन्तु शायद ही वे अपना पूरा नाम प्रयुक्त करते हों। वैरियर एल्विन 29 अगस्त 1902 को डोवर में जन्मा था। एल्विन उच्च मध्यवर्गीय एंग्लों और चर्च के फादरों का परिवार था। वैरियर के दो रिश्तेदार और दो चचेरे भाई तत्कालीन शाही (इम्पेरिअल) प्रशासनीक सेवा में थे। उनके पिता एडमंड हेनरी एल्विन कट्टर ईसाई बिशप थे। पिता के कारण जहां एल्विन में बाईबिल की उपदेश कथाओं और ईसाई धर्म सिद्धांतों के प्रति निष्ठा पनपी, वहीं मां मिन्निए एल्विन ने बालक एल्विन के मन में मसीहाई आदर्श जगाया पिता हेनरी एक तो रहते थे, दूसरा बालक एल्विन के बचपन में ही उनका देहांत होने से मिन्निए एल्विन के व्यक्तित्व ने बालक एल्विन को ज्यादा प्रभावित किया। वैरियर एल्विन परिवार का सबसे बड़ा बच्चा था। वैरियर का एंगलीय बैचारिकता और कर्मकांडीय जकड़ बंदी से मुक्त करने में उनकी नानी फ्लोरा हॉलमन की भूमिका भी बड़ी उल्लेखनीय है।

भारत के कांग्रेसी ए.बी. ठक्कर और जमनालाल बजाज ने भी वैरियर को मध्य भारत के आदिवासियों के बीच काम करने की प्रेरणा दी। इस प्रकार वैरियर ने ठक्कर बाबा, पटेल और बजाज आदि की सलाह और स्वयं की रूचि आदि को ध्यान में रखकर मध्यप्रांत के मंडला जिले के करांजिया गांव में गोंड आदिवासियों के बीच अपना आश्रम किया। मराठी संत तुकाराम भी वैरियर गांधीजी के प्रति निष्ठा रखते हुए भी उनकी आश्रमवादी नियनिष्ठता में क्रमशः अपनी आस्था खोते जा रहें थे। लेकिन कांग्रेस के नेतृत्व में चल रहें स्वाधीनता आन्दोलन में वैरियर अपना योगदान देने को सदा तत्पर रहते थे। वैरियर एल्विन राजनीतिक स्वाधीनता की कांग्रेसी लड़ाई में सक्रिय रूप से हिस्सेदारी नही कर सकते थे अतः अब वे पूर्णतः अपने मित्र शमराओं हिवाले के साथ मिलकर आदिवासियों के कल्याण और उनके अध्ययन में जुट गये।

गोंड आदिवासियों के बीच वैरियर को अपना पहला मित्र एक झाड़–फूंक करने वाला आदिवासी पंडा बाबा मिला था। स्थानीय झारखंडी बोली सीखने के लिए वैरियर इस आदिवासी के संपर्क में आया था। 1938 में वैरियर ऐल्विन ने अपने आश्रम गोंड सेवा मण्डल का नाम परिवर्तित करके "भूमिजन गोंड मंडल" कर दिया ताकि दूसरे आदिवासियों और भूमि से जुड़ी जातियों को इसके दायरे में लाया जा सके।

आदिवासियों के नये–नये समुदायों का अध्ययन करने और सभ्य समाज के सामने उनकी समस्याओं और उनकी वैशिष्टता को प्रस्तुत करने की अदम्व जिजी विषा वैरियर को 1940 में उनकी आदिवासी बाहुल्य बस्तर ले आई। आदिवासियों के हितों के प्रति प्रतिबद्ध बस्तर के दीवान डब्ल्यु० वी० ग्रिगसन की पुस्तक–"The Maria Gonds of Bastar" (1938) ने इस दिशा में निर्णायक प्रेरक भूमिका अदा की थी। बस्तर के तत्कालीन दीवान ई०एस० हाइडे ने वैरियर को बस्तर का सम्माननीय नेतृत्व शास्त्री और जनगणना अधिकारी नियुक्त करके उनकी राह आसान कर दी।

ब्रिटिश प्रशासन द्वारा संरक्षित ''अबुजमांड'' बस्तर के आदिवासियों की स्थिति से वैरियर संतुष्ट नजर आते हैं क्योंकि उनकी सामाजिक, सांस्कृतिक और धार्मिक संस्थाएं और मान्यताएं फलफूल रही थी। बस्तर में परंपरागत आदिवासी अर्थव्यवस्था अभी तक बची हुई थी। बस्तर में रहते हुए वैरियर ने अपनी पहली पुस्तक *मुरिया* आदिवासियों की ''घोटुल'' प्रथा पर केन्द्रीत की। घोटुल इन आदिवासियों की सामाजिक संस्था थी। आदिवासी युवक–युवती घोटुल में रात बिताते हुए अपने समाज की संस्कृति, कला और सामुदायिक परंपराओं में भी दीक्षित हो जाते थे। कोसी की सहायता के बिना घोटुल की रहस्यमयी और बाहरी लोगों के लिए प्रतिबंधित दुनिया का साक्षात्कार वैरियर नहीं सकते थे।

वैरियर एल्विन आदिवासियों की जिंदगी का अध्ययन करने वाले माहिर मानवशास्त्री थे। उनकी किताब ''ए फिलॉस्फी फॉर नेफा(नार्थ इस्ट प्रंटियर एंजेसी –अरूणाचल प्रदेश) को आदिवासियों के विकास का दर्शन कहा जा सकता है, एल्विन लिखते हैं कि हमें आदिवासियों के बारे में आदिवासियों की सोच के मुताबिक होगा, आदिवासीं लोग नुमाइश की चीज या नमूना नहीं है। वे सभी मूलभूत मामलों में ठीक हमारी तरह ही इंसान है। हम उनके हिस्सा हैं और वे हमारा हिस्सा हैं। वे खास हालत में जीते हैं। उनका विकास कुछ खास तर्ज पर हुआ है। उनकी अपनी जीवन दृष्टि है, काम करने का उनका अपना खास अंदाज है।

वैरियर एल्विन ने छत्तीसगढ़ बस्तर के अबुझमांड आदिवासी समाज की महिलाओं के प्रायवेट पार्ट के संबंध में जो बातें लिखी हैं वह हमें एक दूसरी दुनिया में ले जाती हैं, उन्होंने अपनी किताब ''द मिथ्य ऑफ मिडल इंडिया'' में ऐसी बातों का खुलासा किया हैं। बस्तर रियासत के एडमिनिस्टेरटर रहे वेरियर एल्विन घोटुल के बारे में जो कुछ जाना जो कुछ समझा और जो कुछ देखकर महसूस किया उसे बाकी दुनिया के सामने वैरियर एल्विन ने कुछ इस तरह पेश किया कि घोटुल की रंगीनियों को लेकर अजीब–सा, स्वप्न संसार लोगों ने रच डाला। निःसंदेह वैरियर एल्विन को आदिवासियों का अंबेडकर कहा जाता है। मर्मज्ञ लेखक संस्कृति के पोषक हो, शोधार्थी हो, खोजकर्ता हो या सैलानी या फिर यायावर सभी के लिए घोटुल एक अच्छा विषय माना जाता है। बस्तर के अबुझमांड से लेकर बस्तर के अंतिम दक्षिण छोर में कोन्टा की ढलान तक में बसे आदिवासियों चाह मुरिया, धुरवा, परजा, भतरा, या फिर हल्बा सभी के बीच घोटुल के रूप में लोकप्रिय है।

यधपि वनांचल बस्तर एक पिछड़े क्षेत्र के रूप में जाना जाता है। लेकिन देश की जैव सांस्कृतिक विविधता का एक बड़ा हिस्सा यहाँ विद्यमान है। इसकी सांस्कृतिक समृद्धि अपूर्ण है। इस अंचल की बोलियों यथा धुरवी, हल्बी, भतरी, गोड़ी और दोंरली आदि में जनमानस की आशा–आकांक्षो और उसकी सृजनात्मकता विस्तृत रूप से प्रकट हुई है। बस्तर की बोलियों और उनके साहित्य की छद्‌महीन और अकृत्रिम अभिव्यक्तियां आज के औपचारिक ललित साहित्य के अध्ययेताओ को भी अचरज में डाल सकती है। इस तरह बोलियों की समृद्धि को रेखांकित कर लोक साहित्य के विस्तार से हिन्दी साहित्य के विकास में निश्चित रूप से बेहतर होगा। बस्तर के आदिवासियों ने चाहा था कि ब्रिटिश लोगों को बस्तर से बाहर ''बोहार' दें क्योकि वे उनकी संस्कृति को अपवित्र कर रहे थे। औपचारिक शिक्षा और बाहरी सम्पर्क से पूरी तरह बस्तर शून्य था किन्तु उसने आम लोगों को जगाया और समाज के सभी वर्गो का विश्वास और समर्थन प्राप्त किया है।

जिस दिन बस्तर के जनजातियों में लिखने, पढ़ने और चिंतन करने की भूख जागृत होगी, उसी दिन से इनकी समस्त समस्याओं का अंत होना प्रारंभ हो जायेगा। ग्लासफर्ड, एगन्यू एवं इलियट ऐसे अंग्रेज अधिकारी थे जिन्होंने मॉ बाप की भांति आदिवासियों का पालन किया उनके

हितों की रक्षा की, जो शिक्षा के इतिहास के विकास में एक अतुलनीय योगदान है। जनजातियों की शिक्षा के विकास में चुनौतियों को स्वीकार कर प्रस्तुत शोध पत्र इसी कमी को पूरा करने का प्रयास है।

संदर्भग्रंथ सूची

01. केदारनाथ ठाकुर (संस्करण–2012) ''बस्तर भूषण'' शताक्षी प्रकाशन, मार्केट सेन्टर, चौबे कालोनी रायपुर (छ०ग०)

02. हीरालाल शुक्ला (तृतीय संस्करण– 2009) ''बस्तर का मुक्ति संग्राम 1774–1910'', मध्यप्रदेश हिन्दी ग्रंथ अकादमी भोपाल।

03. रामकुमार बेहार (1995) बस्तर एक अध्ययन ''मध्यप्रदेश हिन्दी ग्रंथ अकादमी, रवीनद्रनाथ ठाकुर मार्ग भोपाल।

Chapter - 9

The Agaria, Varrier Elwin

Divya Bharti

The present paper is based on the work on "The Agaria" by Varrier Elwin in the year 1942, published by Oxford University Press, India. The Agaria are the iron-smelters and blacksmiths of the Central provinces of India, presently the States of Madhya Pradesh, Chhattisgarh and Maharashtra. They are most numerous and characteristic in the Maikal Hills and in the lonely zamindaris of Bilaspur. But an Agarian belt may be traced all the way from Dindori to Neterhat. The Agaria probably means a worker in 'ag' or 'fire'. The Agaria burn charcoal and extract iron from ore in small clay furnace. The Agaria use bellows of a particular kettledrum pattern and work with their feet. The Agaria worship tribal gods or demons, who are clearly associated with the ancient Asura, such as Lohasur, Koelasur and Agyasur. The Agaria have an elaborate mythology of which the heroes are Logundi Raja, Jwala Mukhi and Kariya Kuar, but they are ignorant of the Hindu Vulcan, Twasntri or Vishwakarma, the artisan of the gods. Who made the fiery weapon Agueyastra and revealed the Sthapatya –Veda, the science of mechanics and architecture.

The Agarias are short, square-headed, with broad heavy noses, thick-lipped, very dark in colour, with straight hair, the features are coarse. They are dull and heavy. The Agaria are a very hard working people. During the field work Elwin has spent more exhausting days than in their company. He further states that the long tamp through the forest, the cutting of the trees and the tedious and smoky business of making charcoal, the journey home with laden baskets- this alone is no light labour. The pits where iron may be dug are often in the most inaccessible places and required long climbs in the hills, followed by digging with small picks in a confined space. The work of the smithy is heavy enough. He watched the household rise at three or four in the morning and work on till ten or eleven without food or refreshment. The occupation of Agaria are fairly clean and they keep their houses and smithies in good order. They are absorbed in their business. "The Agaria cares not for going here and there, all his intoxication is for his hammer. He is lord in his little smithy. The tongs are yours, the hammer is yours. Hammer away just as you like. Love affairs may be ruinous to his trade. If the hearth is abroad, who will care for the smithy?

Elwin described in his first portion of the book on the origin of the tribe and Agaria belt. He further described that the word Agaria probably means a worker in 'ag' or fire. 'Ag' is the root of Agni the Hindu god of fire of Agyasur, the tribal demon who was born in flame. Agaria belt starts from moving eastward from Mandala. In the Dindoritahsil at the east of that district we find the Patharia Agaria; these may be regarded as standard Agaria. Moving further east to Bilaspur there is Kalha Agaria in foot hills of the Maikal range and in the remote zamindaris of the east. To the south are the God-Dhuka Lohar of Raipur and the Gondi speaking Agaria of Durg. All these are obviously related to the Mandala Agaria. North from Mandla, there are Patharia in Rewa State, some of whom have migrated to Mirzapur. Turning east again we pass through Surguja, Udaipur and Jashpur states into Chotanagpur where we finally reach the Asur groups of tribes; traditionally primitive iron-workers of whom one branch still bears the name Agaria. In Udaipur the blacksmith are called Chokh (which they themselves say is synonymous with Agaria) Mahali or Mahali Lohar. All these tribes have a tradition of the name Agaria and sometimes use it. They erect the same general type of smithy, build the same kind of kiln, use bellows of the same pattern and work with their feet. They all make virgin iron and believe in its power.

In this book Elwin is inclined to think that on the whole the Agaria (known by different names in different places) are ultimately one tribe and something more than a branch or a collection of branches of another tribes or inasmuch as they have the same magic. He further suggests that the Agaria and Asur are descendants of tribes which are represented by the Asura of Sanskrit literature and it is possible that this ancient Asur tribe invaded the Munda country in Chotanagpur, were driven back by the Mundas rallying under the standard of their deity Sing Bonga in to the very border of Bihar (at present Jharkhand) and thence spread west and north through Surguja and Udaipur, Korea and the north of Bilaspur and fettering down to Raipur, until in the Maikal Hills they found a congenial home and a plentiful supply of iron.

The second portion of the book is concerned with the term 'the Asura', Gazetteer and brief organization of the community. Their possible descent from the pre-Aryan Asura is carefully examined and the probability of this descent is quite rightly shown in the book. On the other hand cultural life, religion, customs, etc. vary so much from named sub group to named sub group. Whether the term, Agaria should not be used simply to designate all non-Hindu iron –worker of the area. The chapter on social organization could not help in clarifying the problem.

The main theme of the Elwin book, revolve around the cultural theme of iron, whose role in social organization, myth, magic and economic etc. are carefully examined. The Agaria has shown that he is as well able to present the life of a primitive craftsman and iron-smelter as that of the primitive hunter, agriculturist and poets.

The Agaria myth gives tantalizing glimpses of an earlier technique of iron-smelting. Elwin describes that the making of fire and charcoal the manufacture of bellows, tongs and hammers; the use of change without flux etc. are explained in ancient myth. Religious observance finds their sanction in these stories. The worship of each of the special Agaria demons originates in historical moments and practical necessities; the wind must be honoured the bellows work, fire must be worshipped, or the coal will remain dead and black. The duty of ancestor worship is established in a vivid story from Raipur region.

Elwin in his book "The Agaria" has given a good account of few iron-smelting furnace used by the Agaria community in central India about eighty years ago. Kothi or Bhathi was the term used by the Agaria for their furnace which was a cylindrical kiln. At the top of mouth was made to introduce a blast of air into the furnace. A flame or an aperture was also made for slag to flow out. To push the change special arrangement was made at the top of the kiln called *machan.* It was an inclined bamboo platform on which charcoal an ore could be heaped. The platform was made to slide down to push the change into the furnace.

It is mentioned that the Agaria furnace which was still operating at Raipur region by the end of last century as the simplest form to be found in the world. It was a semi circular construction built of clay and sun dried bricks. Bellows could be operated by a man sitting in a trench made in front of the furnace. The top opening of the furnace acted as a chimney. Separate arrangements were made to tap the slag and to blast the air through two tiers. Charcoal and ore were poured alternately at regular intervals. After certain length of time iron bloom was collected from the bottom.

Elwin introduced to a tribe "The Agaria" that has lived every moment of their lives for an ancient craft and by a living myth. The marriage of myth and craft as the author tells us is the central theme of the book and gives the Agaria great significance. This study of Agaria myths is one of absorbing interest. Elwin shows how the myths lie at the root of the social relations and the religious and economic structure of Agaria society. These myths reveal the fundamental ideas regarding life and nature and sentiments attaching to these ideas in the Agarias minds. Although the age-old rituals of an Agaria are generally found to be a more or less dramatization. Among the Agaria, we can see the strength of the fears which may so easily gather around inanimate objects. In the folktales we see these objects endowed with life and speech and acting in sometimes hostile, sometimes friendly or a way on human affairs. It is a very common for a house which has been the scene of ill-luck or death to be deserted; a bed on which someone has died must not be used again....The Agaria stores suggest some such quite obvious and simple origin for totemism. Someone is bitten by a horse and his children first avoid and then honour the horse so that they will not be bitten again.

The marriage of myth and craft as the another portion in the central theme of the book; Elwin says that "the Agaria are a people absorbed in their craft and their material, they seem to have little life apart from the roar of the bellows and the clang of hammer upon iron. Some of the principal task of iron-smelting done by the Agaria. During the day they collect ore and making charcoal. In evening as the sun sinks to its setting the women of the house go to prepare the smithy for tomorrows work. They remove the lumps of ore from the baskets and break them up into small pieces and clean them of earth. Then they roast them in an ordinary fire of wood and bark. Then a girl brings a basket full of *Kodon chaff* and empties it on the left of the furnace, makes a pile of *hari* clay near it and to the right of the furnace makes piles of sand, earth and the red dust from the broken ore. The iron tools are put in place and one or two water pots. Every thing is prepared with great exactness; the smithy is swept cleaned and tidied. Finally a *mantra* for working the furnace so that good iron will come.

This is the only seminal anthropological study on Agaria by Elwin in the year 1930s, where indigenous iron smelting was recorded in its social context while it was still prevalent. Even after half century ago, the Agaria iron smelting communities are recognized as a good iron ore area for mining by the colour of the site. It may be pointed out that the Agaria people used haematite or magnetite ore, which sometimes occur in association with lateritic rocks or sometimes found in weathered exposures of other rocks. (V. Elwin, 1942 pp.173-176).

The work on Agaria tribe of iron-smelters and blacksmiths found in central India, Elwin shows that though the Agaria shares customs and habits with other tribes, they have a highly developed totemic civilization with its own distinctive mythology affecting every aspects of life. Elwin also scrutinizes the history, demographics, magic and economy in order to provide an analysis of the richness of the craft and culture of this slowly decaying society.

The book revolve around the cultural theme of iron, whose role in social organization, myth, magic, economics etc. is carefully examined. The chapter on craft is most meticulous, and microscopically accurate in detail and extremely satisfying. The term Agaria, used by Elwin as a general designation, covers numerous groups of iron-workers in the studied area. Their descent from Asura is carefully examined and the probability of this descent is quite right.

Lastly.....

Elwin's ethnographic work conveys a personal vision that contrasts the academic standpoint of the formal impersonal and the unemotional. What stands out is Elwin's overarching love and respect for the tribal people, epitomized by his choice to live with them and to share their lot. The appreciation was mutual as the observations recorded by people that knew Elwin well convey a picture of the esteem and love that he inspired... For example, he was widely and affectionately known in the village of Mandla district as 'Bara Bhai' (elder brother in the local dialect in Hindi) observed that there was no standoffish, but an atmosphere of perfect trust and friendliness between the tribal where he worked.

Elwin is without doubt our foremost authority on the so-called aboriginal tribes of the Central provinces of India; his information is sound, detailed and reliable.

Reference

Elwin, Varrier. 1942. The Agaria. Oxford University Press. India.

Chapter - 10

Varrier Elwin and Bastar, Chhattisgarh

Rajesh Roshan

Henry Varrier Holman Elwin was born on 29th August 1902 at Dover, Kent (England). One of the dramatis personae of Indian Anthropology, Elwin came to India in 1927 to join the newly formed *Christa Seva Sangh,* an Anglican Order in Pune (Maharashtra). During the period from 1928 to 1931 Elwin was involved in the national movement an associated with the tribal peoples in India. He lived nearly thirty years of his life with the tribals of India and during this period he observed their life and undertook research on them. In 1946, he was appointed as Deputy Director, Anthropological Survey of India, Kolkata. In the 1950s Elwin was appointed as Adviser to the Governor of Assam on tribal affairs. From 1920s to 1930s, Elwin wrote numerous books, poetry, story, folklore and anthropological and applied anthropological issues, autobiography, natives etc. From the list of his anthropological books, he wrote 26, practically all on tribal peoples of India, 14 of them monographs (mostly solid, well-written accounts), seven general works, two novels and two anthropological studies written with his old friend and collaborator Shamrao Hivale. He spent the better part of three decades doing anthropological studies of Indian tribesmen, most of the time living in or very nearby tribal villages. He produced the largest corpus of data on Indian ethnography which has come from a single hand, and indeed he was one of the most prolific anthropological writers of recent times.

In the year 1940 Elwin was appointed honorary ethnographer to Bastar State. He moved to Bastar in the season of autumn in search of new tribes to write about. They built a home overlooking the spectacular Chitrakot falls on the Indravati river. Over the next three years, they spent the winter months roaming around Bastar, taking to Gonds, Murias, Marias, Koyas and other communities of the region. In hot weather and monsoon, they stayed at home, where Elwin wrote on a desk that faced the Chitrakot falls themselves.

Elwin has written about the beauty of Bastar, according to British Library in London, copy of Elwin's 'Journal of a Tour in Southern Maria Country, November 1941 to March 1942.' States that the *beauty of the countryside, with villages 'surrounded by hills with yellow fields of sirson(mustard) in the foreground and forest everywhere'*. Elwindedicated his life to live with the Maria and Muria tribe of Bastar. Elwin found the tribals of Bastar gentle friendly with no desire for property or power. They were, he wrote to his mother in London. The life led by the Bastar tribals was a great lesion to the world at this time.

Affording his seminal work on the unique institution of the Ghotul among the Murias of Bastar region and understanding the high incidence of murder and suicide among the Maria of Bastar region. Elwin bases his investigation on a hundred homicides committed by Maria of Bastar region. Starting from the police and court –records he studied each cases by taking to the offender, whenever he or she was alive members of his family and to relatives and friends of the victim. Elwin reported that the suicide sex ration among the tribal population of Bastar, 96 per cent of committed suicide by men (Elwin, 1943:48). Elwin notes that the Maria had a bad reputation for violence and drunkenness (Elwin, 1943:37), which was reflected in a homicide rate three times more compared to Gotul Muria.

Elwins data, taken from a sample of 50 cases for which he had detailed information displays a bi-modal distribution. Young adults comprised 42 per cent of the cases. Older adults were 32 per cent of Elwins sample (Elwin, 1943:49). The most common precipitating reason for suicide among the Maria was quarrel with kin. In normally half of the sample (46 per cent) are antagonisms between husband and wife, an intolerable home, resentment at a rebuke or regret for harsh behaviour to someone loved where identified as the antecedent causes (Elwin, 1943: 58). Elwins remarks that the majority of suicides seem to be have caused by a desire to escape from a physical or domestic situation that had become intolerable (Elwin, 1943:58). The large part of Elwin works on Maria and suicide is a detailed analysis of the causes for murder and a Maria believes himself justified in killing his wife (or her lover) caught in the act of adultery. Many of the Maria homicides states Elwin will be recognized not as anti-social crimes, but as expressions of the strongly social instincts of the murderer.

Elwin lived nearly thirty years of his life with the tribals and during this period he observed their life and undertook research to them. In Bastar region regarding the dance of Maria Elwin described (Elwin, 1943:18-19) that the dance as a "superb spectacle". The men in their splendid head dress of Bison Horns and carrying their long drums, move in a large circle with a great variety of turns and changes. The Bison charge and fight each other, pick up rings or leaves on the points of their horns and chase the girl dancer. The girl with a dancing stick in her right hand, form a long line and go round and through the men dancers with many different movements and steps, masked mummers, clowns dressed in straw naked acrobats with enormous genitalia add to the gaiety of the scene. Elwin further remark that "this head dress and the dance is the sole expression of the Bison Horn Maria aesthetic sensibility". Everything they have to say goes into the dance. Typically Elwins hyperbolic enthusiasm for tribal culture, such exaggeration serves to indicate the bias towards the exterior which marks the identification of Bastar Gonds.

During his field work in Bastar region he visited every villages in the area. In a village named Kaklur he attended a tribal dance held in a most romantic spot. The boys were attractively dressed, with 'tassels of red woollen cowries on their *topis',* while the girls were especially beautiful and graceful in their movements. Afterwards Elwin and their hosts drank leaf cups of *Landa,* one of the most potent drinks known to mankind which tasted like liquid dynamite, yet filled one with a spirit of universal benevolence.

Elwinhas also works on the Muria of Bastar region.Varrier Elwin visited the Muria intermittently between 1935 to 1942. The Muria are one of the most famous tribes of India. Their fames extends beyond the boundaries of anthropology into the realm of the Indian public imagination. This position of renown is largely the result of the highly affectionate attention paid to the Muria in both scholarly publication and the popular press by Varrier Elwin. Even now, 70 years after Elwin exuberant affirmations of Muria morality and culture, this group still epitomizes for many non-tribal Indians, the noble savage part of their image of life. This is often articulated by referring to the Muria as exemples of aesthetic and sensual expression which is found lacking in non-tribal culture. More than many any other aspect of Muria society, it is Ghotul (Youth dormitory) which is the source of this high profile image. During this time he collected much ethnographic data. Paying particular attention to the institution of the adolescent "village dormitory" the Ghotul and its relation to Muria culture. Although spending little time in any village, Elwin visited some 347 Ghotul and collected 2000 case histories of Muria individuals through the use of scheduled intended to related Ghotul organization and activities to marriage, family organization, ritual and other aspects of Muria life.

Much like Margaret Meads early research in the South Pacific Elwins writings championed what he saw as the untrammelled yet not irresponsible adolescent sexuality and cultural vigor of the Muria Ghotul as a healthy antidote to twentieth century Hindu Victorianism. It would have been to his chagrin had Elwin realized that this promotions would attract as much or more prurient as admiring interest in the Muria. On the other hand, perhaps he did so realize or 'uplifer' as well as against the pre textual and disruptive visits of the minor administrative officials actuality intent on his desire "to enjoy as the Indian English euphemism has it". At any rate it has become a standard Muria response to strangers' in quarries to deny strongly the prevalence of any sexuality in connection with the Ghotul.

The Muria Ghotul was "an ideal method of training the youth of the tribe in the civic virtues in eliminating jealously and in teaching everyone to live together as a family" (Elwin, 1943, 38-39). Membership in the Ghotul of Muria villages is composed of unmarried preadolescent and adolescent boys and girls who after initiation into Ghotul life, assume graded responsibilities associated with Ghotul titles and related to an internal division of labour. As a corporate group, the Ghotul membership is important in the performance of village rituals; the Ghotul compound is imbued with ritual significance associated with its mythical founder, the culture here is Lingo Pen. Elwin contends that Ghotul experience is regarded by the Muria as a means of co-education for activities important to adult life and that it results in a healthy adjustment and a satisfying natural way of life.

Victor Turner (1967:181) stated that Elwin's approach to research was that of an eclectic ethnographer rather than that of a social analyst. He was, as well a romantic. The value of his work to anthropologist lies in the data& his works provide rather than in the use he himself makes of it. The Ghotul itself is described but not systematically related to the socio-cultural milieu in which it exists. The different types of Ghotul are not analysed either in terms of distribution throughout the area or with respect to other social variables. Elwin indicates that children of different endogamous groups in the village participate equally in the Ghotul, but he gives no description of such groups for particular villages.

Varrier Elwin's research in Bastar focused on Muria and their institution (the Ghotul). Ramchandra Ghua (1999), observed that "Training the young in the art of sex and the conventions of social life, the Ghotul was also a stimulus to artistic expression. Its walls were painted with models of motiaries and tigers, its pillars carved with animals fighting or trials dancing.... The art of combing and comb-making was highly developed". Muria prepared cat's footprint, necklace, rat's bead belt, two horn combs, wooden spears apparatus for extracting toddy juice etc. for their use in daily life.

According to A. Prasad the Muria and the Ghotul is a triumphant illustration of Elwin's modern representation of tribal life style. The Ghotul is an arena of encounter and friendship of play, music and dance with chelik (boy) and motiari (girl). The life in a Ghotul was regulated. Chelik and motiari were expected to come everyday, to keep the dormitory clean, to share in the common labour. In defending the Ghotul from the obvious criticism of the so-called civilized world. Elwin pointed out that there were virtually no cases of venereal disease among the Muria. Prostitution, rape and child marriage, so visibly present in more advanced societies were all to absent in Muria community. Muria are trained handicraft as presented and recorded by Elwin is a clear mark of modernity as there is an extra ordinary presence of 'newness'. Moreover Ghotul life is a distinct departure from the age-old traditional life style of the tribal people.

Varrier Elwin, tribal reserve area and Bastar

A self-taught anthropologist Elwin's ideas and research had an overwhelming influence on Nehru's vision and policies on India's tribes. Pt. Nehru had a liking and faith in Elwin and many of policies relating to the tribes were based on the thoughts of Varrier Elwin.

An ordained priest in the Pune (Maharashtra) based Christa Seva Sangh, Elwin gave up his commitment to proselytize and dedicated his life to research and to help preserve tribal life and culture. In his later writings, Elwin took care to stress that he was not against assimilation of tribals into the mainstream. He only wanted such assimilation to occur at a pace and on terms that suited the tribals. Varrier Elwin has always been associate with the issue of the integration of tribal societies with the greater Indian society. Such an integrationist stance was initially opposed by him, when he proposed that tribals should be left alone instead of being constantly interfered with and acculturated. This gave him the national parks for trials. Such national parks he called 'tribal reserve area'. Elwin felt that the tribals are a very special people who must be kept separate from the rest of Indian society in order to conserve and preserve their ethnic identity, their social structure, their culture and their way of life. He strongly believes that contact with the rest of India would place the tribals in an unequal contest with the non- tribal people and would expose them to virtually unlimited exploitation.

In a way this is a policy which the American government followed vis-à-vis their own indigenous American population, who were confined to earmarked reserves and kept from assimilation into mainstream American society. It is almost as if these people were an endangered species of wild life whose habitat had to be shut away from ordinary society. The fact that mainstream America was the guilty party and that the American Indians were an endangered species because of threat of extermination held out by the new settlers seems to have been lost sight of.

In Bastar the size of the district, its remoteness, the density of the forests and the entirely Gond tribal nature of its people had kept the district fairly isolated from the rest of Chhattisgarh and adjoining states. However, roads were built, settled administration did penetrate the region and a degree of interaction between tribal and non-tribal did take place. So long as the pace was evolutionary it did not present many problems. However two major development took place which completely transformed the district. The first was settlement of large number of refugees from East Pakistan (Now Bangladesh) in the Dandakaranya area of Bastar and adjoining Koraput district of Orissa. In Bastar the largest such development has in the Pakhanjor area of the north and west of the district. Vast areas of forest land were cleared and whereas the tribal, were not allotted land the refugees were settled on it, thus causing simmering resentment amongst the tribals. The second major development was the discovery of what is perhaps the finest iron ore in the world, the blue dust of Bailadila. The forest of this region, which is drained by the Dankani and Shankhani rivers, represented semi moist deciduous and evergreen forests of Central India at their climax. It has been reported that as late as the second half of the nineteenth century Bailadila was an abode of the one horned Indian rhinoceros. The people of Bailadila were very backward as their exposures to non-tribal society were negligible. Suddenly into this region was unleased the National Mineral Development Corporation (NMDC) with its huge machines such as excavators, front end loaders, dumphers, large drilling rigs and explosives for blasting. The tribals had never seen such equipment's, they were quite unprepared for the influx of a whole army of workers from outside the region. Virtually in the twinkling of an eye their forests were destroyed, their land pitted and cratered, their rivers polluted, their homesteads gone and their farms rendered useless. They received some cash compensation but they were totally untrained to handle cash and soon the money was gone. That can only be called an act of barbarism, the tribals were rendered homeless, without work, their tribal society structures broke down as the people were scattered. This is the inevitable fate of any group of people.

Which finds that the cocoon around it has been shattered and the people rendered helpless by the relentless blows of external factors. Indian government not adopted a policy of keeping the tribals in designated reserves known as Tribal Reserve Area nor does constitution allow it to deny any Indian the opportunity for progress and therefore Varrier Elwins thoughts ultimately proved fatal to tribal society.

Varrier Elwin in his "The Tribal World of Varrier Elwin" writes that: I have said that it is not easy to speak of a culture of the Gonds as they are today. And yet what is culture? It is not something moreover he liked to describe the philosophy of his life as the philosophy of love. The talismanic spell of ecological romanticism is resounded in the own voice... Love and the duties it imposes is the real lesson of the forest. Among very poor and exploited people there was the need to maintain those imponderable values that give dignity to the life of man; to restore them their self-respect, the feeling of being loved...There was the need for reverence, reverence for all life. 'Reverence for all life' is the prime essence of all forms of ecological romance. Elwin's description, receding and representation of aboriginal people and their surroundings strictly followed this revelation. There is a very true culture that depends mainly on character, and in this sense the Gonds are highly cultured people. They have royal blood in their veins and even the poorest and simplest of them has a strength of purpose a dignity, redeeming sense of humours and a courage in the face of disasters life that anyone may fancy.

Varrier Elwin found the Bastar tribal at peace but at present they are in stress and strain. Outsiders who occupied their area and the original settlers became landless in their own land. Growth of industrialization has greatly affected indigenous livelihood and caused displacement from their habitats. Big industries had grabbed fertile and forest land. The ecological niches provide food, shelter, fuel, medicine etc. similarly the potential strength of the ecology support their life line. The right of the people was known as *nistar* rights were an important arrangement devised to meet the survival needs of the people and ensure in return that the communities conserved the forest. But due to large way of deforestation in the area the surviving strategies of indigenous people are fading. Lastly each village is split down the middle, clan pitted against clan, family against family. Had Elwin seen these?

Varrier Elwin has played crucial role as advisor to the colonial and native princely rulers on various tribal issues. Pt. Nehru appointed him as anthropologists' adviser to the government of India implanting the adivasis welfare programms particularly in northeast. Thus both Nehru and Elwin have contributed to the tribals development discourse in India. In Nehruian poverty formulation, the concept of caste, tribe and minority were put on a common platform. But Elwins concept of poverty was strictly confined to the tribals. His approach thereof resorted to multi-pronged interventions. On one such occasion, he described tribal poverty to a large audience in the Rotary Club of Bombay. He asked for some chapatti and fish curry made like city style. They give it to him and he ate half of it with great enjoyment then wrapped the remainder up in the left plate and gave it to the jailor telling him that this little son was waiting outside the prison door. The boy had never tasted such a delicacy but he should have it now. In Elwin opinion 'poverty is not only the epitome of material deprivation'; it is also an indicator of a lapse of human compassion. For Elwin it was the colonial rulers, Hindu money lenders and landlords who uprooted the tribes from their indigenous production system and put them into the peasant production network.

Notes

* Rajesh Roshan. Research Officer (SS). Office of the Registrar General, India, Social Studies Division, North Wing, First Floor, Sewa Bhawan, R.K. Puram New Delhi.

Reference cited

Ali, Irshad. 2011. Dr. Varrier Elwin and Assam. The NEHU Journal. Vol. IX. No. 2.

Bera, Gautam. K. 2008. Passage through aboriginal India: Anthropological profile of Varrier Elwin. The Oriental Anthropological Series III. Allahabad. The Oriental Institute of Cultural and Social Research

Elwin, Varrier. 1947. The Muria and their Ghotul. Oxford University Press. London.

Elwin, Varrier. 1950. Maria Murder and Suicide. Oxford University Press, Bombay.

Elwin, Varrier. 1951. The Tribal Art of Middle India: A Personal Record. Oxford University Press.

Elwin, Varrier. 1958. Leaves from the Jungle: Life in a Gond Village. Oxford University Press.

Elwin, Varrier. 1964. The tribal world of Varrier Elwin: An Autobiography. Oxford University Press. New York and Bombay.

Gregory, C.A. Chhattisgarh: At the crossroads. Australian National University and University of Manchester.

Guha, R. 1999. Savaging the civilized: Varrier Elwin, His Tribals and India. Oxford University Press. Delhi.

Prasad, A. 2011. Against Ecological Romanticism: Varrier Elwin and Making of an Anti-Modern Tribal Identity. 2nd Ed. Three Essays.

Turner victor, W. 1967. Aspects of Saora ritual and Shamanism. In the craft of social anthropology. A.L. Epstein, ed. Tavistolk Publication. London.

Obituary on Varrier Elwin. 1964. An obituary and bibliography published in MAN LXIV July-August. P.P. 114-115.

http://www.thehansindia.com/posts/index/2015-05-18/Adivasi-Welfare-Relevance-of-Elwin%E2%80%93Nehru-model-151629.

http://www.southasiaanalysis.org/node/1357.

Chapter -11

Nutritional Status of the Murias of Bastar, Chhattisgarh – a well discussed tribe by Verrier Elwin

Sanjay Shukla

Introduction

Verrier Elwin popularly called by central Indian tribals as "Bara Bhai" among the Muria of Bastar. Tribal communities in independent India did not make any sense, because the facts and figures of independence did not bring freedom from poverty and exploitation to some extent even today, as they continue to remain alienated from the resources on which their survival depends. The study of nutrition and culture under the helm of applied and action Anthropology in India started from the time of British colonial administration and name of Verrier Elwin comes in the front row with Russell and Hiralal, Grigson and Hutton and many such stalwarts who not only undertook administration but contributed in understanding the tribal communities of India.

The integrated concept of nutrition and health in human society is very old. Thought not attempted the approach of Varrier Elwin to study health and nutrition had definitely been in the direction of culture, environment and its relation to food.

In India Tribals, in general are inhabited in divergent physical, biological and socio-cultural environments, often lacking modern health care facilities. While health is an important aspect of development, the nutritional status of a population is considered to be the vital measure of health. Malnutrition has emerged as a major health problem of many tribal groups (Rao et al., 1986: Basu et al., 1989) In view of this and the National Healthcare Policy (NHP) studies on nutritional status have been asserted of extreme importance. As per national health policy it is vital for the planners and policy makers to understand the food and nutritional status of triabal population in order to evaluate and implement effective measure for the well being of these tribal populations. Informations in this direction among Bastar tribes are lacking, therefore the present study is aimed to assess the nutritional and health status of Muria tribals of Bastar.

The word "Muria" under study means aboriginal (Elwin, 1991) and they are subgroup of Gond and may have been derived from the word "Mur" meaning "root'. Murias are well built, coarse black hair and belong to proto-Austroloid group. The Muria are generally cultivators and they practise settled cultivation. They also work as agricultural labourers and daily wage worker in government agencies.

Material and Methods

A total of 50 Muria adult males and 50 females aged 20-45 years are randomly selected from Karli village. Weight (in kg), height, arm circumference and chest grith (in cm) are recorded. From these measurements Weight-Height index (Roy et al., 1982) Pigent index (Ivanovsky, 1923) are calculated.

Results and Discussion

Mean values of different measurements and indices are presented in (Table 1), while the subsequent tables show the distribution of measurement and indices.

Mean weight of the male and female are 47 kg and 41.96kg respectively. The body weight distribution (Table 2) indicates that 66 per cent of the male fall within the range of 42 to 55.5 kg. Average heights of male and female are found as 158.9 cm and 150.7 cm respectively. Mean arm circumference in male and female are observed as 22.31 cm and 22.38 cm respectively while chest circumference in male is 76.38 cm. Mean weight-height value of the Muria male and female are 29.51 and 27.70. Index value below 30 is an indication of under nutrition (Roy and Roy 1982). In the present study 66 per cent males and 90 per cent of the females have the index value below 30 indicating high prevalence of under nutrition (Table 3). Ivanosky (1923) has opined that pignet index value above 31 is an indication of very weak physique. Among the Muria male, average pignet index value has been observed as 32.48 which can be classified as 'very weak' physique and 70 per cent of them having the index above 31 indicating week physique of the community (Table 4).

Body mass index (Table 5) indicates that 48 per cent male and female in chronic energy deficiency stage. BMI value less than 18.5 is an indication of chronic energy deficiency syndrome and above 25 is an indication of obesity (Gamowil 1982).

Table 1: Mean values of anthropometric measurements and indices the Muria

	Male (N=50)		*Female (N=50)*	
Measurements	*Mean*	*SD*	*Mean*	*SD*
Height (cm)	158.86	5.38	150.68	4.9
Weight (kg)	47	4.58	41.96	3.88
Arm Circumference (cm)	22.31	4.61	22.38	1.3
Chest Girth (cm)	76.38	2.69	not Taken	not Taken
Pigent Index	32.48	5.51	not Taken	not Taken
	29.51	2.48	27.7	2.59
Body Mass Index	18.62	1.46	18.5	1.9

Source: primary, data – 1995.

Table 2: Percentage distribution of body weight of the Muria

Range (Kg)	*Male (N=50)*	*Female (N = 50)*
	Percent	*Percent*
Up to 34.5	0	0
35.0 - 38.0	4	16
38.5 - 41. 5	10	32
42.0 - 45.0	22	38
45.5 - 48.5	22	12
49.0 - 52.0	22	0
52.5 -55.5	14	2
56.0 - 59.0	6	0
59.5 - 62.5	0	0
63.0 +	0	0

Source: primary, data – 1995.

Table 3: Percentage distribution of Weight-Height index in adult male and female Muria

Range	*Males* %	*Females* %
X-22.0	0	0
22.1-25.0	4	20
25.1-28.0	22	36
28.1-31.0	50	36
31.9-34.0	18	6
34.1-x	6	2

Source: primary, data – 1995.

Table 4: Percentage distribution of Pignet index value among the adult Muria males

Age Range	*Class*	*Percent*
(X - 10.0)	Very sturdy	0
(10.0 to 15.0)	Sturdy	0
(15.1 to 20.0)	Good	0
(20.1 to 25.0)	Average	10
(25.1 to 30.0)	Weak	20
(30.1 to 35.0)	Very weak	36
(35.1 to 40.0)	Poor	24
(40.1 +)	Very poor	10

Source: primary, data – 1995.

Table 5: Percentage distribution of body mass index in adult male and female Muria

Range	*Class*	*Males* %	*Females* %
Less than 16.0	CED III	4	8
16.0-16.9	CED II	14	20
17.0-18.4	CED I	30	20
18.5-19.9	Low weight normal	52	52
20.0-24.9	normal	0	0
25.0-29.9	Obesity I	0	0
30.0 & above	Obesity II	0	0

Source: primary, data – 1995.

Conclusion

The present study highlights that while majority of the Muria are under the shadow of malnutrition the condition of female family members show sorry figures as regard to physical features and almost all the health parameter like weight/height index, pignet index and distribution of body mass index as well.

Mention may be made in this context that, Elwin provided a wealth of Anthropological information and insights into the tribal way of life as regard to the richness of their beliefs and practices which can protect the tribal society and health. He recorded extensively their physical appearance, dress, food habits, rituals related to cultivation, hunting, crafts, tools, myths, songs of the Baiga 1939, the Agaria, 1942, the Muria and their Ghotul, 1991 (reprint).

Evaluating the deepest anguish expressed by Elwin regarding the apathy towards tribal communities, appears to be continuing as reflected by the poor nutrition status of the tribe which as expressed by him could be the result of systematic encroachment into their resources and degradation of their social life effected by modernization and so-called superficial planning without understanding and evaluating their social value.

The cultural dimension of shearing food and work load in tribal families has made special focus to understand nutritional status of a tribe which cannot be measured in metric parameters. Therefore, the assessment of nutritive value of nutrition in tribal families always remain a question because of gender equality of labour but unequal distribution of food as reveled in the current study. The present findings indicate that majority of Muria tribals are found to be malnourished and effective nutritional trails or programme may be advocated for well being of these tribals.

Reference

AGRAWAL, P. C. 1979: Human Geography of Bastar district, Allahabad, Carga Brothers.

Basu, S., Jindal, A. Kshatriya, G. Singh, Paramjit, Roy, P. and Sharma K.K.N. : Genetic and Sociocultural Determinants of Tribal Health. Bastar Tribal Groups of Madhya Pradesh (Research Report) NIHFW, New Delhi (1989).

Elwin, Verrier: The Muria and Their Ghoutul. Oxford University Press, Delhi (Reprint) (1991).

Ivanosky, A. : Physical modification of the population of Russia. Am. J. Phys. Anthrop., 6: 331-353 (1923).

Rao, H. D., Mathur, Y. N., Radhaiah, G. and Rao P.N.: Health and Nutrition Status of Tribals of Madhya Pradhesh, (Research Report) NIN, Hyderabad (1986).

Roy, J. K., Bhattacharya, K.K. et al. : Diet and Nutritional Anthropological of Santhals of PurliaDistt. W.B. Bull. Anth. Survy. India, 31 : 45-71 (19820.

Singh. I. P. and Bhasin, M.K.: Anthropometry. Kamla-Raj Enterprises, Delhi (1989).

Visweswara Rao, K.: Anthropometry for the assessment of various forms of malnutrition-available approaches and their relatives merits. Man in India, 75: 195-207 (1995).

Chapter - 12

Verrier Elwin and Tallurmuttey – Concept of Earth Goddess among the Muria

Amitabha Sarkar

Part-A

Verrier Elwin was a student at Oxford, Elwin (1902-1964) took keen interest in the Indian culture. He was a devout Christian and underwent formal training as a missionary. He came to India 1927 to spread the gospel and joined the Christian Service Society in Pune. During his work, he was greatly influenced by Hindu philosophy and by Ravindranath Tagore's writings. At that time, the freedom movement was intense in India under the leadership of Mahatma Gandhi. Elwin exchanged with views and ideas with Congressmen such as Nehru and Patel which irked the British Government. He took to travel with Vallabhabhai Patel and Jamanlal Bajaj across India and deeply felt the suffering of the people. Then he met a very capable volunteer by the name of Shamrao Hivale and together by they studied the Gond tribe of Central India (today's Madhya Pradesh).

However, the church objected to Elwin's social service agenda and he resigned to his missionary post in 1931. During the subsequent years, he started an ashram in Karanjiya village. He started living like a tribal to understand them better, but tried to eliminate the myth, superstition, and ignorance from the tribals. He taught them agriculture and opened a pharmacy.

- He worked as a Research Associate in Sir D. Tata School of Social Sciences, Bombay in the late thirties during his studies among the Baiga.
- Professional career in anthropology began in 1940 with the honorary appointment as Census Officer and Ethnographer in Bastar State.

- In 1942 he was awarded the **WELCOME MEDAL** and he was credited with the honour that for the first time this medal was awarded to any person in India.
- He remained as one of the editors of Man in India, the first anthropological journal of the country along with W.G. Archer and Ramesh Chandra Roy-the second son of Rai Bahadur Sarat Chandra Roy.
- In 1944 he was Sectional President for Anthropology and Archaeology of the Indian National Science Congress association.
- He was appointed as Anthropologist in 1945 by Government of India.
- In **1946 he was appointed as Deputy Director of Anthropological Survey of India, called as Dept. of Anthropology and continued till 1949.**
- The Royal Anthropological Institute of London awarded him the **RIVERS MEDAL** in 1948.
- In 1951 he was awarded the **Annandale Medal by the Asiatic Society of Bengal** and was elected as a Fellow there.
- The Govt. of India appointed him as a **ADVISER for Tribal affairs** to NEFA in 1953.
- **The turning point was marked in his life in 1954 when he became an Indian citizen**.
- For his outstanding contribution in tribal studies in India he was conferred upon the Degree of Doctor of science (D. Sc) by the Oxford University.
- In 1960 he was awarded the **Campbell Gold Medal by the** Asiatic Society of Bombay; and in the same year he was appointed as Member of SC and ST commission to look after the welfare of these people.
- In 1961 he was honoured with **Padma Bhusan** –one of the highest civilian awards conferred upon to any person by the Govt. of India.

Due to his close association with the tribals, he became an authority on their lifestyle and culture. He dedicated his life and money to their betterment.

Verrier Elwin's famous work in Bastar was among the Muria entitled "**Muria and the Ghotul**" which was later during 1968 published from Oxford University Press as abridged volume - '**Kingdom of the Young**'.

Elwin was born in 29.08.1902 and died on 22.02.1964. He was a good friend of Pt. Jawaharlal Nehru. Nehru's philosophy of North-east Indian tribes was influenced by Elwin.

Part-B

Now, I will come to my subject. Here I am speaking of undivided Bastar district. Now Bastar is divided into number of districts viz. Kanker, Naryanpur, Dantewada, Bastar, Sukma etc. Our field work was in various pockets of Bastar till 1998 when Bastar was a single district.

Bastar is the cradle of tribal habitat which is very much territorially demarcated. The Muria are living in Naryanpur area. The following map will speak of tribal distribution at Bastar. In course of our field work we have categorized the deities prevalent among the tribals of Bastar viz,-

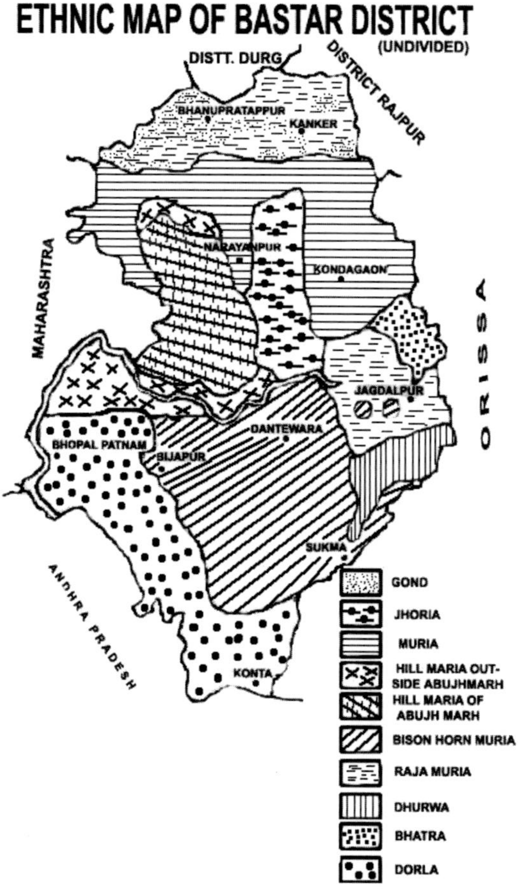

II

Religion cannot be seen but is only felt through empathy. Outward manifestation of religion comes through its active part that is through the performance of rituals and festivals. These are the ways to propitiate and show honour to the supreme authority to appease him for blessing. A person gets mental strength out of it. Ritual is the process of propitiation of deities (Sarkar and Dasgupta, 1996).

In course of our field work we have categorized the deities prevalent among the tribals of Bastarviz,

(i) Earth goddess

(ii) Lineage deity

(iii) Matagudi

Each and every village in Bastar all the ethnic groups propitiate these three categories of deities where ethnic boundary is not taken into consideration. The earth deity is referred as *bhumormati-deo* or *mutak* or *murtal*or*tallin* or *tallurmuttey*. Abujhmaria and Muria refer her as *tallurmuttey*, while, *tallin* by Dandami Maria or Bison-horn-Maria, *mutak/ murtal* by Dhurwa of Kangerghati and *bhum/mati-deo* by Bhatra, Halba and people of neighbouring village of Jagdalpur. The earth deity includes spirits of river, forest etc.

Now in the following lines my discussion will be restricted on Muria. The field work carried out in Benur/Vannur (in Gondi) pargana in which there are 46 villages. We carried out empirical study at Devgaon(in Gondi it is called as Pennar) Remawand, Niyanar, Onnapar, Matavand, and Munjmatta. Except Devgaon, all the villages are under geographical terrain of Benur or Vannurpargana. Devgaon is situated in western part of Benur or Vannurpargana boundary. The present speech highlights on the role of earth deity among the Muria and its intricate relation with Muria life and culture of Bastar where Ghotul also plays a significant role. Now the existence of Ghotul is almost nil and due to such social vacuum the impact of their social situation is ascertained. The essence of this deliberation lies chiefly around their traditional institution which was considered as a platform for their enculturation process where social rules, incest relations, taboos and values were taught for sustainable living.

III

According to Muria pantheon *tallurmuttey* is a feminine and frequently is characterized as the daughter of *Bhagavan*whom they identified as

Ispuriyal, is a masculine being. Both *Ispuriyal* and *tallurnuttey* have creative functions in the formation of living things whereas *Ispuriyal* is incapable of bringing life into the world, on the contrary *tallurmuttey* is capable of revealing it. According to Muria *tallurmuttey* is the mother and producers, an active power manifesting life. *Tallurmuttey* can also be a benevolent mother assisting in the development of crops and humans.

Role of *tallurmuttey* in Muria life

It has been observed from our studied villages that their clan are clustered and distributed into some vans or phratries, viz, *Nagvans* (serpent), *Baghvans* (tiger), *Kacchim* (tortoise), *Bakra* (goat), *Bodmink* (a kind of fish), etc. In each vans there are number of clans which are exogamous in nature and considered as brother-clan or *dadabhai* group and marriage within such *dadabhai* group is tabooed. In contrast to *dadabhai*, there is *akomama* which is considered as wife's clan, i.e. wife can be brought from such *vans* and clan, that is *vans* exogamy is the rule.

It is also reported from Ghotul *Sardar/Sirdar* (supreme post of Ghotul), *Diban* (he is most intelligent member of Ghotul), *Musban* (he is responsible to keep the Ghotul clean and tidy), *Kotwar* (he keeps daily attendance at Ghotul), *Barapahadar/Nanipahadar* (attends the seating arrangement for visitors like us and offer them mat to sit), *Sipahi* (he is guard of the village), *Baid* (actually a medicine-man), *Belosa or Dulosa* (she is the leader of motiyaris of Ghotul), *Motiyar*i (girl member of Ghotul) and some *Cheliks* (male member of Ghotul) (Dasgupta and Sarkar, 2011) that during the meeting between two villages at the cross-road between the settlement–men from both villages as well as the adolescent boys and girls (*Cheliks* and *Motiyaris*) of the Ghotul also meet on this occasion. The parties sit facing each other and the youth of one group pour *darango* (liquor of *mahua*) for the men and youth of the other group. Some men from the village offers *darango* stand up in turn and ask the recipient to raise and voice of any grievances or anger. They exchanges alternately between the groups until all the spirits is consumed. The ceremonial exchange is concluded amid assurances that no one is angry after which the parties return to the village. Manifest expressions of anger in the village are not tolerated since the same create social tensions in village, if chance, blood by oozes upon the earth during the overt expression of anger; it angers *tallurmuttey* and causes the entire village in anger (the loss of life-giving blood during an accident is not regarded as potentially dangerous but as an expression of passion and feminine power associated with *tallurmuttey* it is dangerous).

Villages within a pargana are often uni-clan distribution. It is also observed that all agricultural ceremonies are held at the *manda* (religious centre) of the pargana, the *bhumgayta* gives offering to *tallurmuttey* on behalf of all villagers of the pargana, while the *pen pujari* lays offerings before the *angan* symbolizing *Barha pen* (who is regarded as their senior ancestral deity) and each of the ancestral deities which must be brought from their natal villages' *manda* for the occasion. People of all ethnic groups of Benurpargana brought the ancestral deities or *pen-anask* to the *manda* of village Matavand, as it is believed that it is abode of the original settlers of the pargana and the parents of all *pen-anask* in the area.

The *pen pujari* of Vadde is assisted in the performance of his duties by members of his clan (*katta*) who themselves have specialized functions depending upon their village. Similarly, *gaytatonda (*the earth master lineage*)*have a different function during ceremonies at the sacred religious centre (*manda*). The Pattav *bhumgayta* (the earth master of the territory) comes from the village of Matavand and is assisted in preparing and cooking the offerings for *Tallurmuttey* by his clansmen. Durva clansmen from the village of Kursnar who are attached themselves to the Pattav clan and who are considered as **'sons of the earth master'** are said to be like storekeepers who keeps account of the grain and animals provided for the offerings and feasts. It is also found that Gota clansmen are the *gaytatonda* (the earth master lineage) and are said to be the **Durpe** (one of the vans) brotherhood's (*dadabhai*) Pave. The Pave of a *manda* are generally feared and looked down upon for they are said to steal pieces of cloth, hair and fingernails from the people of other *manda* and offer those to *tallurmuttey* as a substitute form of human sacrifice.

All clans, lineage segments that occupy villages within Durpe territory are required to bring their 'ancestral–deities' represented by *anga, kola* or *doli* to the *manda* of Matavand village whether or not they belong to the same brotherhood during any ceremonies like new eating ceremonies etc. Local clans, lineages that have settled in Durpe territory but consider themselves as part of a different *manda* and they also bring their *doli* who represents both their 'Village Mother' and 'ancestral-deity'. Thus, the corporate nature of *manda* (religious centre) is very much evident.

Numerous genealogies given by the Muria and lack of consistency suggest that the agnatic groups united by these ancestral deities are subject to a process of segmentation. Moreover, it is particularly apparent in the pargana that the 'ancestral deities' can be thought of as a single undifferentiated group with each 'ancestral-deity' being more or less equivalent.

Lastly, it can be said that in each *manda* appears as a religious, territorial brother-hood with two principal descent groups who know themselves to be descendants of an original 'ancestral-deity' and who are identified by different and complimentary ceremonial functions. The relationship between the two descent groups is further extended since Pattav clan and those local clan, lineages that have attached themselves to it stand in an *akomama* relationship to the Vadde clan. It is observed that 'earth master *tonda*' (lineage) and the ancestral-deity sacrifice *tonda* of a *manda* stand in a relationship of maternal uncle and nephew are related through woman. It suggests there is a preference for exchanging sisters and daughters with families who are within the territorial limits of pargana and the earth jointly settled by the two affinal clans.

The Muria recognize the ancestral deities (*pen-anask*) and *Barha pen* whom they equate with *tallurmuttey* as a source of life while the 'ancestors' (*anask*) and ghosts appear as troublesome reflections of their fears and desires concerning the continuation of life.

Muria view to *tallurmuttey* that it is the producers of all sufferings and their opinions indicate that illness is made apparent for moral reasons. Suffering develops when *tallurmuttey* becomes angry. The Muria consider those illnesses like smallpox, chicken pox, measles and a varieties of skin rashes commonly appear during summer season are collectively called as *Yayalmuttey*. The name *yayalmuttey* translates as 'mother of females' and synonymous to *tallurmuttey*. This deity almost regularly possesses someone in the village and is the only form of 'illness' treated by the earth master or *gayta* rather than by the *leske.*

Conclusion

The above discussion on Muria social system where the role of *tallurmuttey* plays a key role in each and every sphere of life. It is also evident that concept of *tallurmuttey*—the earth goddess has an intricate relationship from their birth to death and the division of labour of *gayta, bhumgayata, leske* are very much defined and they learnt to these from the enculturation process at Ghotul.

Now-a-days the existence of Ghotul is almost disappeared due to rise of some external political phenomenon which ultimately creates social unrest in this region. But the question arises the Muria youth of present day are not so aware of their value loaded traditional intricate social behaviour and relation, which are the product of enculturation at Ghotul, which will also help them not only to sustain but will encourage or foster their culture for posterity. "**The arbitrary suppression of all traditional customs, ceremonies, dances is a short-sighted and retrograde policy. Practically it strikes at the root of the whole social structure of the people and its effects are apt to prove disastrous**" (Balfour, H. 'Foreword' to Mills, The AoNagas, 1973).

The vacuum of Ghotul institution among the Muria is replaced by some external hard core political institution, as a result the whole territory became a fearful zone and various developmental programme of Government is not properly executed. Finally, the laundering of money is very much evident in these tribal pockets in the name of developmental programme.

I am personally as a Social Scientist is in favour of the 'existence of Ghotul Institution' of Muria because it is the only learning institution approved by their age-old traditional customs. There is a proverb–"**Idle mind is the devil's workshop**". In absence of Ghotul the tribal youths of the Muria of this region are diverted to other activities for immediate material aspiration and which is the product of modernization.

Literature consulted

Dasgupta, Samira and Amitabhasarkar. 2011 'Ghotul and Muria: An Institutional Cultural Heritage', Man in India, Vol.91. No.3-4.

Elwin, Verrier. 1968. The Kingdom of the young, London: Oxford University Press.

Mills, J.P. and J.H.Hutton.1973 (Original in 1926). The Ao Nagas, Bombay: Oxford University Press.

Sarkar, Amitabha and Samira Dasgupta. 2010. Religious Beliefs and Practices: A Portrayal of the Integrative Process, New Delhi: Agam Kala Prakashan.

Muria-Ghotul Pillow

Motiyaris—the Ghotul girls
at Niyanar Village

Chapter - 13

बस्तर की आदिवासी संस्कृति व सामाजिक स्थिति

भुनेशवर लाल साहू

सार संक्षेपः छत्तीसगढ़ प्रदेश में गोंड जनजाति का सर्वाधिक संकेन्द्रण बस्तर संभाग में है। इनके सर्वाधिक प्रचलित गोत्र में नेताम मरकाम व टेकाम हैं। गोंड प्रजातियों की कुल 30 शाखाएं हैं। जिसमें प्रमुख रूप से अबुझमाड़ियां, दंडामी मारिया आमत गोंड, सबरिया गोडे एवं गोंड मुरिया इत्यादि हैं।

यह छत्तीसगढ़ प्रदेश का दक्षिणी भाग है अपनी विशिष्ट आदिवासी संस्कृति वन्य बहुलता खनिज संसाधन के कारण इस क्षेत्र में राष्ट्रीय स्तर पर पृथक पहचान बनायी है। इसकी क्षेत्रफल 1060 वर्ग कि. मी. है इसकी ढ़लान पहले पश्चिम उसके बाद दक्षिण की ओर है। बस्तर की सबसे ऊंची चोटी बैलाडिला है। (नंदिराज 1210 मी. ऊंची है।) इसकी अपवाह तंत्र गोदावरी अपवाह तंत्र में शामिल है। व इसकी जलवायु मानसूनी, ऊष्णार्द्र शुष्क पर्णपाति बन पाए जाते हैं। बस्तर का निर्माण धारवाह, ग्रनाईट एवं नीस चट्टानो से हुई है। लौह अयस्क की प्राप्ति इन्हीं चट्टानों से होती है।

बस्तर की आदिवासी संस्कृति व सामाजिक स्थिति

गोड़ः–छत्तीसगढ़ के जनजातियों में गोड़ सबसे बड़ी जनजाति है। जो कि राज्य के दक्षिण हिस्से में निवास करती है। गोंड़ जनजाति में विवाह के अवसर पर जब लड़की वाले बारात लेकर लड़के वाले के घर आते हैं, तब ऐसे विवाह को पठौनी विवाह कहते हैं। गोंड़ जनजाति में ममेरे, फुफेरे, लड़के लड़कियों के विवाह को दूध लौटावा कहते है जनजाति में प्रचलित अपहरण विवाह को गोड़ जनजाति में पायसोतुर कहतें है।

गोंडो की अर्थव्यवस्था कृषि व वनों पर आधारित है। कृषि इनकी जीविका का प्रमुख साधन हैं गोंडो की एक प्रजाति पहाड़ी माड़िया आज भी परिवर्तनीय कृषि करते है। गोंड प्रजाति मूल रूप से एक ईमानदार प्रजाति मानी जाती हैं। इनका सामाजिक, सांस्कृतिक जीवन उन्नतशील एवं सभ्य है।

हल्बा बस्तर में हल्बा, भानुप्रतापपुर, कांकेर, केशकाल की ओर बस है। इस जनजाति की कई उपशाखाए हैं। जैसे नायक, भण्डारा, परेत, सुरेत, नरेवा। हल्बा अधिक प्रगतिशील है। हल्बा अपने को महादेव–पार्वती द्वारा उत्पन्न मानते हैं। तथा इनकी बोली हल्बी है।

बस्तर के हल्बा में टोटम को बरग कहते हैं। हल्बा जनजाति में कई वर्ग कबीर पंथी के होते है। हल्बा जनजाति के लोग पारम्परिक रूप से किसान है। अधिकांश कृषि कार्य पर निर्भर रहते हैं। इनकी गणना सम्पन्न कृषकों में की जाती है। इनमें एक ही गोत्र में विवाह नही होता है। विवाह निश्चित होने पर अगर घर में किसी की मृत्यु हो गई हो तो विवाह चार अथवा महुआ वृक्ष के साथ करते हैं। हल्बा जनजाति में दशहरा, दीपावली, होली तथा नवाखानो पर्व मनाया जाता है। इस जनजाति में छुआ–छूत का अत्यधिक महत्व है।

माड़िया:–यह जनजाति प्रमुख रूप से बस्तर में निवास करती हैं। पहाड़ी क्षेत्रों मे रहने वाले माड़िया जनजाति दुनिया की सभ्यता से पूर्णताः अलग है। इनमें अनेक अबूझमाड़ की पहाड़ियो में रहते हैं। अतः इन्हें अबूझमाड़िया भी कहते हैं।

माड़िया का एक वर्ग गौर माड़िया कहलाता है क्योंकि ये लोग जंगली भैंस के सींग की बनी टोपी पहनते है। दण्डामी माड़िया का वर्ग प्रसिद्ध है। यह वर्ग प्रमुखरूप से दक्षिण दंतेवाड़ा, कोटा, बीजीपुर, व जगढ़लपुर में पाया जाता है। ग्रीयसेन ने इस प्रजाति का गंभीर अध्ययन कर इनके विषय में सूक्ष्म जानकारी उपलब्ध करायी है।

इनके गांव जंगलों में नदियों के समीप या पहाड़ी ढलानों पर पाए जाते हैं। जंगलों में प्रत्येक व्यक्ति को उसकी आवश्यकतानुसार भूमि प्राप्त होती है। सामाजिक व्यवस्था के तहत ग्राम का मुखिया भूमि का वितरण ग्राम वासिरयो के मध्य करता है। इनके मकान अस्थायी होते हैं और अवसर पांच–सात वर्षों में यह पुनः नवीन मकान बना लेते हैं।

इस प्रजाति के लोग जंगल से कंदमूल, फल एवं उबला भोजन एवं आग से भुना हुआ भोजन अधिक पसंद करते हैं। मद्यपान इनके संस्कार में है। मुख्य रूप से लांदा, सल्फी व शराब सव्रप्रिय है।

माड़िया जनजाति द्वारा पेद्दा खेती प्रमुख रूप से की जाती है। ये लोग जंगल से कंद–मूल, फल, चिरौंजी, जामुन, आम, तेंदु, शल्फी, आंवला, मांस आदि इकट्ठा कर बेचते हैं। यह लोग बांस की चटाइयां रस्सी एवं टोंकनिया आदि बनाते है। वास्तव में जनजातियों का जीवन अनुशासनप्रिय, एकांतिक व रोमांचक है।

मुड़िया:–मुड़िया गोंडो की एक उपजाति है। यह मुड शब्द से विकसित हुआ है जिसका अर्थ है पलाश का वृक्ष। शाब्दिक दृष्टि से मुड़िया का अर्थ है आदिम। मुड़िया जनजाति अपनी विशिष्ट पहचान कोंडागांव एवं नारायणपुर में बनाये हुए है। यहां इनकी संख्या अधिक है।

ये लोग गोंडी तथा हल्बी बोलियां बोलते है इनकी शारीरिक बनावट मध्यम, रंग सांवला एंव नयन नक्श सुंदर होते हैं। इनके मकान दो कमरों के होते हैं। पुरूष कृषि, मजदूरी, लकड़ी काटना व शिकार आदि का कार्य करते हैं। ये लोग कुदाली से कृषि कार्य करते हैं। मुड़िया परिश्रमी प्रजाति के हैं। इनकी महिलाएं स्वच्छता को पसंद करती है। ये लोग ठाकुरदेव तथा महादेव की पूजा करते है। इनके प्रमुख त्यौहार नवाखाली तथा उत्सवों में पारम्परिक कसार होता है। यह जनजाति अनेक सहगोत्रीय समूहों विभाजित हैं। जिनके अलग अलग गण चिन्ह होते हैं। इनके युवा गृह को घोटुल कहते हैं।

नारायणपुर में मेला के अवसर पर जनजातियों द्वारा प्रसिद्ध एबालतोर नृत्य किया जाता है। यह जनजाति पराशक्तियों पर अत्यधिक विश्वास करती है। यह एक कलाप्रिय जनजाति है जो कि लकड़ी बांस आदि शिल्प कला में प्रवीण है।

निष्कर्षः– उक्त विश्लेषण के आधार पर आदिवासियों का सम्पूर्ण जीवनचक्र धर्म आधारित होता है। इनके पृथक–पृथक देवी–देवता होते हैं। ये लोग नियमों में रहकर अपनी रीति–रिवाज परम्परा के अनुरूप ही जीवन शैली में रहते हैं। इनका जीवन प्रकृति अनुरूप सुन्दर सरल व सहज है।

Chapter - 14

बस्तर की जनजातियों में सामाजिक–सांस्कृतिक परिवर्तन का अध्ययन

राजेन्द्र सिंह,

छत्तीसगढ़ राज्य के दक्षिण में स्थित बस्तर क्षेत्र भारत के प्रमुख जनजातीय क्षेत्र के रूप में विख्यात है। अविभाजित बस्तर जिले या बस्तर संभाग में गोंड जनजाति तथा उसकी उपजाति–मुरिया, धुरवा, परजा, दंडामी माड़िया, राजगोंड, परधान, अबूझमाड़िया, दोरला आदि तथा हल्बा, भतरा, गदबा जनजाति निवासरत हैं। बस्तर की इन जनजातियों के रीति–रिवाज, जीवन शैली, संस्कृति में अनेक समानता के बाद भी कुछ पहलुओं में विशिष्टता दर्शाती है। बस्तर पूर्वकाल से शोधकर्ताओं के लिये जिज्ञासा का केन्द्र रहा है। महान अध्येता वेरियर एल्विन ने बस्तर की जनजातियों के मध्य कार्य करते हुये जनजातीय संस्कृति से संबंधित विभिन्न पहलूओं में व्यापक, गहन व समग्र लेखन किया है।

प्रस्तुत शोधपत्र का उद्देश्य बस्तर की जनजातियों में सामाजिक–सांस्कृतिक परिवर्तन का अध्ययन करना है। इस शोधपत्र हेतु वेरियर एल्विन के ग्रंथों में वर्णित तत्कालीन जनजातीय शोधपत्र संस्कृति को आधार मानकर उसके परिप्रेक्ष्य में हुये बस्तर की जनजातियों में हुये सामाजिक–सांस्कृतिक परिवर्तन का अध्ययन प्रस्तुत किया गया है। बस्तर के आदिवासी क्षेत्र बहुस्तरीय बाह्य संपर्क, विकासीय प्रक्रियाओं, राजनीतिक–प्रशासनिक परिस्थिति आदि के कारण परिवर्तन के दौर से गुजर रहे हैं। बस्तर की जनजातियों में प्रशासनिक, भौगोलिक, भौतिक संस्कृति, विकासीय स्तर, जागरूकता आदि में व्यापक परिवर्तन हुये हैं। इस अध्ययन में बस्तर की जनजातियों में सामाजिक–सांस्कृतिक परिवर्तन, उसके कारक, प्रभाव तथा समस्याओं को प्रस्तुत किया गया है।

परिवर्तन प्रकृति का नियम है। संसार की प्रत्येक वस्तुओं में परिवेश, परिस्थिति तथा काल के सापेक्ष परिवर्तन दिखायी देता है। प्रत्येक जनजाति का निश्चित निवास क्षेत्र व पृथक संस्कृति होती है। गतिशीलता या परिवर्तनशीलता संस्कृति की प्रमुख विशेषताओं में से एक है परंतु संस्कृति में परिवर्तन की प्रक्रिया अत्यंत धीमी होती है। परिवर्तन आंतरिक व बाह्य कारकों से घटित होता है। यह संस्कृति को नवीनता तथा गतिशीलता प्रदान करता है।

छत्तीसगढ़ राज्य के दक्षिण में स्थित बस्तर क्षेत्र भारत के प्रमुख जनजातीय क्षेत्र के रूप में विख्यात है। अविभाजित बस्तर जिले या बस्तर संभाग में गोंड जनजाति तथा उसकी उपजाति–मुरिया,

धुरवा, परजा, दंडामी माड़िया, राजगोंड, परधान, अबूझमाड़िया, दोरला आदि तथा हल्बा, भतरा, गदबा जनजाति निवासरत हैं। बस्तर को इन जनजातियो के रीति–रिवाज, जीवन शैली, संस्कृति में अनेक समानता के बाद भी कुछ पहलुओं में विशिष्टता दर्शाते हैं। बस्तर पूर्वकाल से प्रशासकों, पर्यटकों तथा शोधकर्ताओं के लिये जिज्ञासा का केन्द्र रहा है। महान अध्येता वेरियर एल्विन ने बस्तर की जनजातियों पर गहन शोध कार्य कर जनजातीय संस्कृति से संबंधित विभिन्न पहलूओं में व्यापक, गहन व समग्र लेखन किया है।

उद्देश्य–

प्रस्तुत शोधपत्र का उद्देश्य–**बस्तर की जनजातियों में सामाजिक–सांस्कृतिक परिवर्तन का अध्ययन करना है।**

वेरियर एल्विन ने 1935 से 1942 तक बस्तर के विभिन्न क्षेत्र में शोधकार्य किया। उन्हें 1940 में बस्तर का जनगणना अधिकारी तथा कुछ समय उपरांत अवैतनिक जाति विशेषज्ञ नियुक्त किया गया। उन्होंने बस्तर की दंडामी माड़िया जनजाति पर आधारित "माड़िया मर्डर एंड सुसाइड" (1943), मुरिया जनजाति पर आधारित "मुरिया एंड देयर घोटूल" (1947) तथा तथा अनेक शोधपत्र लेखो। बस्तर की जनजातियों पर आधारित इस शोधपत्र हेतु वेरियर एल्विन के ग्रंथों में वर्णित तत्कालीन बस्तर तथा जनजातीय संस्कृति को आधार मानकर उसके परिप्रेक्ष्य में बस्तर तथा जनजातियों में हुये सामाजिक–सांस्कृतिक परिवर्तन का अध्ययन प्रस्तुत किया गया है।

परिवर्तन के कारक–

उन्नीसवीं सदी के चौथे दशक से वर्तमान तक लगभग आठ दशक में न सिर्फ बस्तर वरन संपूर्ण विशव पटल में व्यापक परिवर्तन हुये हैं। तत्कालीन काल में अंग्रेजों का प्रभुत्व विशव के बड़े भू–भाग पर था, जो धीरे–धीरे समाप्त हुआ। पिछले आठ दशक में जनजातीय समाज में व्यापक परिवर्तन हुये हैं। बस्तर के जनजातीय समाज में हुये परिवर्तन के प्रमुख कारण निम्नांकित हैं–

1. **राष्ट्र की स्वतंत्रता–** अंग्रेजों की दासता से मुक्ति संपूर्ण भारत के लिये अविस्मरणीय घटना है। स्वतंत्र भारत ने लोकतांत्रिक गणराज्य के रूप में सभी दिशाओं में तरक्की की। स्वतंत्र भारत में सभी जाति, समुदाय तथा वर्गों के विकास एवं परिवर्तन का मार्ग प्रशस्त हुआ।

2. **संवैधानिक प्रावधान–** स्वतंत्रता पशचात भारत के संविधान में जनजातीय समुदाय के विकास व संरक्षण हेतु संरक्षी, विकासीय तथा प्रशासनिक प्रावधान बनाये गये। जिसका उदेश्य सुदूर वन तथा पर्वत, घाटियों में निवासरत मानव समुदाय के हितों की सुरक्षा व विकास तथा राष्ट्र की मुख्य धारा से शामिल करना था। यह संवैधानिक प्रावधान न सिर्फ सुरक्षा की दृष्टि से महत्वपूर्ण साबित हुये बल्कि इससे शिक्षा, रोजगार, स्थानीय व केन्द्रीय स्तर के शासन में प्रतिनिधित्व प्राप्त हुआ जिसने समाज की दिशा बदल दी।

3. **जनजातीय विकास की नीति–** स्वतंत्र भारत में जनजातीय विकास हेतु अलगाव या अजायबघर की नीति, जनजातीय समाज का दूसरे समाजों में आत्मसातीकरण तथा राष्ट्र की मुख्य धारा से एकीकरण जैसे विचार सामने आये किंतु जनजातियों के विकास हेतु संस्कृति संरक्षण, सह विकास की नीति अपनाई गई जिसके कारण जनजातीय समाज में परिवर्तन हुआ।

4. **सांस्कृतिक संपर्क–** बस्तर संभाग में स्वतंत्रता के पभचात रोजगार, व्यवसाय, खनिज संसाधनों के उत्खनन, बंग शरणार्थी के रूप में हजारों परिवार बस्तर में आये तथा स्थायी रूप से बस गये। इसी प्रकार अनेक हिंदू तथा इसाई मिशनरियों ने इस क्षेत्र में शिक्षा, स्वास्थ्य, सेवा आदि का कार्य किया। इस प्रकार जनजातीय संस्कृति तथा बाह्य संस्कृति के संपर्क के कारण जनजातीय संस्कृति में निरंतर बदलाव हो रहा है। बस्तर की जनजातियों के रहन–सहन, खान–पान संबंधी व्यवहार, भौतिक संस्कृति, जीवन संस्कार, आर्थिकी, सामाजिक, धार्मिक जीवन, कला व संस्कृति प्रभावित व परिवर्तित हो रही है।

5. **विकासीय प्रयासों का परिणाम–**शासन द्वारा विगत आठ दशकों में बस्तर में शिक्षा, स्वास्थ्य, क्षेत्रीय व आर्थिक विकास हेतु व्यापक विकास योजनायें एवं कार्यक्रमों को लागू किया है। प्रारंभिक अवधि में उन कार्यक्रमों का प्रभाव कम रहा किंतु बाद में उनका व्यापक प्रभाव हुआ तथा बस्तर के सभी जनजातीय समुदाय में विकासीय प्रयासों का परिणाम दिखायी देता है।

6. **राजनीतिक नेतृत्व का विकास तथा सामाजिक संगठनों का गठन–** बस्तर के जनजातियों में विगत आठ दशकों में जागरूकता तथा राजनीतिक नेतृत्व का विकास हुआ है। रियासतकालीन तथा अंग्रेजी शासनाधीन बस्तर में जनजातीय राजनीतिक नेतृत्व व संगठन अपने गांव तथा क्षेत्र तक सीमित था किंतु राष्ट्र की आजादी के पशचात संविधान के लोकसभा व विधानसभा में जनजातीय प्रतिनिधित्व हेतु सुरक्षित सीटों के कारण शनैः शनैः जनजातीय क्षेत्रों में राजनैतिक नेतृत्व व जागरूकता का विकास हुआ। जिससे क्षेत्रीय व स्थानीय मुद्दे राज्य व केन्द्रीय स्तर पर लाये जाने लगे।

   इसी प्रकार शिक्षा व जागरूकता के विकास के कारण बस्तर की अधिकांश जनजातियों में सामाजिक संगठन का गठन किया गया है। यह सामाजिक संगठन समाज को संगठित करने के साथ–साथ सामाजिक कुरीतियों, बुराईयों को दूर करने हेतु प्रयासरत है तथा यह समय–समय पर आदिवासियों पर हो रहे अत्याचार, शोषण, गलत नीतियों के विरूद्ध मजबूती से विरोध करते रहे हैं।

7. **पंचायती राज व्यवस्था–** बस्तर की जनजातियों में परंपरागत जाति पंचायत व्यवस्था व्याप्त थी। शासन द्वारा सत्ता को विकेन्द्रीकृत कर ग्राम पंचायत व्यवस्था लागू की गई। इसने जनजातियों की परंपरागत जाति पंचायत व्यवस्था को प्रभावित किया। 1994 से लागू त्रिस्तरीय पंचायती राज व्यवस्था तथा पेसा अधिनियम–1996 ने जनजातीय क्षेत्रों की राजनीतिक व्यवस्था को व्यापक रूप से प्रभावित किया। अनुसूचित क्षेत्र में लागू पेसा अधिनियम–1996 के तहत ग्राम पंचायत, जनपद पंचायत तथा जिला पंचायत के प्रमुख पद अनुसूचित जनजाति के लिये आरक्षित होने के कारण जनजातियों के राजनैतिक नेतृत्व का विकास हुआ। शिक्षित जनजाति युवा वर्ग की बढ़ती राजनैतिक जागरूकता व आकांक्षाओं के कारण पूर्व की तरह निर्विविरोध निर्वाचन के स्थान पर चुनाव होने लगे। ग्राम विकास हेतु ग्राम पंचायत की बढ़ती भूमिका के कारण वर्तमान में परंपरागत जाति पंचायत व्यवस्था की भूमिका अत्यंत सीमित हो गयी है।

   इसी प्रकार नवीन त्रिस्तरीय पंचायती राज व्यवस्था में महिलाओं के लिये सीटें आरक्षित हैं, जिससे महिलाओं की राजनीतिक व्यवस्था में सक्रियता तथा भागीदारी में वृद्धि हुई

है। जनजातीय महिलाओं को संसद, विधानसभा व त्रिस्तरीय पंचायती राज व्यवस्था अंतर्गत राजनीतिक अधिकार प्राप्ति व सत्ता में भागीदारी, जनजातीय समाज व्यवस्था में व्यापक परिवर्तन का प्रतीक है क्योंकि परंपरागत जनजातीय पंचायत व्यवस्था में महिलायें राजनैतिक अधिकारविहीन थीं।

8. **संचार तथा आवागमन के साधनों का विकास**—बस्तर संभाग में संचार व आवागमन के साधनों का व्यापक विकास हुआ है। वर्तमान में बस्तर संभाग में राष्ट्रीय राजमार्ग 63, 30, 1300 तथा 163 गुजरते हैं, यह बस्तर को देश के शेष भाग से जोड़ते हैं। इसी प्रकार रेल सुविधाओं का भी विकास हो रहा है। विगत दशक में बस्तर में रेडियो, मोबाइल नेटवर्क का व्यापक विकास हुआ है। ज़िससे सूचना का आदान प्रदान व आवागमन तथा सामग्रियों का परिवहन आसान हुआ है। जिससे बस्तर में विकास एवं परिवर्तन की गति तीव्र हुई।

9. **प्राकृतिक संसाधनों का दोहन**—बस्तर संभाग मेंवन तथा खनिज संसाधनों के व्यापक तथा प्रचुर भंडार हैं। अंग्रेजों के शासन काल से इनका दोहन जारी है, बस्तर के उत्तर पूर्वी क्षेत्र के वनों का दोहन करने के उद्धेशय से अंग्रेजों ने रेल लाइन बिछायी थी, जो वर्तमान में बंद है किंतु उसके अवशेष वर्तमान में व्याप्त हैं। बस्तर के बैलाडीला क्षेत्र में उच्च कोटि के लौह अयस्क का भंडार है, जिसके दोहन हेतु 1970 के दशक से जापान के सहयोग से रेल मार्ग का निर्माण कर विशाखापट्नम बंदरगाह से जापान को लौह अयस्क भेजा जा रहा है। वर्तमान में देश के औद्योगिक घराने लौह उत्खनन कार्य कर रहे हैं। बस्तर के वनों का दोहन भी जारी है।

10. **गैर सरकारी तथा स्वैच्छिक संगठनों के प्रयास**—बस्तर संभाग के निवासियों को पिछड़ापन, अशिक्षा, स्वास्थ्य व गरीबी जैसी समस्याओं को दूर करने के लिये माता रूक्मणी सेवा संस्थान, रामकृष्ण मिशन, गायत्री परिवार, वनवासी कल्याण आश्रम, इसाई मिशनरी आदि संगठन कार्यरत हैं। जिन्होनें बस्तर के जनजातियों की समस्याओं को दूर करने तथा विकास की ओर अग्रसर करने में महत्वपूर्ण योगदान किया है।

11. **नक्सलवादी आंदोलन तथा उन्मूलन के प्रयास**—जनजातियों की गरीबी, समस्याओं, भ्रष्टाचार, शोषण, विकास तथा प्रशासनिक नियंत्रण के अभाव ने 1980 के दशक से नक्सलियों को बस्तर में जमने का अवसर दिया, जिसने बस्तर के अधिकांश भाग को प्रभावित किया। नक्सलियों के आंदोलन के बदलते स्वरूप तथा हिंसा ने बस्तर के निवासियों को व्यापक रूप से प्रभावित किया था। नक्सली तथा नक्सली उन्मूलन प्रयासों के कारण हुये हिंसा ने बस्तर को कशमीर से भी अधिक हिंसा प्रभावित क्षेत्र में बदल दिया। नक्सलियों ने मिलिट्री बटालियन, नक्सली दलम, संघम सदस्य तथा विभिन्न नक्सलियों के संगठन में बस्तर वासियों को शामिल कर बस्तर के शांतिपूर्ण परिवेश को हिंसक परिवश में बदल दिया। अंदरूनी क्षेत्रों के बाजार बंद हो गये तथा अंदरूनी क्षेत्र बाहरी दुनिया से कट गये। नक्सलियों के विरोध में हुये सलवा जुडुम अभियान के कारण नक्सल प्रभावित क्षेत्र के 600 से अधिक गांवों के निवासियों को सलवा जुडुम शिविर में रखा गया। बस्तर के आदिवासी की स्थिति दो पाटों के बीच पिसने जैसी हो गयी। नक्सलवाद ने बस्तर के जनजातियों का स्वाभाविक जीवन व संस्कृति को व्यापक रूप से प्रभावित किया।

12. **जागरूकता**– बस्तर में विगत आठ दशकों में जनजातियों में व्यापक रूप से जागरूकता का विकास हुआ है। विकासीय गतिविधियों, सांस्कृतिक संपर्क, संचार व आवागमन के साधनों का विकास, राजनैतिक चेतना आदि ने बस्तर के आदिवासियों में जागरूकता विकसित की है। पूर्व में बस्तर के ग्रामों में बाहरी व्यक्तियों के आने पर उनसे चर्चा करने में घबराते थे या वन में भाग जाते थे किंतु वर्तमान में यह परिदृशय पूरी तरह बदल गया है, गांव के व्यक्ति भी बाहरी लोगों से बिना झिझक चर्चा करने लगे हैं।

बस्तर की जनजातियों में सामाजिक–सांस्कृतिक परिवर्तन

बस्तर की जनजातियों में उपरोक्त कारणों से जनजातीय जीवन, संस्कृति, विकास, विचारधारा पर व्यापक असर हुआ है। बस्तर की जनजातियों में सामाजिक–सांस्कृतिक परिवर्तन की उपरोक्त पृष्ठभूमि के आधार पर वेरियर एल्विन के अध्ययनकाल पशचात् विगत आठ दशकों में व्यापक परिवर्तन आये हैं, जिनका विवरण निम्नांकित है–

1. **शासन एवं प्रशासनिक व्यवस्था**–वेरियर एल्विन के अध्ययनकाल में बस्तर राजशाही शासन तथा अंग्रेजों की शासन व्यवस्था के अंतर्गत प्रशासित था। यह पूरा क्षेत्र बस्तर तथा कांकेर रियासत तथा सेन्ट्रल प्रोविंसेस एवं बरार के अंतर्गत शामिल था। राष्ट्र की स्वतंत्रता के पश्चात् मध्यप्रदेश राज्य में बस्तर तथा कांकेर रियासत को मिलाकर बस्तर जिला बनाया गया तथा 1981 में इसे बस्तर संभाग बनाया गया। बस्तर जिला को 1998 में तीन पिले तथा बाद में इसे सात जिलों बस्तर, कांकेर, कोंडागांव, नारायणपुर, सुकमा, दंतेवाड़ा तथा बीजापुर जिलों में विभाजित किया गया।

भारत के संविधान में भारत के पिछड़े तथा जनजातीय क्षेत्र को विशेष दर्जा प्रदान किया गया। इसके तहत् बस्तर क्षेत्र को पांचवी अनुसूची में शामिल करते हुये अनुसूचित क्षेत्र का दर्जा दिया गया। बस्तर में पंचायती राज में पेसा अधिनियम–1996 लागू है।

2. **भाषा/बोली**–वेरियर एल्विन के अध्ययनकाल में बस्तर में हल्बी, गोंडी, भतरी, दोरली, परजी, धुरवी, माड़ी, गदबी आदि बोलियों का प्रचलन था। हल्बी बोली को लिंग्वा फ्रेंका अर्थात संपर्क भाषा का दर्जा प्राप्त था, हिंदी भाषियों की संख्या कम थी। वर्तमान में शिक्षा के प्रसार के कारण हिंदी संपर्क भाषा का दर्जा प्राप्त कर चुकी है तथा जनजातीय बोलियों के वक्ता कम हो रहे हैं।

3. **भौतिक संस्कृति**–स्वतंत्रता पूर्व तथा वर्तमान बस्तर की जनजातियों की भौतिक संस्कृति में व्यापक परिवर्तन हुआ है। भौतिक संस्कृति का कोई भी पक्ष अछूता नही है। भौतिक संस्कृति में हुये परिवर्तन का विवरण निम्नांकित है–

3.1 ग्राम–

3.1.1 **जनसंख्या व सामुदायिक स्थिति**– वेरियर एल्विन के अध्ययनकाल में बस्तर के ग्राम कम जनसंख्या तथा वनक्षेत्रों में पहुंच मार्ग से दूर हुआ करते थे। ग्राम एक जनजातीय, एक गोत्रीय परिवार की बहुलता होती थी, वर्तमान में ग्राम में जनसंख्या की बहुलता होने लगी है। ग्राम में बहुजातीय–जनजातीय सदस्य निवास करने लगे है।

3.1.2 **बाजारों पर निर्भरता**–पूर्वकाल में आवागमन के साधनों तथा ग्रामों में दुकान व वस्तुओं की अनुपलब्धता के कारण जनजातीय समाज नमक, लोहे के औजार, वस्त्र आदि

वस्तुओं के कय तथा वनोपज के विनिमय हेतु साप्ताहिक बाजार, वार्षिक मेले–मंडई पर निर्भर थे। दूर–दूर ग्रामों में निवासरत परिवार पदयात्रा कर एक दिन पूर्व बाजार में पहुंच जाते थे तथा रात में बाजार स्थल पर रूक कर अगले दिन बाजार से अपनी आवश्यकता पूर्ति हेतु वस्तु प्राप्त कर अपने ग्राम प्रस्थान करते थे। मुरिया जनजाति के क्षेत्र में नारायणपुर, अंतागढ़, कोंडागांव, केशकाल बाजार तथा दंडामी माड़िया के क्षेत्र में जगदलपुर, तोकापाल, कोड़ेनार, गीदम, बारसूर, दंतेवाड़ा बाजार थे। वर्तमान में जनजातीय समाज में बाहरी वस्तुओं का उपयोग, परिवर्तित आर्थिकी तथा क्रय शक्ति में वृद्धि के कारण बस्तर के ग्रामों में शासकीय राशन दुकान, किराना व अन्य दुकान खुले हैं जिससे जनजातीय सदस्यों की दैनिक उपयोगी वस्तुओं पर बाजार की निर्भरता कम हो रही है, किंतु वनोपज, अनाज, फल–सब्जियों के कय–विकय हेतु बाजार पर निर्भरता यथावत है। अनेक ग्रामों में बाजार प्रारंभ हुये हैं तथा मनोरंजन हेतु मुर्गा लड़ाई बाजार बनाये गये हैं। अंदरूनी क्षेत्रों के बाजारों में नक्सली–पुलिस के मध्य कई हिंसक घटनायें घट चुकी हैं। इस प्रकार स्पष्ट है कि बस्तर के जनजातीय क्षेत्र में बाजार के उपयोगिता के स्वरूप में परिवर्तन हुआ है।

3.1.3 **शासकीय हस्तक्षेप का अभाव–** वेरियर एल्विन के अध्ययनकाल में बस्तर के ग्राम क्षेत्रों में शासकीय हस्तक्षेप कम था, विशेष कारण या अवसर पर पुलिस, राजस्व तथा वन विभाग तथा रियासत के अधिकारी–कर्मचारी गांवों में जाते थे, वर्तमान में समग्र विकास की अवधारणा के तहत ग्रामों में शिक्षा, स्वास्थ्य, पोषण, खाद्य, राजस्व, वन, पंचायत आदि विभागों के केन्द्र स्थापित किये गये हैं जिसमें संबंधित विभागों के कर्मी ग्रामों में ही निवास करते हैं। इस प्रकार ग्रामों में शासकीय प्रभाव में वृद्धि हुई है।

3.1.4 **मौलिक सुविधाओं का अभाव–**पूर्वकाल में बस्तर के ग्रामों में शिक्षा, स्वास्थ्य व पोषण, पेयजल जैसी मौलिक सुविधाओं का अभाव था। जिससे बस्तर के जनजातीय सदस्यो अनेक रोग व समस्याओं का सामना करना पड़ता था। वर्तमान में बस्तर के ग्रामों में मौलिक सुविधाओं का विकास हुआ है, यद्यपि यह पर्याप्त नही है। किंतु सुधार हुआ है। शासन द्वारा तय गाइडलाइन के अनुरूप अंदरूनी ग्रामों तक स्कूल, स्वास्थ्य व आंगनबाड़ी केन्द्र, पेयजल हेतु कुएं, हैडपंप स्थापित किये गये है।

3.2 आवास व दैनिक जीवन से संबंधित भौतिक संस्कृति–

बस्तर में जनजातीय आवास के स्वरूप में वृहत परिवर्तन हुंआ है। पूर्व में अधिकांश जनजातीय परिवार झोपड़ियों में निवास करते थे तथा कम संख्या में मिट्टी के कच्चे तथा छोटे आवास या मध्यम आकार के आवास होते थे। वर्तमान में जनजातीय आवास में झोपड़ियों की संख्या नगण्य है, अधिकांश कच्चे मकान हैं। आर्थिक स्थिति में सुधार होने तथा आवास संबंधी शासकीय योजना से लाभ के कारण कच्चे तथा अर्धपक्के आवास बनाये जा रहे हैं। निवास के आधार पर देखा जाय तो संयुक्त परिवार के आवास के स्थान पर एकल तथा विस्तृत परिवार आवास की बहुलता हो गयी है।

पूर्व में अनाज का भंडारण घर से पृथक मचाननुमा कमरे में या घर के अंदर भंडार कक्ष में बल्लियों से चबूतरा तथा उसके ऊपर चौकोट कोठी बनाकर किया जाता था। दलहन व बीज को सियाड़ी व अन्य पत्तों के गोल पात्र में रखा जाता था किंतु वर्तमान में अनाज को बांस के पात्र, कोठी, प्लास्टिक के ड्रम, टिन के कनस्तर तथा दलहन व बीज, बांस की टोकरी, पॉलीथीन के पैकेट आदि में रखते हैं।

पूर्व में अनाज कूटने के लिये ढेंकी, मूसर एवं दलहन के लिये चक्की, पीसने के लिये कूटन व सिल–बट्टा का उपयोग करते थे किंतु वर्तमान में मिल में कूटा अनाज उपभोग कर रहे हैं। पारंपरिक साधनों का लोप हो रहा है।

पूर्व में जनजातीय परिवारों में रसोई व घरेलू उपयोगी अधिकांश वस्तुयें स्थानीय परिवेश में उपलब्ध वस्तुओं से निर्मित थी जैसे–दोना–पत्तल, मिट्टी के बर्तन, चटाई, झाड़ू, कूटने–पीसने की वस्तुयें आदि। वर्तमान में बस्तर के जनजातीय समाज में आधुनिकता दस्तक दे चुकी है। वे स्टील व अन्य धातु के बर्तन, प्लास्टिक के सामान, कुर्सियां, आधुनिक संचार व मनोरंजन के साधन आदि उपयोग करने लगे हैं।

3.3 भोजन –

पूर्व में जनजातीय समाज के भोजन परंपरागत कृषि पर आधारित देशी उत्पाद जैसे– कोसरा, कोदो, मक्का, मंडिया, देशी चांवल, कुल्थी, मूंग, उड़द, स्थानीय भाजियां, सब्जियों पर आधारित था किंतु वर्तमान में चांवल की नयी किस्में, आधुनिक बीजों तथा खादों से उत्पादित दाल व सब्जियों का उपभोग कर रहे हैं। जनजातियों की खाद्य आदतों में परिवर्तन हो रहा है।

3.4 पशु शाला–

जनजातीय क्षेत्रों में पशु को संपत्ति माना जाता है। इस कारण अधिकाधिक पशुपालन किया जाता था किंतु जनजातियों का निवास वन क्षेत्रों में होने कारण वन्य प्राणियों से पालतू पशुओं की रक्षा करने के लिये गाय, बैल, भैंस पशुशाला घर से जुड़े हुये या समीप होता था, बकरियों को मचाननुमा पशुशाला में रखा जाता था, मुर्गे–मुर्गियों को घर के अंदर रखा जाता था। वर्तमान में अंदरूनी क्षेत्रों के ग्रामों में पशुशाला पूर्वानुसार हैं किंतु शेष ग्रामों में कृषि कार्यों में निर्भरता की कमी व पशु चराने की कठिनाई के कारण पशु पालन में कमी आने के साथ–साथ पशुशाला में परिवर्तन आया है।

3.5 वस्त्र विन्यास–

जनजातीय परिवारों के वस्त्र विन्यास पूरी तरह परवर्तित हो गये हैं। पूर्व में जनजातीय पुरूष कमर में मात्र एक लंगोटी धारण करते थे, स्त्रियां प्रायः एक ही साड़ी लपेटे हुये रहती थी। कन्यायें कमर के नीचे वस्त्र लपेटे रहती थीं तथा वक्षस्थल पर कपड़े ढांक लेती थी। छोटे बच्चे पेंट या चड्डी पहने रहते थे।

वर्तमान में वस्त्र धारण व्यवहार में व्यापक परिवर्तन आया है। पुरूष शर्ट, लुंगी, बनियान, हाफ पेंट, टी शर्ट पहनने लगे हैं। जबकि स्त्रियां साड़ी, ब्लाउज, पेटीकोट धारण करती हैं। कन्या स्कर्ट, कमीज, सलवार कुर्ता, फ्राक पहनने लगे हैं। छोटे बच्चों को हाफ पेंट, टी शर्ट, शर्ट, फ्राक आदि पहनाया जा रहा है। स्थानीय दुकानों या बाजारों में वस्त्र आसानी से मिलने लगे हैं। मौसम के अनुरूप वस्त्र तथा शारीरिक सुरक्षा साधनों का प्रयोग कर रहे हैं। स्पष्ट है कि बस्तर के जनजातीय समाज में आधुनिकता के साथ–साथ परिधान व ओढ़ने–बिछाने के वस्त्रों का उपयोग बढ़ा है।

3.6 आभूषण व श्रृंगार–

आभूषण व श्रृंगार सुंदरता, आकर्षण तथा प्रदर्शन हेतु सहज मानवीय प्रवृत्ति है। बस्तर के जनजातीय समाज स्त्री–पुरूषों के आभूषण व श्रृंगार में परिवर्तन आया है। जनजातियों में परंपरागत

आभूषण जैसे– सिक्कों की माला, चांदी या एल्यूमिनियम तथा अन्य धातुओं से निर्मित विभिन्न प्रकार की माला, बांहटा (बांह में पहनने का आभूषण), ऐंठी व अन्य प्रकार की चूड़ियाँ, पैड़ी व अन्य प्रकार के पैरों के आभूषण, सिक्कों की अंगूठी आदि परंपरागत आभूषणों में कमी आयी है तथा अनेक प्रकार के आभूषण प्रचलन में नहीं हैं। तेल, काजल, कंघी, बांस के क्लिप जैसे परंपरागत श्रृंगार सामग्री में बदलाव आया है। वे सोने, चांदी के साथ ही आधुनिक, सस्ते व हल्के आभूषण धारण करने लगे हैं। श्रृंगार सामग्री में परिवर्तन आया है, वे लिपिस्टिक, क्रीम, पावडर, नेल पालिश आदि का उपयोग करने लगे हैं।

पूर्व में जनजातीय समाज में गोदना महत्वपूर्ण स्थायी शारीरिक श्रृंगार माना जाता था। पुरूष चेहरे, कलाई में तथा स्त्रियां चेहरे, छाती, बांह, कलाई, पैर में गोदना गुदवाती थीं। गोदना अंकन करवाने के संबंध में अनेक धारणायें तथा मान्यतायें समाज में प्रचलित हैं लेकिन गोदना अंकन के निशान आजीवन बने रहते हैं, इसलिये गोदना गुदवाने की परंपरा धीरे–धीरे गोना कम हो रही है।

3.7 आवागमन एवं परिवहन के साधन–

विगत आठ दशकों में बस्तर क्षेत्र में आवागमन व परिवहन के साधन पूर्णतः परिवर्तित हो चुके हैं। पूर्व में जनजातीय क्षेत्र में पैदल, बैलगाड़ी द्वारा आवगमन तथा सिर पर टोकरियों में, कांवड़, बैलगाड़ी द्वारा वस्तुओं का परिवहन होता था। मुख्यमार्ग में ट्रक, बस, जीप, ट्रैक्टर यदा कदा मिल जाते थे। वर्तमान में बस्तर के अधिकांश क्षेत्र में पक्की सड़क, सीमेंट–कांक्रीट सड़क, कच्ची सड़क बन चुके हैं। इस कारण जनजातीय सदस्य सायकल, मोटर सायकल, ट्रेक्टर, ऑटो, बस, जीप, टैक्सी आदि साधनों द्वारा आवागमन तथा वस्तुओं का परिवहन करते हैं।

4. जीवन संस्कार–

मानव समाज में जीवन के प्रारंभ से पूर्णता तक होने वाले विशेष घटना या बदलाव को स्मरणीय बनाये रखने व सामाजिक स्वीकृति हेतु नियमों, रीति रिवाजों व संस्कारों का पालन करता है। यह रूढ़ियॉ समाज के स्वरूप को एकरूपता, निरंतरता तथा स्थायित्व प्रदान करते हैं। जीवन संस्कार के विभिन्न रीति–रिवाज, रस्म, सामग्रियॉ, क्रियाकलाप, समाज व संबंधियों की सहभागिता गहन अर्थपूर्ण होते हैं। बस्तर की जनजातियों के जीवन संस्कार व परिवर्तन को निम्नांकित बिंदूओं में प्रस्तुत किया गया है–

4.1 जन्म संस्कार– बस्तर के जनजातीय समाज में गर्भकाल, प्रसव तथा प्रसव उपरांत जन्म संस्कार में परिवर्तन आया है। पूर्व में गर्भकाल में चिकित्सीय जांच का अभाव था। प्रसव घर पर परंपरागत दाई/सुईन द्वारा कराया जाता था। नाल काटने हेतु चाकू या तीर या खपरैल आदि का प्रयोग किया था। गर्भकाल में विशेष देखभाल की कमी के कारण प्रसूता तथा नवजात में कुपोषण की समस्या व्याप्त थी। शिशु मृंत्यु दर तथा प्रसव के दौरान मृत्यु दर अधिक थी। वर्तमान में आंगनबाड़ी एवं स्वास्थ्य केन्द्र के माध्यम से गर्भकाल में जांच, दवाईयॉ तथा पोषण आहार दिया जा रहा है। संस्थागत प्रसव या प्रशिक्षित दाईयों द्वारा प्रसव किया जाता है। नाल काटने हेतु ब्लेड का उपयोग किया जाता है। प्रथम संतान हेतु पुत्र की चाह में वृद्धि हुई है।

नाल झड़ने के बाद 'छठी' संस्कार किया जाता है। इसमें देव पूजा, नवजात का नामकरण व भोज किया जाता है। पूर्व में जनजातीय समाज में मौसम, वार, मास, शारीरिक लक्षण के आधार पर नामकरण किया जाता था वर्तमान में बाह्य संपर्क के कारण आधुनिक नाम रखे जाने लगे है। 'छठी' संस्कार में दिये जाने वाले भेंट या उपहार के स्वरूप में परिवर्तन हुआ है।

4.2 विवाह संस्कार– बस्तर के जनजातीय समाज में विवाह संस्कार में परिवर्तन हुआ है। पूर्व में अल्पायु में विवाह होता था जैसे– लड़कों का विवाह 15–16 वर्ष में तथा लड़कियों का विवाह 13–15 वर्ष में होता था। वर्तमान में विवाह उम्र में वृद्धि हुई है। विवाह हेतु ममेरे–फूफेरे विवाह को प्राथमिकता दी जाती थी, यह प्रथा वर्तमान में जारी है किंतु इसमें शिथिलता आयी है। एकल तथा बहुपत्नी विवाह वर्तमान में जारी है किंतु बहुपत्नी विवाह कम हो रहे हैं। विवाह से पूर्व सात–नौ सगाई का रिवाज था किंतु वर्तमान में तीन–पांच सगाई की जा रही है। विवाह अवधि पांच–सात दिनों के स्थान पर तीन दिनों में किया जा रहा है।

जीवन साथी चुनने की विधियों में सहमति विवाह, पलायन विवाह, हठ विवाह, विनिमय विवाह, लमसेना विवाह, अपहरण विवाह प्रचलित थी। वर्तमान में हठ विवाह, अपहरण विवाह, लमसेना विवाह में कमी आयी है।

जनजातीय विवाह के प्रमुख पक्ष वधू मूल्य प्रचलित है, जिसके स्वरूप में परिवर्तन हो रहा है। सक्षम वधू पक्ष वर को उपहार देने लगे हैं।

विवाह संस्कार में आधुनिक वस्तुओं का समावेश हो रहा है। साउंड स्पीकर, आधुनिक गीत, ढोल बाजा का प्रयोग हो रहा है। विवाह में पारंपरिक गीत, नृत्य आदि का लोप हो रहा है। विवाह खर्चीले होते जा रहे है।

4.3 मृत्यु संस्कार –जनजातीय समाज में मृत्यु को जीवन की पूर्णता माना जाता है तथा शव को जलाने व दफनाने की प्रथा है। इस कार्य में विवाह संबंधियों की भूमिका महत्वपूर्ण होती है। मृत्यु के तीसरे, पांचवे या दसवें दिन मृत्यु संस्कार करते हैं। इस दिन संबंधियों तथा ग्रामवासियों के साथ स्नान, अनुष्ठान व भोज किया जाता है। कुछ जनजातीय समाजों में भांजा को विशेष दर्जा देते हुये दान देने की परंपरा है। वर्तमान में हिंदू व इसाई क्रियायें जनजातियों के मृत्यु संस्कार को प्रभावित कर रही हैं।

बस्तर की जनजातियों में शव दफन/दाह स्थल या समाज द्वारा नियत स्थल पर मठ, काष्ठ या पाषाण के स्मृति स्तंभ, पत्थर के टीले बनाये जाने की परंपरा रही है। वर्तमान में मुरिया जनजाति में पाषाण के स्मृति स्तंभ तथा ईंट, सीमेंट से पक्के मठ बनाये जा रहे हैं। दंडामी माड़िया जनजाति में पेंट से चित्रित पत्थर के स्तंभ तथा ईंट, सीमेंट से पक्के मठ बनाये जा रहे है।

5. सामाजिक जीवन–

बस्तर के आदिवासी समाज में विकासीय प्रक्रिया के कारण परिवार के स्वरूप में परिवर्तन हो रहा है। संयुक्त परिवार के विघटन के कारण एकल परिवार की संख्या में वृद्धि हुई है। परिवार में स्त्रियों का दायित्व व प्रभाव में वृद्धि हुई है।

जनजातियों में रक्त संबंधी तथा विवाह संबंधी नातेदारी पाये जाते हैं। वर्तमान में नातेदारी शब्दावली में परिवर्तन हो रहा है। शिक्षा, अन्य समाजों तथा भाषाओं में संपर्क में आने के कारण हिंदी या अंग्रेजी के नातेदारी का शब्दावली का प्रयोग हो रहा है। जैसे– मम्मी–पापा, चाचा–चाची आदि।

बस्तर के ग्रामों में जन्म, खान–पान तथा व्यवसाय के आधार पर जातियों में सामाजिक स्तरीकरण पाया जाता है। जिसमें जातियों को उच्च, समान व निम्न रूप में वर्गीकृत किया जाता है। वर्तमान में जातियों में स्तरीकरण व्याप्त है किंतु खान–पान संबंधी निषेध शिथिल हुए है। इसी प्रकार जनजातियों तथा जातियों में कार्य विशेषीकरण तथा कार्य आश्रितता के आधार पर जजमानी संबंध पाये जाते हैं। वर्तमान में जाति आधारित कार्य में परिवर्तन तथा कार्य आश्रितता कम होने के कारण जजमानी संबंध का लोप हो रहा है।

घोटूल–बस्तर के मुरिया तथा अबूझमाड़िया जनजाति में घोटूल नामक अत्यंत महत्वपूर्ण सामाजिक संस्था पाई जाती है। ग्राम के बच्चे तथा अविवाहित युवक–युवतियों इसके सदस्य होते हैं, विवाह उपरांत सदस्यता समाप्त हो जाती है। घोटूल, जनजातीय सामुदायिक मनोरंजन सह प्रशिक्षण केन्द्र है। इसमें युवक–युवतियों को समाज के रीति–रिवाज, परंपरायें, सामाजिक–आर्थिक–राजनैतिक–धार्मिक जीवन एवं संपूर्ण जीवन पद्धति की शिक्षा दी जाती है, जिससे युवा सदस्य समाज के अनुरूप नागरिक बन सके। वेरियर एल्विन ने "मुरिया एंड देयर घोटूल" (1947) ग्रंथ में अपने अध्ययनकाल में कोंडागांव तहसील में 278, नारायणपुर तहसील में 244 तथा कांकेर क्षेत्र में 80 घोटूल कुल 602 घोटूल का उल्लेख किया है। उन्होनें यह भी उल्लेख किया है कि वास्तविक संख्या अधिक हो सकती है। वर्तमान में अधिकांश घोटूल बंद हो चुके हैं या बंद होने की स्थिति में है। घोटूल का विलुप्ति के कगार पर होना बस्तर के जनजातीय जीवन में मुख्य परिवर्तन में से एक माना जा सकता है।

6.आर्थिक जीवन

बस्तर के जनजातीय समुदाय का आर्थिक जीवन पर्यावरण एवं कृषि पर आधारित है। बस्तर के जनजाति संकलन, शिकार, पशुपालन, अस्थायी तथा स्थायी कृषि पर आधारित थे जो वर्तमान में संकलन, पशुपालन, स्थायी कृषि एवं मजदूरी पर आधारित हो चुके हैं।

पूर्व में खाद्य संकलन की अधिकता थी जबकि वर्तमान में वनोपज संकलन की अधिकता है। पूर्व में वन्य पशुओं का शिकार किया जाता था, वर्तमान में शिकार प्रतिबंधित है। पशुपालन किया जा रहा है। पूर्व में बस्तर में स्थानांतरित कृषि की जाती थी वर्तमान में अबूझमाड़िया जनजाति आंशिक रूप से हैं स्थानांतरित कृषि में कर रही है। शेष भागों में परंपरागत स्थायी कृषि शेष की जा रही है। इन जनजातियों में कुछ परिवार वर्तमान में हल बैल की कृषि के साथ–साथ आधुनिक कृषि यंत्रों जैसे– ट्रेक्टर, उडावनी पंखा, पंप के साथ आधुनिक कृषि व बहुफसली कृषि करने लगे हैं।

पूर्व में बस्तर में बेगार की परंपरा थी, वर्तमान में मजदूरी कार्य जनजाति अर्थव्यवस्था का प्रमुख अंग है। जनजातीय सदस्य कृषि मजदूरी, स्थानीय मजदूरी, शासकीय कार्यों में मजदूरी तथा मौसमी पलायन मजदूरी में संलग्न हैं। जनजाति के कुछ सदस्य शिक्षा प्राप्त करने के पश्चात् शिक्षक, शिक्षाकर्मी, ऑगनबाड़ी कार्यकर्ता, चपरासी आदि पदों पर नौकरी करने लगे हैं। नौकरी के कारण जनजातीय परिवारों की आर्थिक स्थिति में सुधार हुआ है।

बस्तर की जनजातियों की आर्थिक क्रियाओं में परिवर्तन को निम्नांकित रूप से दर्शाया जा सकता है–

तालिका क्रमांक–1

जनजातियों की आर्थिक क्रियाओं में परिवर्तन का विवरण

क	*जनजाति*	*पूर्व*	*वर्तमान*
1.	मुरिया	संकलन, शिकार, पशुपालन, मछली मारना, स्थानांतरित कृषि (कम), स्थायी कृषि	संकलन, पशुपालन, मछली मारना, स्थायी कृषि, मजदूरी। नौकरी व व्यवसाय (अल्प संख्या में)
2.	अबूझमाड़िया	संकलन, शिकार, पशुपालन, मछली मारना, स्थानांतरित कृषि, स्थायी कृषि।	संकलन, पशुपालन, मछली मारना, स्थानांतरित कृषि (आंशिक क्षेत्र में जारी),स्थायी कृषि। मजदूरी, नौकरी व व्यवसाय (अल्प संख्या में)
3.	बायसन हार्न माड़िया	संकलन, शिकार, पशुपालन, मछली मारना, स्थानांतरित कृषि (पेंदा, दिप्पा, डाही), स्थायी कृषि	संकलन, पशुपालन, मछली मारना, स्थायी कृषि, मजदूरी। नौकरी व व्यवसाय (अल्प संख्या में)

बाजार एवं वस्तु विनिमय – बाजार, जनजातीय अर्थव्यवस्था एवं सामाजिक जीवन का हिस्सा रहा है। पूर्व में नमक, वस्त्र जैसे आवश्यकता की पूर्ति हेतु साप्ताहिक बाजारों पर अत्यधिक निर्भरता थी। **बाजार में वस्तु विनिमय की परंपरा थी, जो आर्थिक शोषण का मुख्य माध्यम थी। वर्तमान में वस्तु विनिमय की परंपरा समाप्ति पर है। वर्तमान में जारी वस्तु विनिमय कीमत आधारित हो गई है।**

7. राजनीतिक संगठन

मानव समाज में संगठन तथा व्यवस्था बनाये रखने के लिये सामाजिक प्रतिमान तथा सामाजिक नियंत्रण के अनेक साधन होते हैं। सरल समाजों में ये साधन अनौपचारिक, अचेतन, अप्रत्यक्ष एवं सहज होते हैं। इन समाजों में सामाजिक व्यवस्था को बनाये रखने के लिए विशिष्ट राजनीतिक संगठन पाया जाता है। जो प्रथाओं तथा धार्मिक रीति के सामंजस्य से कार्य करता है।

बस्तर की जनजातियों में ग्राम स्तरीय तथा परगना स्तरीय परंपरागत राजनीतिक संगठन पाया जाता है। परंपरागत जनजातीय पंचायत में स्त्रियों की सहभागिता नही होती थी। वर्तमान में बस्तर की जनजाति पर आधुनिकता, बाहरी संपर्क, पंचायती राज तथा अन्य समाज के प्रभाव के कारण परंपरागत जाति पंचायत का प्रभाव कम हो रहा है।

आधुनिक पंचायत व्यवस्था में महिला आरक्षण के कारण ग्राम, जनपद तथा जिला पंचायत स्तर पर स्त्रियों का प्रतिनिधित्व व सहभागिता हो रही है। यह उल्लेखनीय परिवर्तन है।

ग्राम पंचायत, जनपद पंचायत, जिला पंचायत, विधानसभा व लोकसभा हेतु सीट आरक्षित होने के कारण जनजातीय समाज को प्रतिनिधित्व प्राप्त हो रहा है।

वर्तमान में जनजाति के शिक्षित, जागरूक तथा प्रगतिशील सदस्यों द्वारा समाज को जागरूक, संगठित तथा विकास मार्ग पर अग्रसर करने हेतु आधुनिक जातीय सामाजिक संगठन का गठन किया गया है।

8. धार्मिक जीवन

बस्तर का जनजातीय धर्म तथा देवी–देवता प्रकृति, आत्मा, अलौकिक शक्ति के विश्वास पर आधारित है। जनजातियों में गृह स्तर, ग्राम स्तर, क्षेत्र स्तर तथा सार्वभौमिक स्तर पर देवी–देवता पाये जाते हैं। इन देवी देवताओं की पूजा देवगुड़ी ग्राम में या जंगल में या किसी मुख्य स्थल पर होती है, जिनका पूजनकार्य पुजारी, गायता आदि करते हैं। जनजातियों के त्यौहार प्रकृति तथा आर्थिक कार्यों के सापेक्ष जुड़े हुये हैं।

बस्तर की जनजातियों के धर्म के क्षेत्र में परिवर्तन हुआ है। सांस्कृतिक संपर्क के फलस्वरूप हिंदू धर्म का प्रभाव जनजातीय धर्म पर हुआ है।

बस्तर की जनजातियों में इसाई धर्मान्तरण का प्रभाव हुआ है। बस्तर के जनजातीय क्षेत्रों में इसाई मिशनरियों के प्रचार तथा प्रभाव स्वरूप अनेक जनजातीय सदस्य इसाई धर्म ग्रहण कर रहे हैं। जिससे जनजातीय समाज में कई अवसर पर विवाह व मृत्यु संस्कार के दौरान विवादपूर्ण स्थिति निर्मित होने लगी है।

बस्तर के जनजातीय पर्व में परंपरागत आदिम पर्व के साथ–साथ हिंदू व इसाई त्यौहार भी शमिल हो गये हैं।

9. लोक कला संस्कृति–

बस्तर की जनजातीय के परंपरागत लोक गीत, संगीत, नृत्य में परिवर्तन आया है। अनेक महत्वपूर्ण गीत, संगीत, नृत्य का लोप हो रहा है। नर्तक दलों के पारंपरिक वेश भूषा, आभूषण, वाद्य यंत्र का लोप हो रहा है तथा वे नये प्रकार के वस्त्र व बाहरी आभूषण, वाद्य यंत्र का प्रयोग करने लगे है।

बस्तर के जनजातीय समुदाय बहुस्तरीय बाह्य संपर्क, विकासीय प्रक्रियाओं, राजनीतिक–प्रशासनिक परिस्थिति आदि के कारण परिवर्तन के दौर से गुजर रहे हैं। बस्तर की जनजातियों में प्रशासनिक, भौगोलिक, भौतिक संस्कृति, विकासीय स्तर, जागरूकता आदि में व्यापक परिवर्तन हुये हैं। यह परिवर्तन जनजातीय संस्कृति को नयी दिशा प्रदान कर रहे हैं। बस्तर के जनजातीय समाज में व्याप्त परिवर्तन से वह भौतिक प्रगति की ओर अग्रसर हैं किंतु स्वाभाविक जीवन, खुशी, स्वच्छंदता, प्रकृति से समीपता, निश्चिंतता में कमी आयी है।

संदर्भ ग्रंथ

1. बेहार, आर.के. (1995): बस्तर–एक अध्ययन. म.प्र. हिन्दी ग्रंथ अकादमी भोपाल
2. सिंह, आर. (2003): अबूझमाड़िया आदिम जनजाति के विकास कार्यक्रमों का मानवशास्त्रीय मूल्यांकन. अप्रकाशित शोध प्रबंध, मानवविज्ञान अध्ययनशाला, पं. रविशंकर शुक्ल विश्वविद्यालय, रायपुर.
3. एल्विन, वी. (1947): द मुरिया एंड देयर घोटुल. ऑक्सफोर्ड युनिवर्सिटी प्रेस, लंदन.
4. एल्विन, वी. (1943): माड़िया मर्डर एंड सुसाइड. ऑक्सफोर्ड युनिवर्सिटी प्रेस, लंदन.
5. ग्रिगसन, डब्ल्यू. वी. (1938): द माड़िया गोंड्स ऑफ बस्तर. ऑक्सफोर्ड युनिवर्सिटी प्रेस, लंदन.
6. जगदलपुरी, एल.(2000): बस्तर–इतिहास एवं संस्कृति. म.प्र. हिन्दी ग्रंथ एकादमी भोपाल.
7. विद्यार्थी, एल.पी. एवं रॉय, बी.के.(1976): द ट्राइबल कल्चर ऑफ इंडिया, कान्सेप्ट पब्लिशिंग कम्पनी नई दिल्ली.

नोट

डॉ. राजेन्द्र सिंह, अनुसंधान सहायक, आदिमजाति अनुसंधान एवं प्रशिक्षण संस्थान, जगदलपुर (छ.ग)
मोबाइल–9424282782, 8827160789- ई–मेल–dr.rajsingh@rediffmail.com.

Chapter - 15

मुरिया जनजाति के जीवन में घोटुल का महत्व

बीना विष्वकर्मा

प्रस्तावना

मानव सामाजिक प्राणी है। प्रत्येक जाति और जनजाति अपने समुदाय के अनुसार एक क्षेत्र में समूह में रहना पंसद करती है। प्रत्येक समुदाय को अपने समूह के प्रति विषेष लगाव होता है। हर समुदाय के अपने पारंम्परिक राजनैतिक, रीति–रिवाज, धार्मिक और सामाजिक नियम होते है। यह व्यवस्था समुदाय के हित के लिए बनाई होती है जिसका उस समुदाय के प्रत्येक व्यक्तियों का पालन करना कतर्व्य होता है। जिससे समुदाय में आपसी प्रेमभावना, विश्वास व सहयोग की भावना बनी रहती है। समाज द्वारा बनाये गये नियमों के। कोई लिखित प्रमाण नही होते है। पंरतु समुदाय इन नियमों का पालन अपने समाज के हित के लिए करता है। प्रत्येक समुदाय स्वयं को सुरक्षित और व्यवस्थित रखने के लिए संस्था बनाता है। इस संस्था के उद्देष्य को पूरा करने हेतु समुदाय द्वारा विषेष कानून व्यवस्था होती है। विभिन्न समुदाय अपनी पारम्परिक संस्कृति, सामाजिक, धार्मिक, राजनैतिक व्यवस्थाओं के बनाये रखने हेतु स्वयं की संस्था बनाया करते है। अतः इस प्रकार की व्यवस्था विष्व के भौगोलिक क्षेत्रो के आधार पर निवासरत जाति व जनजातियों जैसे मलेषिया, आस्ट्रेलिया, बर्मा, अफ्रीका और भारत इत्यादि देषों में सामाजिक व्यवस्थाएँ देखी गई हैं।

इस प्रकार कुछ समुदाय में अपनी संस्था व्यवस्था होती है, जो अपने समुदाय की युवा पीढ़ियों के लिए बनाते है। जो उस संस्था में रहकर अपने समाज के प्रति कर्तव्य से परिचित होने और समुदाय के हित के लिए बनाये गये है। वयस्क जीवन में कदम रखते ही संस्थाओं में षिक्षा ग्रहण करने के लिए भेजा जाता है। इसी प्रकार भारत में निवास करने वाले विभिन्न क्षेत्रों के आधार पर जनजातीय समुदाय में पारम्परिक ज्ञान का केंद्र संस्था के रूप में देखा गया है, यह संस्था लिंग के आधार पर कहीं एक साथ और कही अलग–अलग भी होते हैं। लड़के और लड़कियाँ विवाह के पूर्व इस संस्था में रहकर अपने समाज की संस्कृतियों, और राजनैतिक व्यवस्था, धार्मिक और आर्थिक व्यवस्था से सम्बधित ज्ञान अर्जित करते है। इन संस्थाओं को भौगोलिक क्षेत्रों और भाषाओं के आधार पर विभिन्न नामों से जाना जाता है। जैसे भारत देष में निवासरत नागाओं में युवा गृह लिंग के आधार पर होता है, जिसे **इखईची** और **इलुइची** कहते है। हिमालय प्रदेष में भोटिया जनजाति में युवा गृह को **रगंबग** कहा जाता है। छोटा नागपुर क्षेत्र में निवासरत **मुण्डा** और **हो** जनजाति में **गितिओरा** और उड़िसा व झारखण्ड की उरांव जनजाति में युवागृह को **धुमकुड़िया** कहते है। इसी प्रकार छत्तीसगढराज्य के अर्तगत बस्तर जिला में मुरिया और अबूझमाडिया जनजाति में भी यह युवागृह संस्था होती है जिसे यह लोग **घोटुल** कहते है।

शोध का अध्ययन क्षेत्र एवं विधि

प्रस्तुत शोध बस्तर भू–भाग के अर्तगत निवास करने वाले मुरिया जनजाति के "**मुरिया जनजाति के जीवन में घोटुल का महत्व**" पर केन्द्रित है। इस शोध हेतु नारायणपुर जिला के अंतर्गत देवगाँव, उड़ित गाँव, गढ़बंगाल और लालसुनहार गाँव में शोध अध्ययन किया गया है। द्वितीय तथ्यों के संकलन हेतु पुस्तकालय और शोध से संबधित पुस्तकों का अध्ययन किया गया है। इस शोध अध्ययन हेतु मुरिया जनजाति के घोटुल से संम्बधित तथ्यों का संकलन के लिए साक्षात्कार, सामूहिक साक्षात्कार, छायाचित्र और अन्य विधियों का प्रयोग किया किया गया है।

मुरिया जनजाति

मुरिया जनजाति अधिकांशतः नारायणपुर, कोण्डागाँव और बस्तर के अन्य क्षेत्रों मे निवास करती है। यह जनजाति पीढ़ी–दर–पीढ़ी घने जंगल और पहाड़ों में निवासरत है। लोक मान्यता अनुसार मुरिया शब्द का अर्थ **मुर** है। जिसका शाब्दिक अर्थ मूल निवासी माना जाता है। यह जनजाति मुख्य रूप से आखेट, संग्रहण, पशुपालन, और कृषि से अपना जीवोकापार्जन करती है। इनके मुख्य त्यौहार अमूस, नयाखानी, दीयारी, गडोंजी, जात्रा, नवाखानी, आमा जोगानी, चाड (माटी त्यौहार), पारधी है, इनके साथ पूवजों की स्मृति पर स्मारक लगाने की परम्परा है, जिसे गाता खुटा कहकर सम्बोधित करते है। इनका पारम्परिक लोक नृत्य ककसाड नृत्य, चरहे नृत्य, टीटो (गेडी) नृत्य, कोलांग नृत्य, विवाह (मरमिंग नृत्य) प्रचलित है। मुरिया जनजाति में महिला और पुरुष दोनो वर्ग श्रृंगार प्रेमी होते हैं। महिला शरीर के विभिन्न अंगो को आभूषणों जैसे पयडी, चूडी, चाँदी का सूता, लाल–पीला माला, बाँहटा, नेक माला और गोदना से अंलकृत करती हैं, और पुरुष वर्ग हाथ में खाडु, गले में साने की माला, रंग–बिरगे मोतियों की माला इत्यादि अपने शौक के अनुसार अंलकृत करते हैं। इनमें विवाह संबंध विषमगोत्र पर आधारित होता है।इनमें घोटुल व्यवस्था होती है। जनजातियों में घोटुल एक पवित्र संस्था के रुप में मानी जाती है। जहाँ अविवाहित युवक–युवतियाँ अपने समाज से सम्बधित संस्कृति, सामाजिक रीति–रीवाज, धार्मिक क्रिया–कलाप, राजनैतिक व्यवस्था का ज्ञान अर्जित करते हैं। घोटुल के सदस्य युवक को चेलिक और युवती को मोटियारी के नाम से सम्बोधित किया जाता है। मुरिया जनजाति हस्तकलाओं जैसे पारम्परिक लोकचित्र कला, काष्ठ नक्काशी में निपुण होते है।

घोटुल

मुरिया जनजातियों का पहाड़ों, घनें जंगलों के मध्य आवास होता है और कुछ क्षेत्र में अपने समुह में बिखरे और आस–पास घर बनाया करते हैं। अतः वे अपने बसाहट गाँव के पास ही कुछ दूरी पर घोटुल बनाया करते है। जिससें गाँव की युवापीढ़ी वहाँ जाकर सामाजिक, सांस्कृतिक, धार्मिक संस्कारों की शिक्षा ग्रहण कर सके।

घोटुल मिट्टी, लकड़ी, बांस और खपरेल से बनी घर के समान संरचना होती है जिसमें दो कमरे होते हैं। जिसमें रात में युवक–युवतियॉ विश्राम किया करते हैं। इसके समीप एक खुले संरचना का चौकोरनुमा घर बना होता है, जिसमें बैठकर मोटियारी और चेलिक एक दूसरे से प्रतिदिन चर्चा किया करते हैं। घोटुल की देख–रेख का कार्य यहाँ के सदस्यों की जिम्मेदारी होती है। चेलिक जंगलों से लकड़ी, बांस इत्यादि लाकर घोटुल की मरम्मत किया करते हैं, और मुटियारी प्रतिदिन घोटुल की लिपाई–पोताई और साफ–सफाई करती है। घोटुल को बहुत ही कलात्मक कलाओं से सजाया जाता है। दरवाजों और खंभों में पशु–पक्षियों, जानवरों, और अपनी संस्कृति से

जुड़ी विभिन्न क्रियाकलापों का चित्रण और नक्काशी किया करते है। इस चित्रण और नक्काशी को देखकर हर नयी पीढ़ी अपने घोटुल व्यवस्था और अपने पारम्परिक संस्कृति से परिचित होती है।

घोटुल की सदस्यता

मुरिया जनजाति में किशोर अवस्था बारह या चौदह उम्र के युवा–युवतियाँ को घोटुल की सदस्यता दी जाती है। घोटुल प्रवेश के दौरान घोटुल के युवक (चेलिक)–युवतियाँ (मुटियारी) जिसमें लड़कों में सुबेदार और लड़कियों में बेलोसा मुखिया होती है। घोटुल में नए सदस्य का चुनाव अपने घोटुल के नियमों के अनुसार करते है। नए सदस्य को कुछ दिनों के लिए घोटुल की व्यवस्था और अनुशासन से परिचित कराया जाता है। जब कोई नए युवक–युवती घोटुल का सदस्य बनने की इच्छा रखते हों, तब घोटुल के मुखिया को भेंट के रूप में महुआ की शराब देते हैं। जब तक नए सदस्य को घोटुल की सदस्यता प्राप्त नही होती है तब तक वह घोटुल के मुखिया सूबेदार और बेलोसा के आदेशानुसार कार्य करता है। उनके कार्य से प्रसन्न होकर जब नए युवक को घोटुल की सदस्यता दी जाती है। तब घोटुल के मुखिया नए चेलिक को घोटुल के नए नाम से सम्बोधित करते है। इसके पश्चात् घोटुल के चेलिक का वास्तविक नाम घर और परिवार में लिया जाता हैं। घोटुल से प्राप्त नाम का प्रयोग उसके घोटुल के सदस्य ही किया करते हैं। घोटुल में सदस्यता मिलने से नया चेलिक खुशी जाहिर करते हुए घोटुल के मुखिया और अन्य सदस्यों को शराब और तम्बाकू भेंट करता है। घोटुल में विभिन्न सदस्यों के नाम अलग–अलग होते हैं। जैसे प्रमुख नेता में सुबेदार, कोटवार, दिवान, चौकीदार, तहसीदार इत्यादि और लडकियों में बैलेसा, दुलैसा, अलियारों, मलियारों, जान्कों, झम्मकों इत्यादि इन नामों के आधार पर उन्हें घोटुल की जिम्मेदारी सौंपी जाती है। अर्थात घोटुल में मुखिया बनने हेतु एक युवक–युवती को ईमानदार, कर्तव्य निष्ठा, मेहनती, स्नेही होना चाहिए। अपने घोटुल के मुखिया का चुनाव सभी चेलिक और मोटियारी मिलकर उनके आचरण को देखकर करते हैं। इसके पश्चात् सूबेदार के सहायक के रुप में कोटवार और बैलेसा की सहायिका दुलैसा का भी चयन किया जाता है। जिसे सूबेदार अपनी पगड़ी कोटवार को पहनाता और बेलौसा अपनी अंगुठी दुलैसा को पहनाया करती है। इस प्रकार चुनाव होने पर उन्हें घोटुल के बाकी सदस्यों की जिम्मेदारी दी जाती है। कि घोटुल के बनाये गये नियमों के आधार पर सभी से समान व्यवहार करोगे, क्योंकि सभी आपके पद चिन्ह के आाधार पर चलेगे इसलिए घोटुल के नियम के विरुद्ध कोई कार्य नही करोगें, और किसी धार्मिक अनुष्ठान और सामाजिक कार्यो में जाने पर सभी की सुरक्षा एवं ध्यान रखोगे। इस प्रकार की प्रतिज्ञा भी घोटुल के मुखिया के द्वारा दिलाई जाती है।

घोटुल का अनुशासन

घोटुल का अनुशासन कठोर होता है। जिसका पालन वहाँ के प्रत्येक सदस्य के लिए अनिवार्य होता है। इन नियमों के पालन हेतु घोटुल के मुखिया सूबेदार और बेलौसा अपने अन्य सदस्यों से घोटुल से सम्बधित विभिन्न कार्य भी करवाते है। घोटुल के प्रत्येक चेलिक और मोटियारी को प्रतिदिन घोटुल पर अपनी उपस्थिति देनी होती है। अगर किसी कारण वश वह नही आता तो इसकी सूचना अपने मुखिया को देना होता है, नही तो उसे घोटुल के अनुशासन न मानने पर दण्ड दिया जाता है। कोई चेलिक–मोटियारी अपने मुखिया के आदेश का पालन न करता हो और घोटुल व्यवस्था को भंग करता हो तब बैठक सभा बुलाकर उसे दण्डित किया जाता है। घोटुल की मोटियारी के साथ अगर कोई चेलिक उसकी इच्छा के बिना या अन्य किसी के साथी के साथ उससे शारीरिक सम्बंध बनाने के लिए कोशिश करे तो उसे कठोर दण्ड दिया जाता है साथ ही

जुर्माना भी लिया जाता है। इनमें अगर घोटुल के मुखिया भी घोटुल के नियमों के विरुद्ध कार्य करता हो तो उसे भी दण्ड देने का प्रावधान उनके अन्य सदस्य के द्वारा होता है। इस प्रकार देखा गया है, कि घोटुल की अनुशासन व्यवस्था सभी के लिए समान रुप से होती है। और घोटुल के अनुशासन के माध्यम से युवक–युवतियाँ अपने जीवन में अनुशासन के महत्व को समझते है।

सामाजिक जीवन में घोटुल का महत्व

घोटुल मुरिया जनजातियों के अनुशासन और समाज से सम्बधित सामाजिक, आर्थिक, धार्मिक और राजनैतिक शिक्षा का केन्द्र रहा है जहाँ अविवाहित लड़के और लड़कियाँ जीवन को व्यवस्थित ढंग से जीना सीखते है। यहाँ अपने मुखिया सुबेदार और बेलौसा के मार्ग दर्शन के माध्यम से जीवन में अनुशासन, परिवार के प्रति स्नेह, एक दूसरे के प्रति मदद की भावना इनमें समाहित हो जाती है। और जब वह घोटुल से विवाहित होने के बाद अपनी सदस्यता खत्म करता है। तो अपने साथ घोटुल से प्राप्त गुणों को जीवन भर आत्मसात किया होता है। अतः घोटुल के चेलिक और मोटियारी घोटुल में रात्रि में अपना समय बिताते हैं। पंरतु वह समुदाय में होने वाले विभिन्न अवसरों में भी अपना योगदान देते है।

जन्म संस्कार

मुरिया जनजातियों में जब किसी परिवार में नवजात शिशु का जन्म होता है। तब बच्चे के जन्म के बाद विभिन्न संस्कार जैसे छठी संस्कार और नामकरण संस्कार बहुत ही उत्साह के साथ करते है। इस अवसर पर घोटुल के चेलिक–मोटियारी भोजन व्यवस्था, लोकन नृत्य, लोकगीत गाते है। और नए शिशु का स्वागत बहुत ही हर्षो उल्लास से करते हुए उसके अच्छे जीवन की कामना करते है।

विवाह संस्कार में सहयोग

मुरिया जनजातियों में लोकमान्यतानुसार विवाह जीवन में आवश्यक माना जाता है। विवाह के बिना जीवन सार्थक नहीं होता है। विवाह के पूर्व मृत्यु हो जाये तो व्यक्ति की आत्मा भटकती है। और अन्य अविवाहित युवक–युवतियों को परेशान करती है। इस प्रकार इस तरह वे विवाह और परिवार को सार्थक बनाने हेतु इसकी शिक्षा घोटुल से प्राप्त कर लेते हैं। यहाँ युवक–युवतियाँ घोटुल में एक दूसरे से प्रेम भावना से जुड़ने लगते हैं। और घोटुल के मुखिया सूबेदार और बेलौसा के माध्यम से विवाह के पूर्व वैवाहिक जीवन जीने की शिक्षा प्राप्त करते है।

मुरिया समुदाय में जब किसी का विवाह होता है। तब यह विवाह घोटुल के सदस्य चेलिक–मोटियारी का प्रेम विवाह हो या परिवार के पंसद से हो घोटुल के चेलिक– मोटियारी की महत्वपूर्ण भूमिका विवाह संस्कार में होती है। विवाह के लिए वर–वधू के लिए मंडप तैयार करना जिसके लिए चेलिक–मोटियारी का जंगल से सेमुर और महुआ के पेड़ की डाल लाना, मंडप में चावल आटे का रंगोली बनाना इत्यादि शामिल है। वर–वधू को अविवाहित युवक–युवतियाँ ही हल्दी लगाने का कार्य करते है। आपस में प्रेम भावना और परिहास का सम्बन्ध होने के कारण विवाह के दौरान वे एक दूसरे से हंसी–मंजाक करते हुए वर–वधू से भी परिहास करते हुए चिढ़ाया करते है। विवाह के दौरान घोटुल के युवक–युवतियाँ खुशी जाहिर करते हुए नृत्य और लोकगीत, विदाई गीतों की तरह होती है, जो घोटुल में साथ बीते हुए हर पल से संम्बधित होता है, कि घोटुल के दौरान उसका जीवन कैसा था, आज वो वैवाहिक जीवन से जुड़ रहा है, विवाह के बाद उसकी घोटुल से भी

विदाई हो जाएगी यह सभी भावनायें उनके गीतों में शामिल होती है। इस प्रकार विवाह संस्कार में भोजन व्यवस्था में भी घोटुल के सदस्य भोजन बनाने, खाने हेतु पत्तों का दोना बनाना, मेहमानों को भोजन वितरण करना इत्यादि कार्य में भी सहयोग करते हैं।

मृत्यु संस्कार में सहयोग

मुरिया जनजातियों में जब किसी की मृत्यु प्राकृतिक कारण वश या दुर्घटनावश होती है तब मृत व्यक्ति के शरीर को जलाया या दफनाया करते है। साथ ही मृत व्यक्ति की आत्मा की शान्ति के लिए विभिन्न प्रकार के मृत्यु संस्कार भी करते है। ये अपने पूवर्जो से बहुत ही भावनात्मक रुप से जुड़े होते है। और उनकी आत्मा शांति हेतु क्रियाक्रम, बरसी और पूवर्जो का गाता खूंटा संस्कार करते है। यह संस्कार गोत्र के आधार पर होता है। पर मृतक संस्कार में होने वाले सभी रीति–रिवाजों को अन्य गोत्र के सदस्य जो उन परिवार सम्बन्धी हो, वे ही इस कार्य को करते है। इन मृतक संस्कारों में घोटुल के सदस्य भी मृतक के परिबार के साथ सहयोग के रुप में अतिथियों की देखभाल, भोजन व्यवस्था, रिश्तेदारों की विदाई की व्यवस्था इत्यादि कार्य करते है।

धार्मिक उत्सवों में सहयोग

मुरिया जनजातियों का जीवन विभिन्न अलौकिक शक्तियों की अवधारणक देवी–देवताओं के लोक मान्यताओं पर आधारित होता है। यह अपने जीवन की विभिन्न क्रियाकलापों का सम्बन्ध इन देवी–देवताओं के आधार पर मानते है। शुभ–अशुभ लक्षणों के संकेत अलौकिक शक्तियों की देन मानते है। इस प्रकार अपने घरों, गाँव और परिवार की सुरक्षा हेतु देवी–देवताओं की पूजा अर्चना समय–समय पर करते रहते है।

मुरिया जाति में घोटुल भी धार्मिक केन्द्र के रुप में ही माना जाता है। लोक मान्यनुसार घोटुल की स्थापना महानतम् शक्तिशाली लिंगोपेन देव के द्वारा माना जाता है। घोटुल एक प्रवित्र स्थल पर स्थापित होता है, जहाँ किसी भी प्रकार का अनिशट कार्य करना निषिद्ध होता है। इनकी मान्यनुतासार यह देव उनको किसी भी जादु–टोना और अनहोनी से इनकी रक्षा करता है। साथ ही घोटुल में लिंगों पेन देव का वास भी माना जाता है। इस लिए कई धार्मिक त्यौहारों के दौरान घोटुल में धार्मिक अनुष्ठान भी किया जाता है। घोटुल में उन्हें धार्मिक ज्ञान भी दिया जाता है। कई धार्मिक अनुष्ठान नए धान की पूजा, आमुस, करसाड़, देव जात्रा, कोलांग इत्यादि त्यौहारो में चेलिक–मोटियारी सहयोग करते है। जैसे चेलिक द्वारा देव स्थान की सफाई करना, विभिन्न गाँवों से आए देवी–देवताओं को रखने हेतु स्थान बनाना, पूजा में होने वाली सामाग्रियों की व्यवस्था करना, भोजन बनाने हेतु जंगल से लकड़ी लाना, भोजन पकाना, वितरण करना और मेाटियारी वर्ग अपनी क्षमता अनुसार जंगल से पत्ते लाकर दोने और पत्तल बनाते हैं। धार्मिक उत्सवों में घोटूल के चेलिक–मोटियारी मिलकर लोकगीत गाते हुए विभिन्न त्यौहारों जैसे ककसाड नृत्य, चरहे नृत्य, टीटो (गेडी) नृत्य, कोलांग नृत्य करते हैं। धार्मिक त्यौहारों में घोटुल के सभी सदस्यों का आना अनिवार्य होता है। अगर घोटुल का सदस्य किसी भी कार्य में सहयोग न करे इसके लिए घोटुल कानून व्यवस्था के अनुसार दण्ड दिये जाने का प्रावधान होता है।

आर्थिक कार्यो में घोटुल का महत्व

मुरिया जनजाति पहाड़ों और घने जंगलों में निवास करती है। इनको जीव कोर्पाजन का साधन यहां से प्राप्त कंदमूल, शिकार और द्वितीय रुप से कृषि और पशुपालन होता है। आर्थिक कार्यो में किस प्रकार अपने परिवार का सहयोग करना यह एक युवक–युवती घोटुल के परिवेश में रह कर अपने मुखिया के मार्गदर्शन में सीखता है। इस प्रकार वे अपने घर के कार्यो के साथ–साथ

कई बार घोटुल के चेलिक–मोटियारी गाँव के लोगों की सहायता करते है। निर्बल और आर्थिक रुप से कमजोर लोगों के घर बनाने या खेत में टूटे मेड जोड़ना, धान बोआई, कटाई का कार्य निःस्वार्थ किया करते हैं। जिसके बदले उस घर का व्यक्ति प्रसन्नता व्यक्त करते हुए घोटुल के सदस्य को मांसाहारी भोजन, और महुआ की शराब दिया करते हैं। इस प्रकार घोटुल के सदस्य अपने समुदाय की कई प्रकार से आर्थिक व्यवस्थाओं में सहयोग किया करते हैं।

राजनैतिक कार्यो में घोटुल का सहयोग

सभी समुदाय में अपनी एक राजनैतिक व्यवस्था होती है। इस प्रकार मुरिया जनजाति में भी राजनैतिक व्यवस्था होती है। जिसका प्रथम चरण वह घोटुल की सदस्यता काल में सीखना शुरु कर देता है। घोटुल योग्य व कुशल शिष्टाचारी, कर्तव्यनिष्ठ युवक–युवती को तैयार करता है। इसकी शिक्षा अनुशासन में रहकर अपने मुखिया के द्वारा घोटुल का हर सदस्य सीखता है। प्रत्येक गाँव का एक घोटुल प्रमुख केन्द्र होता है, जहां गाँव में होने वाले सामाजिक, धार्मिक, आर्थिक व्यवस्थाओं को लेकर बैठक इनके प्रांगण में किया जाता है। और समाज से जुड़े विभिन्न कार्यो का दायित्व घोटुल के सदस्य लेते है। और किसी प्रकार का मतभेद या लड़ाई–झगड़ों का समाधान वे उम्र के आधार पर समाधान या दण्ड तय करते है। घोटुल के सदस्य सदैव अपने गाँव की सुरक्षा की जिम्मेदारी लेते हैं। इस प्रकार घोटुल में होने वाली सामाजिक बैठक में युवा और वृद्ध वर्ग दोनों ही सम्मिलित होते है। इस प्रकार बैठक के दौरान दोनों पीढ़ी के विचारों को समान रखते हुए समाज से सम्बधित सभी निर्णय लिये जाते हैं। घोटुल का अनुशासन और दंड व्यवस्था अत्यंत सक्रिय होते है जिसका दबाव घोटुल के प्रत्येक सदस्यों पर बना रहता है। जिसके फलस्वरुप इनमें आपसी मतभेद व अपराध की प्रवृति कम देखी जाती है।

वर्तमान में समुदाय व घोटुल स्थिति एवं अवलोकन

मुरिया जनजाति अपनी संस्कृति, परंम्पराओं लोकनृत्य, लोकगीत, धार्मिक, सामाजिक, राजनैतिक व्यवस्थाओं के लिए अपनी एक पहचान बनाए हुए है। परंतु वर्तमान स्थिति में यह भी आधुनिकता के दौर से अछूता नहीं रहा है। आज इनके परिवेश में पारम्परिक संस्कृतियों में बदलाव होने लगा है, और बाहरी संस्कृतियों की झलक इनकी पारम्परिक सामाजिक, धार्मिक, राजनैतिक गतिविधियों में देखने को मिल रही है। इस समुदाय का वरिष्ठ वर्ग ही अपनी संस्कृति को मौखिक रूप से बचाये हुए है। नई युवा पीढ़ी नई संस्कृतियों को आत्मसात करने लगी है जिससे उनकी स्वयं की संस्कृति के कई भाग लुप्त होने की कगार पर हैं। पहले घोटुल एक समुदाय को जोड़कर रखता था, जिससे सभी में आपसी प्रेम, सहयोग की भावना हुआ करती थी। परंतु वर्तमान में घोटुल की व्यवस्था को लोग गलत दृष्टिकोण से देखने लगे और उसे गलत ढंग से लोगों के सामने पेश किया जाता है, जिससे घोटुल व्यवस्था टूट गयी है, और वर्तमान में घोटुल अब लुप्त हो चुका है। कुछ गाँवों में घोटुल बचा है, उसका स्वरुप बदल कर अब सामुदायिक केन्द्र के रूप में प्रयोग किया जाता है। इसके साथ उनके लोकनृत्य और लोकगीत वर्तमान में अन्य लोगों के लिए मंनोरंजन और पैसा कमाने का माध्यम बन चुके हैं। नई युवा पीढ़ी शिक्षित होने और आधुनिक विचारों के कारण अपनी संस्कृति के प्रति रुचि कम ले रहे है। इसके साथ धर्म परिवर्तन और नक्सली गतिविधियों के कारण पारम्परिक संस्कृतियों और घोटुल व्यवस्थाओं में हस्तक्षेप हुआ जिसके परिणाम स्वरुप इनके जीवन में काफी बदलाव हुआ है। वर्तमान परिस्थिति में इनमें आपसी सहयोग, प्रेम भावना, पारम्परिक संस्कृतियों के विश्वास में काफी परिवर्तन हुए है। वर्तमान में मुरिया जनजाति अपनी ही अमूल्य संस्कृति से दूर होती जा रही है।

मुरिया जनजातियों की इस अमुल्य धरोहर को सुरक्षित करने हेतु हम सभी को प्रयास करना चाहिए। और उनकी संस्कृति को बचाने हेतु मुरिया जनजाति की युवा पीढ़ी को भी आपकी अमूल्य सांस्कृतिक धरोहर के बारे में उनके पूर्वजों एवं बुजुर्गो के द्वारा अवगत कराया जाना चाहिए जिससे आधुनिकता के परिवेश के साथ व यह विचार और प्रयास करें ताकि लुप्त होती उनकी स्वयं की संस्कृति, बोली, परंम्परा को बचाया जा सके।

सर्दभ सारणीः–

वेरियर, एलविन 2008: **मुरिया और उनके घोटुल.** प्रथम,भाग राजकमल प्रा.लि. प्रकाशन,

वेरियर, एलविन 2008: **मुरिया और उनके घोटुल.** द्वितिय भाग राजकमल प्रा.लि. प्रकाशन,

जगदपुरी, लाला 1994: **बस्तर इतिहास एवं संस्कृति,** मध्यप्रदेश हिन्दी अकादमी, भोपाल,

जी, ग्लार्फोड 1862: **रिर्पोर्ट आन द डिपेनडेन्सी आफ बस्तर**, सिरोंचा,

शुक्ला, हरीलाल 2007: **आदिवासी बस्तर का वृहद इतिहास,** बी.आर. प्रकाशन दिल्ली,

ठाकुर, केदार नाथ 1908: **बस्तर भूषण**, नवप्रकाशन, कांकेर,

गोसाई,सुमन,बन्गवाल,के.के.चन्द्र, बी.एस 2008: **बोक्सा जनजातियों की सामाजिक–सांस्कृतिक स्वरुप,** वन्याजाति आदिमजाति सेवक संघ, न्यू दिल्ली,

Chapter - 16

World View of Abujh Maria: Katta-Pen Relationship with Celestial belief System

Samira Dasgupta

The Abuj Maria or Abujh Maria, a lesser known tribal community live in the Abujh Marh hill tract of presently Chhattisgarh. Etymologically the word Abuj Marh or Abujh Marh means unknown hills. The inhabitants of the area are generally identified and recognized as Abujh or Abuj Maria. The name Abujh Maria is probably been given to them by the outsiders holding the name of the place. They generally introduce or prefer to introduce them selves as Meta Koitor. Here Meta means hills and the term Koitor means man. Koitor is used by all the Gond people as their generic name. The Koitors are of two types the Meta Koitor and the Dor Koitor. Those who live in the hilly tract or Meta bhum are Meta Koitor and those live in the plains or low land are Dor Koitor. As the Abuj Maria live in the hilly tracts, they are Meta Koitor. The Abuj Marh hills are situated in the north-western part of Bastar district of undivided Madhya Pradesh, presently Chhattisgarh. The Abuj Marh area of the district is an extensive hilly terrain of 3900 Sq.Km. Presently Bastar is divided into Kanker, Dantewada, Sukma, Narayanpur to districts etc. and comes under Chattisgarh state. Abujh Marh, the place of present study is at present under the jurisdiction of Narayanpur district. Chhote Dongar village check post is the gate of Abujh Marh region. The present treatise will discuss on undivided Bastar district.

The Abujh Maria are distributed in 236 villages, of which 189 villages are under Narayanpur tehsil, 39 villages under Bijapur tehsil, 8 villages are under Dantewada tehsil and they number 19250 as per 1981 Census.

ETHNIC MAP OF BASTAR DISTRICT
(UNDIVIDED)

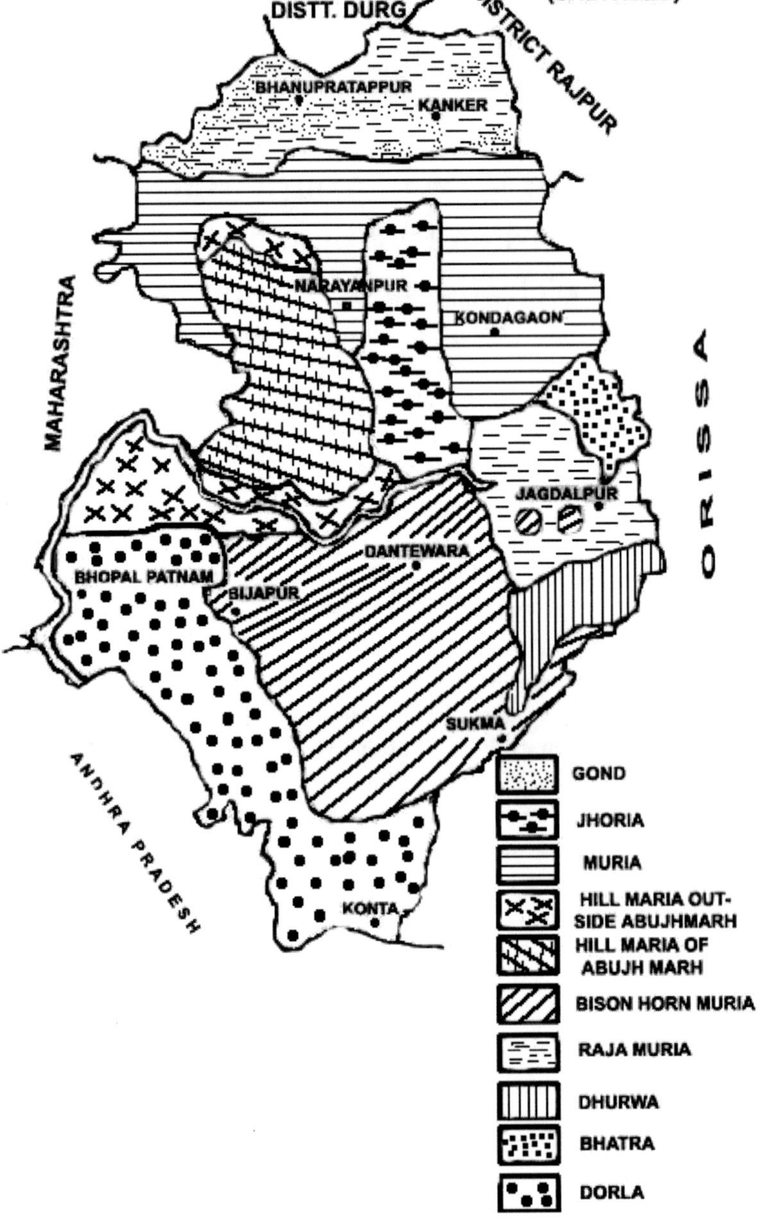

Abujh Marh area is covered extensively with hills and hillocks, with streams and dense forest.. Abuj Maria culture is nourished within the undisturbed eco-system. The area is very less connected with outer world other than with Marh area; it is ill communicated and also is declared as restricted area by the State Government. It is reported that they belong to Proto-Australoid group and their dialect is under Dravidian family. They speak in Gondi.

Economic life

As they live in the surrounding forest, they get plenty of forest products which are very important in their day to day life. Collection of those is one of their very important occupations. They collect those not only for their consumption but they also either sell or exchange the excess portion of collection in the market. They collect various types of roots, fruits, tubers, shoots, flowers, seeds, honey, leaves, leafy vegetables for cash earning. They get seasonal tasty items, from the forest such as *putu* or mushroom, *basta* or young bamboo shot etc. They generally sell tamarind and phool *jharu* for earning cash. Mahua is an important item of their collection grown abundant in their locality. It has both economic and religious importance. They are not allowed to eat any new *mahua* flower without performing it's ritual-Irpu Pandum. It is an essential item of offering to their deities and ancestors in rituals and festivals.

Mahua and *salphi* juice are favourite juice of Abujh Maria people.

Traditionally the people are *penda* (slash-and-burn or shifting hill) cultivators. As they inhabit the hilly terrain, full of jungle, *penda* is the most suitable and easy process of cultivation. Till date they have been practising *penda* as their primary source of earning. They produce various types of cereals and millets such as Kolha, Kosra etc. Along with *penda,* presently they are engaged in settled plough cultivation, but penda is the most preferred type of cultivation. Rice is the chief crop from plough cultivation.

Impact of celestial life

Bastar is such a place which is completely full of various types of myths. Right from the creation of earth they have several stories in connection with their life and culture which are transmitted from generation to generation through oral tradition. These are known as myths.

The Abujh Maria society is very unique and interesting in both of its structure and function and from the origin of Abujh Maria society, they have various types of stories, tales and myths.

According to their myth on their social life and social organization, Bhagwan lives in *upor* or *swarg* that is heaven or supernatural world. In the supernatural world along with Bhagwan, their other deities also live. There, in the supernatural world, the deities are related with each other either through blood relation or through marriage relation. In supernatural world, inter-relationship between the groups in marriage regulations and the relationship of the presiding deities of all the exogamous divisions is strictly followed by them in the terrestrial world.

They believe that once the almighty Bhagwan, after creating earth suitable for habitation, to please his wife, created two sets of brothers and sisters named Nelariya and Nelire and Bumeriya and Bumire and put them to live in the hills and forests of this area long back. As time passed, children grew-up. Nelariya was married to Bumire and Bumariya was married to Nelire. Gradually they had got children and formed two sets of social groups.

In reality when further studies are done, it is observed that instead of two exogamous groups, there are several other groups which are also exogamous in nature. Again in a myth it is told that in heaven there are several gods and goddesses who are the children of Bhagwan and obviously they are subordinate to him .They are called as *pen.* They are related with each other either through *bhaiband* or blood relation or through *akomama* or marital relation. It is believed that the Abujh Marias are their children. Each of the *pens* has one or more village in the terrestrial world under his or her control presented by the heavenly father. As per the wishes of the heavenly father he or she is the authority of those villages. The Abujh Maria children or each Abujh Maria traces his /her descent from a *pen.* They also call those deities as *pen* deities and in short *pen*. Again each *pen* deity has some smaller divisions which are called as *katta*. It can be said that all the Abujh Maria under a *pen* are distributed among it's *kattas.* Here the *pens* may be considered equivalent to lineage and *kattas* are clan like structure. The Abujh Maria people of a particular *pen* are divided and distributed among the *kattas*

Furthermore, in their celestial world the *pen* deities are again having genealogical relations; marriage within *dadabhai* relations of *pen* deities is tabooed. Descent is traced through father. They are patri-potestal. Among them monogamy is the rule, polygyny is also allowed.A genealogical chart of the *pen* deities is drawn where the relationship of the *pens* is neatly cited.

It is believed that among the pens, Pat Raja or Raja Dokra is the oldest *pen* deity in Abujh Marh area. He is married with Pat Rani. After marriage as a rule of patriarchal society, she was brought to her husband's place at

Informant : (a) Tonderamusendi, vill. Orcha. Male, 75
(b) Koriya Jodi, vill. Ader, Male, 70
(c) Senior Male members of Gudari Village

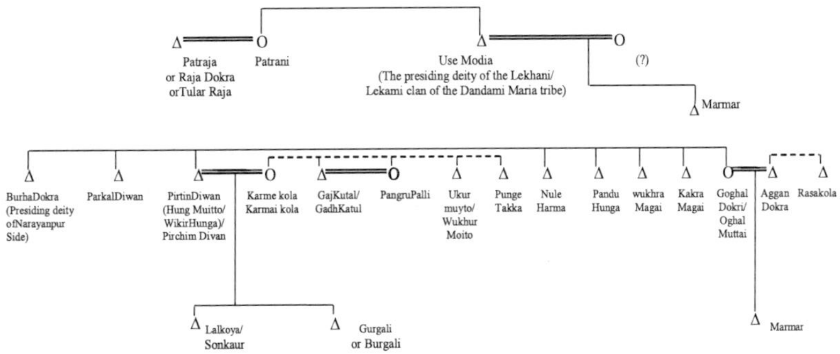

Figure 1: Genealogy of Patraja-The Supreme Authority in Celestial World

Mohonar village of Mangnar pargana. They have seven sons and they are Burha Deo, Paikal Deo, Pirtin Dewan/Wikir Hunga/Hunga Muitto, Nule Harma, Pandu Hunga, Wukhra Maghai, and Kakra Maghai. They are all the *pen* deities of the Abujh Marias of Abujh Marh. Each of them was married, got children and formed their own families which are obviously exogamous. Again each of the *pens* has a number of smaller divisions or branches which are known as *katta.*

The present work is done in village Orcha where the *pen* deity Pirtin Dewan is the in charge. Pirtin Dewan is also known as Parkal Deo. He is the in-charge of both the villages Orcha and it's neighbouring village - the village Gudari. The *pen* deity Pirtin Dewan lives in the village Orcha which is permanent abode and occasionally used to visit the village Gudari specially during their problems, crisis and also during festive occasions. Once there was disputes and quarrel between the villagers of the two villages. The point of demand and dispute is to install the *pen* deity in their village Gudari instead of Orcha. The inhabitants of Orcha had not agreed and not accepted the demand of the villagers of Gudari village .Then as a measure of compromise; Pirtin Dewan decided to divide himself into two equal halves. It also got life and became Pat Raja or Pat Deo's another son named Paikal Dewan. Paikal Dewan is established in Gudari village and Pirtin Dewan in his original place village Orcha.

It is told that establishment of new *pen* god and repairing and construction (when the structure of Pat Deo gets old then repairing or construction of new one is done.) It is a very lengthy process having several risks also. If there is a little bit of mistake, misfortune definitely comes in the village. In this occasion, several rituals and sacrifices are offered to the deity. In establishment of new Pat Deo, one life is needed. So they selected two people especially old who construct the deity and Pat Deo is established by them. It is believed that after the whole process is completed, within few days a person among the two will die.

All the *pen* deities are named as Pat Deo suffixing with their own name.

Following the marriage rules in the celestial world, the Abujh Maria community of terrestrial world is endogamous in nature with a number of exogamous *pens* who live in heaven. Each of the *pens* has some smaller branches which are called as *katta*. The *kattas* are probably equivalent to clans. The *kattas* of a *pen* are *dadabhai* or *saga* (consanguineal kins or brother clan) with each other with a *bhaiband* tie. They are prohibited to have any marital relationship with a person of a *katta* of same *pen* and even with other brother *kattas* of different *pens*.Marriage can be solemnized in the *katta*s of other *pens* only who are related by marriage ties which are known as wife's clan; that is; *akomama* (*ako* means mother's and *mama* means brother). Their *kattas* or clans are named after some animals, fruits, flowers, birds, fishes, generally available in their locality. They worship their *pens*, and trace their descent from their respective *pens*.

In the genealogical chart (Figure: 1) it is observed that Pat Raja's wife belongs to Dandami Maria group. Pat Rani's borther's name is Use Modia who is the presiding deity of Kekhami Katta of Dandami Maria group of Ghotpal. There are several stories which tell that in ancient days the Abujh Maria and the Dandami Maria used to have marital relationship but afterwards due to some disputes between the two groups they were separated and stopped to have any such marital alliance.

A list of *kattas* under control of the respective *pens* of Abujh Marias is now given-

Kattas under the control of respective *pens* (deities)

Name of the pen	***Kattas under control***
1.PatRaja	(a)Jaterom/Jate(of Chote Dongar and Mangar Parganas), (b)Hukur(only Mongnar Pargana) (c)Alami,(do) (d)Nonde(do)
2.Pirtin/DewanDokra WikirHunga and/ParkalDewan(pat Raja's son	(a)Usendi, (b)Wadder, (c)Erme, (d)Korami, (e)Deda,

(*Contd...*)

	(f)Dodi, (g)Dol (h)Gecha, (Chote Tondabera village area) (i)Ahkal(Gudari Village), (j.)Demor
3.Nule Harma(Pat Raja's son)	(a)Deda, (b)Parsa, (c)Ete(Kurmer Village), (d) Boke(kurmer Village) (e) Kodo
4.Pandu Hunga(Pat Raja's son)	Katlami
5.WukhraMagai(Pat Raja's son,Pen deity of villageTakveda)	Vetti/Wetti.
6.Kakra Magai(Pat Raja's son)	Netam
7.Sonkuar(Pirtin and Karmaikola's son. Chalcher village)	(a). Parsak /Parsal (b).Kodlo
8.Karmaikola Muttai	(a).Jugho/Karme, (b).Jodi/Juri, (c). Mador, (d).Kohanaka, (e).Ichami/Hichmi, (f).Badebako/Barbako, (g)Nighaku, (h).Dondaku, (i)Korami
9.Reka Mudia(Jatlur village)	(a).Jatah/Potam/Poyami, (b).Gota
10.Maramar	(a).Marvi(Taktoli village of Mangnar Pargana)
11.GogalDokri/Oghal Muttai	(a).Dhurwa, (b)Dheorai, (c).Dhodi, (d).Vadde.

The Abujh Marias prefers to practise marriage by exchange and specially cross-cousin marriage. Generally they prefer to arrange marriage from a nearby village due to physical inaccessibility or difficulty to travel to a long distance. Another reason for the preference of cross-cousin marriage (or *dudh lotana*) is due to bride-price system. In such cases, automatically the bride price becomes less.

In such marriages, one man gets back the bride-price which he paid as bride-price to his wife's parents during his marriage. That amount he gets back during his sister's marriage. It is primarily known as marriage by exchange and commonly found among the cross cousins.

The present study is done in the villages Orcha and Ader of the Chote Dongar pargana of the Abujh Marh. Each of these two villages has its respective *pen* deity. In Ader village the *pen* deity is Karmaikola Mutte and in Orcha the *pen* deity is Pirtin Dewan; He is also known as Wikir Hunga or Hunga Muitto and popularly known as Dewan Dokra. Among several myths, there is a myth that about Dewan Dokra's family, his relatives, ancestors and friends. They believe that he is Pat Raja's son and married with Karmaikola mutte the *pen* deity of Ader village. (See genealogical chart of the family – Figure 1).

During field work it is found that their social structure is very complicated. It does not support the concept of moiety organization (Jay Edward, 1968) .On the contrary it may be phratry organization (Grigson, 1991-reprinted).

Here an example is given.

The Abujh Maria society beside the *pens* Pirtin Dewan and Karmaikola Mutte (they are husband-wife), there are several other *pens* who are at the same time *akomama* or *dadabhai* with both Pirtin Dewan and Karmaikola Mutte.

1. Both *pen* Waram Mari and *pen* Kapatdar have *akomama* (marital relation) with both Pirtin Dewan and Karmaikola Mutte.But Karmaikola Mutte is related with Pirtin Dewan through marital relation and have several *kattas* under her control. Pirtin Dewan also has several *kattas.*
2. Kapatdar, another *pen* deity considers Waram Mari and Ukhra Magai as *dadabhai(* brother clan group*)* and Pirtin Dewan and Karmaikola are their *akomama* (but Pirtin and Karmaikola are related through marital ties).So it is thought that Waram Mari and Ukhra Magai should be *dadabhai* to each other if it is a moiety organization but in reality Waram Mari and Ukhra Magai do not have *dadabhai* relation but they are *akomama* with each other. There are example, of several such cases which gives the thought of phratry organization instead of moiety organization.

Bhaiband Akomama

Pirtin Dewan————————————————Karmaikola

Pat Raja and all his sons ——————————Waram Mari

> Kapatdar

> Karmaikola

Bhaiband——————————————————————Akomama

Karmaikola ——> Waram Mari

> Kapatdar

Bhaiband ——————————————— Akomama
Waram Mari ——————————————— Wukhra Magai
With
Kapatdar
Bhaiband ——————————————— Akomama
WukhraMagai ——————————————— Waram Mari
With
Kapatdar

It is thought that as Wukhra Magai and Waram Mari both are *bhaiband* with Kapatdar then they should be also *bhaiband* but in reality Wukhra Magai and Waram Magai are *akomama* with each other.

It is already mentioned in their myth that Bhagwan divided the area or land of Abujh Marh among the *Pen* deities as per his wishes. Each *pen* is the owner of his or her portion. Further the *pens* divided and then distributed their own individual portion among their subdivisions or *kattas*. In fact the Abujh Marh hills are also marked out in terms of *katta* and *pen*.

In the terrestrial world, the Abujh Maria people obey the mythical division and distribution of land. The work is done in the village Orcha, which is under the control of the *pen* deity Dewan Dokra or Pirtin Dewan. He, they believe, had divided the land of Orcha village, which is under his control, among his *kattas*. The Abujh Maria progenies of the village are the owner of the land under their Katta's control.

In this way, they believe that, their ancestors got the land which are inherited by them generation after generation. Nobody of other *pens*, even the *kattas* of the same *pen* are allowed to get right over land under the control of a particular *katta*. They have no dispute on any issue of land as they believe it is the order of the *pen* deity which they must obey and must be satisfied with his portion of land.

Penda or slash and burn or shifting hill cultivation is very popular to them. Interestingly it is seen that after two or three or at the most four years cultivation in a land, they leave the land for a long gap of fifteen to twenty years. After that they again come to the part of land and cultivate. It is done as due to repeated cultivation in a land, it's productivity is less and the cultivable product is not at all healthy.. If the land is left fallow again it regains it's fertile capacity, nitrogen balance etc.

When Abujh Maria are asked why they leave the land fallow, they informed that as per the order of *pen* deity they do so. Dharti, known as Tallur mutte is their mother. She gives birth of seven types of cereals and millets, who are her children, to feed them. In repeated delivery she will be sick and the children also will be weak. It is a torture and a serious offence for Abujh Marias who are *pens*' children. Their *pen* deity will never tolerate such a crime and he/she will severely punish them. As they have a vast land, they can easily shift from one to another land where they can cultivate for another three to four years and again after that in another land. In this way they shift from one to another land and after 15/20 years they again come to the land where they cultivated 15/20 years ago. By this time the land will rejuvenate and be healthy and can produce crop for next three/ four years. Here also their *pen* deities, as they believe, instructed them to get better crop.

Now a few cases are observed that Dandami Maria people occupied some of their lands. After repeated enquiry they told that the Dandami Marias is very cunning. They tried to satisfy some *pen gaita* (priest) by offering drinks and after they are drunk they gave some portion of lands to the outsiders which are against their customary law. The Abujh Marias are not happy with it but could not oppose. According to them Dandami Marias are very ill tempered and dangerous so they have no courage to oppose against it.

Conclusion

In Abujh Marh, land is vast and on the contrary the population size is small. So during the field work it is observed that till the time of field work they had no crisis of land .They said that there is no demarcation of land for each family of a *katta*. They informed that the portion which a man can clear, that portion becomes the man's portion for the year and he is allowed to cultivate that portion for the year.

Their *pens* are so important to them and at their villages there is a place which is regarded as the seat of their *pen* god is known as *pen-rawars*. It is a special shed under an *aden* tree and the place is full with vegetation. They are not allowed to cut many other trees for various social, economic and religious reasons. The Abujh Marias has an annual festival of their *pens*. It is performed in village Orcha once in a year. It is known as *madai* or *mandai*. In this festival the *pen* deities of different villages assemble and rituals are done in their honour. In this festival, the *pens* meet with each other. It is the festival the villagers from far off villages bring their *pen* deity on their shoulder to the place of performance.

These deities not only regulate their social structure, marriage system and as a whole total social organization. They are also responsible in land division and distribution. These are done according to the particular laws of the *pen* deities, but the *pen* deities look after many other things of their villages. The pen deities are responsible to keep the members together. They keep tiger and other ferocious animals far from the reach of the village and villagers along with Tallur mutte – the mother deity and their ancestors. They also protect the village and the villagers from all the evils. They are the protector of their Abujh Maria children.

They, prior to the beginning of any ritual or festival, at first carry their *pen* deity (the log god) to the place of the ritual or festival to check the place whether there is any evil spirit or person who may spoil the ritual and also to spoil the place. So to sanctify the place and also to protect the ritual performances they are brought by four persons of the village on their shoulder.

If there is any theft in the village, the *pen* deity is brought and is requested to identify the actual culprit. They say it is miracle; the *pen* deity really detects the culprit person. Not only the thief, they also detect the witches, persons who may do any harm, bring sickness etc. Their *pens* have very important position in their life. They control the whole group of people and their society by their religious orders. Sometimes they order through dreams, sometimes through possessions etc. Their *pens* have very important position in their life. They control the whole group of people and their society by their religious orders. Sometimes they order through dreams, sometimes through possessions etc.

The *pen* deities are very important in their life. Their world view is that their *pens* are their guardians. Their land, their crops, their social, political and religious life, and all the worldly objects are controlled by their *pens*. Each *pen* has village or villages under his or her control. But they are directly linked with the Supremo— the heavenly father.

Reference

Dasgupta, Samira and Amitabha Sarkar 2003. 'A New Dimension on Social Organisation of Abujh Maria of Tribal Bastar: Communion between Celestial and Terrestrial life', in Journal of Indian Anthropological Society, Vol.38, pp.41-54.

Dasgupta, Samira and Amitabha Sarkar 2005. Reflection of Ethno-Science: Study on the Abujh Maria, New Delhi: Mittal Publications.

Grigson, Sir Wilfrid (reprinted). 1991. The Muria Gonds of Bastar, Delhi: Vanya Prakashan and Oxford University Press.

Jay Edward, J. 1968. A Tribal Village of Middle India, Calcutta: Anthropological Survey of India, Memoir no. 21.

Chapter - 17

Socio-economic and Cultural Life of the Baiga: A Dicronic Study in Achanakmar-Amarkantak Biosphare, Chhattishgarh

Raj Kishor Mahato

An attempt has been made in this paper to testify the impact of science and technology, impact of urbanization, spread of modern education and fast communication on Baiga tribe of Achanak-Amarkantak Biosphere, Bilaspur. The present paper intends to know about their change of socio-economic and cultural life of the Baiga tribe in two different time frames. To understand the impact, different parameters were incorporated in the study which includes the social, economic, religious and educational level of Baiga tribe.

The field work was carried for a period of one month during 2008. The primary data was collected with the help of interviews, schedules, observations and photography. Focused Group Discussion was carried out simultaneously to get the knowledge of the existing situation.

Area and the people

Achanakmar-Amarkantak Biosphere Reserve lies between latitude 20°15' to 22°58' N and longitude 81°25' to 82°25' E having an area of 3835.51 Sq. Km. partly falling in Madhya Pradesh and partly in Chattisgarh state. This Biosphere Reserve is demarcated into two zones i.e. Buffer Zone and Core Zone.

Buffer Zone: The area of this zone is 3283.96 Sq. Km. of which 1124.98 Sq. Km. falls in Dindori and Anuppur district of Madhya Pradesh and rest 2058.96 Sq. Km. area falls in Bilaspur district.

Core Zone: Achanakmar wild life sanctuary is the core area and its area is 551.15 Sq. Km. Core zone entirely falls under the jurisdiction of Chattisgarh state. There are only twenty-two villages in the core area of this biosphere as per official record of the Bilaspur forest division. But the study reveals existing twenty-four villages.

In tribal heritage of Achanakmar Biosphere Reserve only six tribes, namely, Baiga, Dhanwar, Gond, Kawar, Kol and Oraon are living. Among all these tribes the Baigas are found in each and every villages of the core area of the biosphere reserve. So, they are having special identity. Ethnically, they primarily belong to proto-Austral racial stock and linguistically to Dravidian family of languages, but most of them have, however, given up their original mother language and speak in local dialect of regional language i.e. Chattisgarhi.

The Baiga is one of the Particularly Vulnerable Tribal Group (PVTG) in Chhattishgarh. They are also referred to as Panda. Etymologically, the term Baiga means a priest. They believe that they are the descendents of mother earth. According to another legend, the community descended from a man called Nanga Baiga. They are village priests and medicinemen, distributed in the forest hill tracts of Bilaspur, Shahdol and Durg of Chhattisgarh state. According to the 1981 Census, the population of the Baiga was 2,48,949, out of which 97.12 per cent are returned from rural areas. The local dialect, Parshi bhasha or Govali bhasha, a corrupt form of Hindi, is spoken by the Baiga. Hindi language and the Devanagari script are used for inter-group communication (K. S. Singh: 1994:79-82).

The Baiga people used to practise shifting cultivation and subsisted on collection of non-timber forest produce/minor forest produce. Of late, they have taken up settled cultivation and they continue to collect non-timber forest produce/minor forest produce.

Since shifting cultivation in forest areas has been completely banned, the Baiga now depend on agriculture, collection of non-timber forest produce/minor forest produce and wage labour. The Baiga are categorized as Particularly Vulnerable Tribal Group as they are agriculturally, technologically, socially and economically very backward. To elevate the socio-economic status of the Baiga, the Government of India has introduced several developmental programmes keeping in view their natural environment.

Baiga Population in the Core Area

The total populations of core villages are 8918 and out of this population the tribal population is 7489 which constitute 83.9 percent of the population.

So, it appears that core area of Achanakmar-Amarkantak Biosphere Reserve has a sizable number of tribal populations. From the table given below it appears that Baigas are dominant as well as ranking on the top among the tribal communities. Their total population is 3400 which constitute 45.4 percent. Unfortunately I am unable to show an analysis of the variation of population of the Baiga during the Census of 1981, 1991 and 2001 and further comparison with my data due to non-availability of the Census data.

Table No. 1 Distribution of population in the core area

Sr. No.	*Tribe*	*Male*	*Female*	*Total*	*%*
01.	Baiga	1725	1675	3400	45.4
02.	Dhanwar	73	64	137	1.8
03.	Kawar	112	115	227	3.0
04.	Kol	119	188	382	5.1
05.	Gond	1275	1288	2563	34.2
06.	Oraon	4.4	378	782	10.4

Source: primary, data – 2008.

Big villages like Chaparawa, Lamani, Mahamai, Niwaskar, Rajak, Surhi have maximum under of Baiga families, besides families of other communities. Similarly a few small villages such as Bankal, Chhirhatta, Jalda, Kuba, Samardhasan have hundred percent Baiga families. In other words we can say that these villages are uniethnic villages. In addition to these villages, two hamlet namely Babutola and Ghameri which are now considered as villages and existing Mahamai since 1980 have also a considerable number of Baiga population. The entire area of these two villages was earlier forest.

Table No. 2 Distribution of male-female population of Baiga in the core villages

Sr. No.	*Name of villages*	*Male*	*Female*	*Total*	*No. of household*
01.	Achanakmar	22	21	43	9
02.	Atarija	20	19	39	6
03.	Babutola	31	32	63	12
04.	Bahaud	110	96	206	35
05.	Bamhani	8	6	14	3
06.	Bankal	58	62	120	16
07.	Bindawal	38	36	74	17
08.	Birarpani	33	33	66	12
09.	Bokrakachar	63	47	110	20
10.	Chaparawa	112	108	220	40
11.	Chhirhatta	40	41	81	14

(Contd...)

12.	Dagania	137	143	280	45
13.	Ghameri	116	138	254	45
14.	Jakarbandha	3	6	9	1
15.	Jalda	101	106	207	41
16.	Katami	15	14	29	5
17.	Kuba	101	106	207	41
18.	Lamani	132	140	272	57
19.	Mahamai	55	45	100	21
20.	Niwaskar	175	144	319	55
21.	Rajak	174	187	361	61
22.	Samardhasan	32	26	58	14
23.	Surhi	136	130	266	59
24.	Telaidabara	74	61	135	32
	Total	1637	1727	3400	636

Source: primary, data – 2008.

So they have come and settled down in this village after abandoning their villages of Boiraha (10 Km), Patparha (12 Km), Birarpani (20 Km) etc.

Numerically the Baiga occupies first position in the core area and it may be pointed out that among other societies of the core area they are socially downward. This may be because of ignorance, simplicity and absence of education or skill among them.

Marriage

Socially and economically marriage in a family is very important because necessity of paying bride price is attached to it. So the parents must save for paying the bride price. Generally a Baiga does not take a girl from his own clan. Most of the Baiga of the core area prefer village endogamy and maintain clan exogamy but the rule of clan exogamy are not always maintained. We have seen that now-a-days rule of clan exogamy are not strictly observed and a few marriages have been solemnized within the same clan by violating the rule of clan exogamy. In Baiga society marriage is fixed after attaining puberty and both boys and girls are formally engaged through a ritual called 'sagai' (betrothal). The bride-price known as 'Sukh' is settled by the boy's and girls's father. It consists of cash ranges between Rs.200 – 250/-, clothes 5 sarees, two dhoti and utensils of stainless steel either two or four. After finalization of bride price a feast is arranged by the boy's parent and in this feast the marriage date is also fixed. On a fixed date the wedding procession starts from bridegroom's house which consists of thirty to forty people including musician. At bride's house both the parties embrace each other and proceed to the marriage booth. Here, the bride and the bridegroom throw fried rice at each other until they are tied together. The elderly person of the girl's side performs most of the rituals. At bride's house four round of bhanwar is taken and three round at bridegroom's house.

Among Baiga, widows are remarried under "haldi pani" ritual. Divorced wife may also go through it to get a second husband. This type of ritual is known as 'churi-pairana'. Such marriages ceremony is simple, cheaper and quicker. A little of liquor, turmeric and a few bangles complete the list. The husband puts bangles round his wife's wrist in presence of elder and few friends and then the woman becomes his wife. In case of a poor boy whose parent cannot pay bride price, the boy serves for two to five years in his father-in-law's house. He receives food and clothing. After completion of the period he is married to the girl in a very simple manner. This type of marriage is called 'Lamsena'. If the girl rejects him or runs away with another man, the lamsena is given back in cash or kind depending upon the financial condition of the girl's family.

Polygamy has social sanction in Baiga society. Economic and sexual consideration sometimes prompt a Baiga society of Achanakmar-Amarkantak Biosphere Reserve, polygamy is on decrease and no such type of case has been reported.

Birth

Delivery takes place at home and elderly females help in safe delivery, but now-a-days a few of them call a lady health worker for delivery. She also gives all necessary medicines required during pregnancy for mother and child. Lady health worker attached to Primary Health Centre (PHC) run by Chattisgarh government. They used to visit pregnant lady once in a week. Umbilical cord is cut by them and then they dig a hole in the floor on the spot where the baby was born and bury the cord. They observe three months pollution period for male child and two months for female child. During this period they don't take part in any religious activities of Affinal Kin. When the stump of the cord falls off, the next day they perform 'Chatthi', bathing ceremony is also observed on the same day. A barber is also called to remove the hair of the baby and give them rupees cash or five kilogram paddy. They invite their 'Natphai' (Afffinal Kin) and 'Kutumb Pariwar' (Consanguineous Kin) to celebrate chatthi and a feast is arranged in which they serve Bhat (rice), Dal (pulses) and Allo ki Sabzi (potato vegetable). Naming of the child is also done on the same day. Generally grand parents give the baby his name.

Death

After death the dead body is either buried or burnt. The dead body is given a bath, anointed with oil and turmeric and finally wrapped in a new cloth. The male members of the family and relatives prepare a bier on which the body is laid. Four men of close relatives such as son, brother, father or husband carries to the burial ground. Mostly they bury the dead body. A grave is made waist deep and the head is kept towards the south in the grave. Over the grave a stone is kept erected.

Mourning period is observed for three days and during this period household labour is stopped. Food is supplied by the friends of the family or affinal kin. On the third day the mourners assemble at the burial ground and collects flowers and immersed in the nearby river, then they take bath and members of the family also drink mahua liquor. This ceremony is called 'Tija'. On this day they arrange a feast for their relatives and friends in which simple food is served. After that normal household work is resumed.

Kinship Organization

The kinship system of the Baiga is classificatory type. Baiga regard everyone to whom his father would regard as brother of his father. Similarly all the women to whom his father may marry are his mother. The social custom has also some influence on their terminology. Hence kinship term mama is used for the father's sister's husband and mother's brother. Where there is cross cousin marriage these relationship are combined in the same person. The father-in-law is also called mama. The father's younger brothers are called 'Kaka' and elder brother 'Bade kaka'. Different terms are used for the same class of relatives. According to their age, most men of the same generation, a man's own brother, his mother's brother's son are classed together as brothers. Bhai is used if they are younger than the speaker, dada if they are older.

Dress

Once upon a time the Baiga were nude except a lungoti, but now those days are gone. They are more civilized and presently wear a dhoti, shirt, jacket like other caste cultivators. Earlier Baigas usually did not use foot wear of any kind because they were of the opinion that it will render their feet soft, so it may give them trouble while quick walking in the forest or climbing trees and rocks but now-a-days they are wearing shoes and slippers. The Baiga women are fully covered with sari and blouse known as 'Kpra' or 'Lugra'. Earlier woolen clothes do not form part of their clothing during winter season and during night they were sleeping round the fire kept burning whole night but now they are using woolen clothes and blankets during winter.

The Baigas are considered as a primitive tribe, but they are not devoid of aesthetic sense. They are very much conscious about their personality and dress code. Iron bracelets (Chura) on wrist, ring of fingers and sometimes a necklace of beads are the common ornaments the youth Baiga wears for their better look. The people of older generation with the advancing age devoid of ornaments but the test of decoration finds full expression at the time of dance when the dancer's turban is decorated with "Kalgi" of peacock's feathers and Paijan (anklet) tinkle on the ankle. The Baiga women wear ornament for ear. A necklace of coloured beads called Chutia, the Sutia, large round silver necklace or 'Kanthi' decorate their neck. Rings and bangles are also commonly used by the younger Baiga women on the feet 'Pairi' or anklet and 'Chutki' or toe ring on the toes are also worn. Visits to weekly market greatly influenced their choice of ornaments. Both Baiga men and women take extraordinary interest in tending and dressing their hair.

Now-a-days the youth (boys and girls) are more particular about their appearance and clear looks. They might have cultivated this tendency with increasing contact with outsiders and other people.

Tattooing

Tattooing is one of the important aspects of a Baiga girl. For them it signify an ornamental and decorative device which enhance their beauty in the eyes of a Baiga menfolk. According to them the marks of tattooings are the only thing which is certain to go with them to the graveyard after the death. A girl tattooed on the arm, breast and forehead after getting adolescence and in her legs after marriage. Tattooing is performed by a 'Godanharin'. Women themselves take a great pride in their tattoo marks.

Food and Drink

The staple food of the Baiga is most simple and suited to their economic condition. 'Pej' a sort of gruel prepared by Kutki (Panicum Psilopodium), Kodon (Paspakum Scvobiculatum), coarse grain mainly satisfy their hunger. Sometimes they also use rice to prepare this 'Paj'. The staple food is supplemented with leaves, roots, tubers and fruits. Their food item also include non-vegetarian which consists of mainly fish and chicken. A large variety of roots are entered in their diet either in boiled or original form.

Locally available fruits such as Mango, Jamun, Char, Tendu, Bel, Gowava are very common among them. Their daily time table for food starts with a light meal or 'Pej' which may be taken as their breakfast. The second meal is taken in the noon and third in the night. Women follows men's routine and take their meal after elders but children have no fixed time nor the numbers of meal in a day.

Mahua is also of special significance in the life of Baigas ritual and social aspect. All are habituated of drinking mahua liquor. Now they are also habituated of taking English Daru as it is available for them in the village. The village shopkeepers bring it from Kota or Bilaspur.

Economic Organization

During the time of Elwin's study the Baigas were shifting cultivators, hunters, food gatherers and used to roam in the forest with a "Langothi". But with the changing situation specially in their economic life, there is a change in their every aspects of life. Since the Baigas were shifting cultivators so they used to shift their settlement occasionally in relation to the changing sites of their 'Bewar' land. As a result they were free for new settlement. But today after abolition of shifting cultivation a new economy based on cultivation has been developed in Achanakmar – Amarkantak Biosphere Reserve. Naturally, this new economy has also influenced the growth of settlement and house type. Agricultural land is distributed among the Baiga by the forest department to the different households of a Baiga. So they preferred to construct their settlement near agricultural field and utilize the forest materials in their own way in which they put wooden logs, bamboo, grasses, mud etc. Normally one big room with cooking space was constructed by them. Today examples of the same structure are also available but side by side with the changing economy and development of communication example of new structures can be observed in which different type of building materials are used such as brick, tiles, wooden frames, wooden doors with artistic designs.

Forests and the Baiga

Ecology plays an important role in shaping the mode of livelihood of a people. The Baiga prefer to live nearer to forest and depend considerably on forest produce because for Baiga two important resources of livelihood are land and forest. Forests and the Baiga are culturally and traditionally linked to each other. So, they have to occupy forested regions, where they have been living in isolation from time immemorial. They draw their sustenance from forests. Forests not only provide food but also materials to build their houses, fuel for cooking as well as fodder. Forests also satisfy their deep rooted tribal sentiments, right from birth to death. In time of distress forest was Baiga's last resource. Forest occupies a central position in Baiga economy.

The forest impinges on Baiga's economy in two ways. It provides fruits, flowers, leaves, roots which they collect for their consumption and marketing. Secondly provides wage employment through a number of operating schemes like logging, afforestation, construction of roads, buildings, checkdams and reservoir for storing water for wild animals. The socio-economic life of Baiga is intimately interrelated, intermingled with the forest. Forests and Baigas have become two inseperable words. They have developed a symbiotic relationship with each other.

The Baiga culture has developed around forests and in spite of large scale depreciations of the forests Baigas still thrive in the lap of nature. In this age of transformation of economy the Baigas are cultivators but the importance of the forest on Baiga's economic life is still great and can be understood in the following way.

Forest as a Source of Food

The Baigas take out their subsistence from the extensive forest surroundings. Though, they are cultivators but their individual as well as community life is organized to procure food by collecting roots, tubers, honey, fruits, nuts, flowers, leaves, raw materials such as fibre bark, bamboo etc. for preparing ropes and items of basketry. All around their villages and far into the forests one can find useful fruit trees of different varieties. Mango trees of local variety are most numerous. During summer month of May and June when their food supply dwindles, mango serves as secondary and supplementary food for them. Jack-fruit (Actocarpus Integrifolia), black berry (Eugenia Jam Bolana), tamarind (Tamarindus Indica) and wood apple (Aegle Marmelos) are other useful species of fruits. Mahua (Bassia Latiforlia) tree provides fruits and flowers which can be consumed in several ways. A large variety of leaves, flowers are also collected in different seasons, which forms important items of food during the winter. Different species of edible like mushrooms and tubers are available in plenty during the rainy season.

Forest plays another important role as the only source of providing herbal medicines to the village-folk well as Baiga. Varieties of roots, shoots, leaves and barks are collected by the Baiga medicine-man, who have some knowledge about these herbal medicines. These are the raw materials for certain traditional medicines used to cure different ailments. Now-a-days these herbal medicines are collected and sold in the village market. Since the Baigas are at very low technological level, most of these herbs are brought in their natural form.

Agriculture

It is almost obvious that the Baiga is extremely backward and poverty stricken. It is because they had in the shifting cultivation stage of economy in the past. As the pressure of the population further grew and also government efforts, agriculture advanced and forest receded into the background with the land coming under settled cultivation it was possible to grow a variety of crops in different fields. But in spite of all, the economic condition of the Baiga cannot be said to be much improved. Agriculture among them has remained backward due to natural, technological as well as institutional factors. The main agriculture produce is rice but the yield of rice per hectare is inadequate due to lack of irrigation facilities.

The Baigas also maintain a Bari (Back garden). In this garden they produce crops like maize, castor and vegetables. They have also planted drumstick, banana, guava etc. In Atariya, Katami, Surhi villages the Baigas are selling drumstick to the traders who appreciate the value of Bari in their home economy and therefore bestow maximum core upon it. The agriculture activities require hard labour and attention. So, the Baigas don't spend much time for carrying on old activities of collecting and gathering wild food. The Baigas of new generation particularly those who have got land and come into contact with ordinary cultivators are not so adopt in collecting and preserving forest products for dietary purposes. Increased attention towards cultivation has diverted Baigas energies from food gathering to agricultural economy.

Wage Labour

Wage earning by employment as labourer is the third important economic resource on which Baiga subsist. It is a regular affair in respect of time as well as amount. Earlier forest department provide them works on an average from 3 to 4 months in a year. During the rainy season this labour force generally engaged by the cultivators (mostly Gonds) for agricultural work (Bani-Bhuti) and are paid in form of agricultural produce i.e. paddy. In forestry operations such as preparation of fire line, repair of forest road, construction of check dams and for that they are getting cash money. Sometimes they also go outside the village in urban areas in search of employment. Employment is not only the reason for them for going outside the village; rather they have other reasons which are as follows:

(01) After introduction of cash money, the Baiga need ready cash as the only way to get money is to take a job in urban area.

(02) There is a desire to see something of new places because they had very little knowledge of distant places.

(03) Wage labour outside village is an escape from village boredom.

When the Baiga go outside their village they meet several people who are not try a particular caste group. This caste group person offers a big opportunity for the Baiga people to change themselves. They go outside their village to earn money as soon as they reach there, they are oriented to customs, ideas, norms, behaviour of that area. All these things led to the emergence of a new type of personality different in many ways from that of their own village.

Basketry

Making basketry from bamboo is also a means of earning livelihood for the Baigas of many villages of Achankmar-Amarkantak Biosphere Reserve. The forest of this biosphere abounds in various kinds of bamboo. So, the Baiga people take full advantage of these natural resources to prepare baskets and other articles of domestic use. They prepare baskets of different shapes and sizes. It is occupation of both male and female. The female-folks utilize their leisure by basket money in order to meet their household requirements. They sell these baskets in the market to earn money. Baskets are used for fishing, winnowing, food collection, marketing, weighing, rituals and worships. The equipment required for the craft is inexpensive. A big knife and a blunt spear is the only toll required by the craftsman.

The technique of basketry is simple. The bamboo work is an individualistic craft. The craftsman may take the help of his family members if he is making articles in large quantity and at quicker speed. Production of basketry is neither a laborious nor a skilled work. So the entire family members are engaged in preparing of baskets and they sell each basket at Rs.20/- to Rs.30/-. They also sell their products to the contractors who are known as Kochia in wholesale. They come from Bilaspur and purchase it from them in very low price. In wholesale they sell each basket @ Rs.10/- or Rs.12/-.

Religion

The Baiga pantheon is exceedingly varied and elastic. Earlier they were near animist (the primitive belief in spirits, technically known as animism). But now in addition to their old primitive belief they also worship all gods and goddesses of Hindu pantheon but special concern is for his own tribal god. Their principal deity is 'Buradeo' who is supposed to reside in 'saj' (Terminilia Tomentosa) tree. He is worshipped once in three years during Holi festival in the month of Phalgun (February-March) with sacrifice of fowls, coconut and mahua liquor. Head of the family worship this god. The legend goes that nanga Baiga took Buradeo to the forest and put him in the stump of a Saj tree. So, the Baiga never cut the saj down to the ground but always leave a stump.

The Baiga also observe Hindu festival like Holi, Dassehra, Deepawali. They celebrate these festivals with feasting, drinking and dancing. For them these festivals are more a recreation than worship as they are not aware of the religious significance of these festivals. 'Nawa Khai' (Harvest thanks giving) is celebrated in which new rice is offered to the Thakur Deo and some is tucked on the door. In this festival for the first time new rice is cooked in the house not by any woman but by the head of the family who has to keep fast on that day. During all these festivals the Baiga will not miss the opportunity of drinking mahua liquor. This mahua liquor is so deep rooted in their culture and society that they have associated mahua liquor in their religious belief in the efficacy and necessity for all his ceremonies.

Education in Baiga

The Baiga have elevated their social status through the process of modernization, transformation and imitating the cultural aspect of their neighbouring communities. Now they are not looking like a tribe from any angle. But so far the education is concerned they are far behind. Education in its true sprit is unknown to them. They never encourage their children to go to school. Education is primarily the responsibility of the state government. So, the state government has opened primary and middle schools in the villages within the radius of 2 to 3 kilometers. In addition to that hostel accommodation is also provided by the government with free lodging and boarding for the Baiga children. In spite of all these facilities the dropouts from the school is very high among them.

Table No. 4 Literacy level of the population

Tribes	*Literate*	*Percent*	*Illiterate*	*Percent*
Baiga	720	21.2	2680	78.80
Gond	997	38.93	1566	61.11
Oraon	312	39.93	470	60.48
Kol	94	34.60	288	75.34
Kawar	149	65.50	78	35.37
Dhanwar	38	27.73	99	72.26

Source: Present Study, 2008

Table No.4 shows that the literacy rate of the tribe in core area and percentage of illiterate is more among the Baiga (78.80 percent) whereas it is low among the Kawar (35.37 percent). The Baiga have a literacy rate of 21.2 percent whereas the percentage is more in Kawar (65.50 percent).

Many explanations have been given by them in not promoting education to their children. According to them girls give every kind of help to their mother at home. They look after small children at home and when they become grown up it is better to give their daughter in marriage. Boys work in the agricultural field with their parents whereas boys and girls both work as daily wage labourers in various development scheme of the village. During seasons they are busy in collecting forest produce, fire wood, watching the crop, bringing water etc. So many parents just cannot afford to send their children to school. On the basis of above mentioned explanations we can conclude that for a Baiga family to send it's grown up boy or girl to school is essentially a matter of economics and entails dislocation in the traditional pattern of division of labour.

Findings

01. It consists of variety of flora and fauna but another most important and interesting character of this area is its cultural entity. Different types of ethnic groups inhabit and represent a homogenous milieu in which the members are almost an undifferentiated kin groups and feels as one.
02. The people of core area have retained and developed their traditional heritage. They also maintain their identity in several significant respects. They all share the same language live in similar types of houses and cultivate the same crop utilizing the same technique.
03. Few villages such as Bankal, Bahaud, Birarpani, Bokarakachar, Chirhhatta and Samardhasan have peculiar characteristic as these villages are located in unapproachable remote tract quite often isolated from the rest of the world.
04. Due to ignorance and innocence of the local people they are prone to serve socio-economic exploitation by the outsiders in several ways.
05. Extensive cultivation and deforestation seriously erodes the soil and affects the ecology.
06. The Baiga is known for its unique culture because they don't access education totally dependent on forest, live for the present

and don't think for the future. These distinguishing characteristic separates them from other tribal groups. Still they are far behind education or skill which makes them non-responsive to various social, economic or welfare programme.

07. Owing to the suitable location and favourable situations big villages of Achankmar – Amarkantak Biosphere Reserve such as Achanakmar, Chaparwa, Lamani and Surhi become weekly market place. These villages naturally led to the better means of transportation and communication. So, the contacts of the Baiga with urban centers increase which have influenced and are influencing their life style.
08. There is a remarkable change in their outlook, in their world view, value system and philosophy of their life. A new model of modernization has emerged before them and lust for material comfort has increased. So changes have taken place in material and non-material aspects of their culture.
09. Paper indicates that their houses are of traditional style but many items of household have got changed. Such as sleeping cots, wooden or plastic chairs, metal utensils, buckets, lot of fancy goods such as torches, TV sets, shoes, slippers, combs (plastic), bathing and washing soap, cream and powder, umbrella have come as essential items for them.
10. Their traditional dress "Langoti" has been disappeared totally. Each male has dhoti or lungi and female has a saree. The young generation used tailored shirt and trousers. The girls wear salwar and kurta, jeans pant and use lipstick. One can easily observe such type of dress during marketing day.
11. For majority of them subsistence agriculture continues to be most important occupation but in some villages inspired Baiga take up cash crop such as banana and papaya and plated trees and a variety of vegetables especially drumstick, brinjal, tomato and other green vegetables are grown. These cash crops give them additional source of income. In addition to that five Baiga families are running grocery shops in Surhi village. It shows that now they are venturing into entrepreneurship.
12. We have observed in Chaparawa, Lamani, Surhi villages that the Baiga have picked up urban habits of visiting road side hotels in their village for tea, distilled liquor, witnessing movies of TV sets, witnessing movies has broken up their traditional code of conduct and social taboos.

13. Now the Baigas are very much conscious about their rights and privileges. The Baigas of Jalda village, which is in the midst of forest, is to be shifted and according to them they are waiting of the shifting since 1975. When the situation became so bad they disobeyed the government law and settled far away from Jalda near Buran for their livelihood.
14. The author had visited many houses of Baiga family where photo of many Hindu god and goddess such as Lord Rama, Siva, Bajrangbali, Durga are hanging on their walls. This shows their ambition to raise in the social scale of the Hindu society. Seeing large number of Hindu villagers going to Amarkantak for piligrimage during Shivratri festival they also accompany them, enjoy the fair and take a holy dip in the Narmada. This has resulted in giving shape to Bhakati cult, which they found among the Hindus.

Bibliography

Articles

Archer, W. G.	1943	Baiga Poetry, Man in India, Vol. 23, No. 1
Baghel, Ramnath	1980	Ek Satya Katha *(in Hindi)*, Vanyajati, Vol. 28, No. 1
Bose, N. K.	1956	Cultural Zones of India, Vol. 18, No. 4, Geographical Review of India
Hiralal	1924	Baiga, Man in India, Vol. IV
Nag, D. S.	1958	Tribal Economy: An Economic Story of Baiga, Bharatiya Adimjati Sevak Sangh
Shrivastava, A. R. N.	1984	Tribals if Madhya Pradesh and Forest bill of 1980, Man in India, Vol. 64, No. 3

Books

Donold, L. Hardestry	1977	Ecological Anthropology. John Wiley and Sons, Canada.
Elwin, V.	1986	The Baiga, Gyan Publishing House, New Delhi.
Fuchs, Stephen	1960	The Gond and Bhumia of Eastern Mandla, Asia Publishing House, New Delhi.
Gadgil, Madhav & Ramchandra Guha	1955	Ecology and Equity, Penguin Books India Pvt. Ltd., New Delhi
Lewis, Michael	2003	Inventing Global Ecology, Orient Longman Private Limited, New Delhi
Mohan, Madan	2000	Ecology and development
Reddy, K. Vishwanatha	2002	(ED) Cultural Ecology of Indian Tribes, Raj Publication, Delhi

Government Publication

Census of India	1961	District Census Hand Book, Bilaspur District, Government of Madhya Pradesh
Census of India	1971	District Census Hand Book, Bilaspur District, Government of Madhya Pradesh
Census of India	1981	District Census Hand Book, Bilaspur District, Government of Madhya Pradesh
Census of India	1991	District Census Hand Book, Bilaspur District, Government of Madhya Pradesh

Chapter - 18

The Muria at Cross Roads

Palash Jalani

Introduction

The Bastar region of Chhattisgarh is one of the most important cultural hotspot in India. Each nook and corner of this region is full of various tribal cultural traditions of different sub-groups of Gond. Muria is one of the well-known sub-group of Gond known for their unique customs and traditions. They are mainly concentrated in the forest region of Narayanpur and Kondagaon district in Chhattisgarh. Their livelihood revolves around the surrounding natural resources. The monumental study of Verrier Elwin, titled "Muria and Their Ghotul" had introduced the unique ghotul culture of Muria community to the outer world. He also presented a brief ethnographic account of the Muria community and their socio-religious life related to ghotul i.e. youth dormitory.

This paper attempts to present the socio-cultural transformation of Muria community after the study of V. Elwin. The fieldwork was conducted through visiting different Muria villages like Lalsunar, Benur, Binjli, Kerlapal, Palki, Bhranda, Bakulbahi, and Garh Bengal which are situated in and around the Narayanpur district. The data was collected by means of observation, interviews, appraisal meeting, focussed group discussion, etc.

Murias as described by Elwin

As per Verrier Elwin the word Muria comes from the Gondi word, '*mur*' means root. At that time the territory north of the Indrawati was divided into three administrative division of these only two namely Kondagaon and Narayanpur tahsils (now each are separate districts) are inhabited by Ghotul Murias. In 1941 their population was near about 100,000. Elwin described settled agriculture as their primary economic source which is supported by collection of forest produce, fishing, hunting, and craft work.

Murias have phratry system. They are divided into several clan and totem such as *buyi* (bullock), *durwa* (goat), *duga* (cobra), *kalo* (cobra), *karanga* (wild buffalo), *kado* (goat and horse), *maravi* (goat), *kassi maravi* (kassi tree), *etikal marabi* (she-goat), *nei nuroti* (dog), *nuroti* (cobra), *partabi* (goat), belong to the *nag* (cobra) phratry. *Kawachi* (got), *komra*, *markami*, *netami* (tortoise and dog), *parchapi*, *poyami*, *tekami*, belongs to *kachhim* (tortoise) phratry, *gaude*, *karhami*, *ori*,*wadde* belon to *bakra* (goat) phratry, *sori* (tiger, buffalo, bod fish), *wadder* (buffalo), belong to *bagh* (tiger) pherity, and *halami* (bod fish), *kachlami* (kassi tree), *kumoti* (kumot bird), *usendi* (usi bird) belong to *bodmink* (fish) pheratry. As per their belief injuring, eating and killing of the totem animal and plants are taboo. Each clan has its own territory called as *bhum* and each *bhum* has a spiritual capital (*pen-rawar* or *pen-kara*), the abode of their *Anga* (clan god). Though many of them live in other *bhum* far away from their *pen-rawar* but happily share the *bhum* of others and live with other clan in same village. All the clans with one phratry call themselves as *dadabhai* and marrying within this relation is strictly prohibited. The marriage is only permissible with *akomama* (clan belong to different clan in different phratry generally, maternal clan).

Generally marriage by negotiation is practised by them but elopement, divorces, widow, remarriages and *ghotul* system of marriage are also practised by them. Family plays the important role in socio-religious life of Muria community. They observe pollution during birth and death and observe life cycle rituals such as name giving ritual, *betrothal* (fixing of marriage), marriage ceremony, death ritual etc., they bury the dead body *of chelik, motiari*, little children, and the victims of small-pox and cremate the others. They erect a stone in the memory of departed person called as *uraskal* or *kotokal* bearing their megalithic cultural tradition.

They prefer to live scattered in plane area and a street connects them with each other. Their house are built of timber or bamboo and plastered with mud and thatched by local grass and leaves. Muria possess few material, belongings which include some utensils like basket, leaf-bundle for daily uses, fish-traps, bows and arrows, drums, wooden log and flutes. An earthen pot for their ancestors is placed in the inner room, inaccessible to the outsider.

Rice is the major crop of permanent cultivation. Besides, they also practise three type of axe-cultivation depending on availability of land which is categorised by them as *penda* (slash and burn cultivation at hill slope without use of plough or hoe), *dippa* or *marhan* or *erka* (slash and burn cultivation in level ground), *parak* or *dahi* (where ploughing and sowing are done after clearing and burning the area). The *penda* is only practised by the inhabitants of Raughat hill and Abujhmar region. They cultivate rice, millets (*kosra, hirma, mandia*), pulses (*rahar, kutki, urad,mung, kulthi*), *sarso* (mustard), *jira* (cumin), gourds, pumpkin, beans etc. with the help of traditional tools namely plough, axe (*kulhadi*), digging stick (*kunj*), hoe, *detai l*(tool), *yerk, garga*, etc. They cultivate variety of vegetables at their kitchen garden (*bari*). As a part of forest produce, they collect various types of tubers, roots, leafy vegetables, mushroom, honey, fruits, flower, bamboo shoots, red ant, lizards, etc. which supplements their livelihood. They also catch fish namely *bodmin, sipa, dandai, nari, bole, dundum, turu, bagum* etc. and hunt birds and animal as game for enjoyment. They also play various game (*karsana*) for recreational purpose such as *wanjing* (husking), *rumela* (grinding), *pindi usna* (grinding flour), *chakki* (grinding stone), *chuerkarsana* etc. Indoor games and *hoydel, baipar-lad, godel-gara, hirka, meriha, donga, min, kor, raja-rani, rajana belori, goihal, hupen-korihan, tedka, mogral, yen, koda, karsana,*etc. as outdoor games. Their excellent craftsmanship and skill of wood curving and painting are found on wall and door of ghotul and houses, combs, flutes, musical instruments, tobacco-box, other wooden utensil and ornaments.

Jawa, a mixture of *kutki*, rice and *mandia* and other millet, is their main food. They take various types of vegetables which are collected from the forest or grown in their kitchen garden. They consume those vegetable after boiling in water or roasting in fire by adding salt and chilli. But sometimes they also used *garaneyi* (mahua oil) for cooking. They prefer chutney with their daily meal. They meet their non-vegetarian food demand by hunting. They also rear some domestic animals like cow, pig, goat, hen, etc. Their women help their male almost in all work along their daily household work. They drink liquor like *mahua* (country liquor), *landa* (rice bear), *salphi* (sago palm juice), *chhind* (date palm juice), which plays a key role of enjoyment in their monotonous life and social and ritual gatherings. They also take tobacco and *bidi* (country cigar). For lighting purpose the use firewood, oil of *karanji, bandgul* or *kusum*.

A loin-cloth is tied round the waist and wear a turban by their men while women wear small cloth in lower part and cover their upper portion of the body by a small strip of cloth. They, both boys and girls pay special attention toward their attractive looking. The common ornament of Muria women are *murgal, hawel, detail,* etc necklaces, aluminium or brass ring, armlets and anklets, glass and lac bangles, neck and head bans, colour beads, *dhar, kinwa, rear ring, kunjar balla* (wooden block to support the hair), *kunjar kota* (hair pin). Similarly, their men also wear few ornaments. Generally, the girls should get tattooed before marriage because if she dies without being tattooed then *Mahapurub* will punish her in the world after death. They take regular bath to keep them clean and tidy. Occasionally rub their body and hair with mud.

During menstruation women are not allowed to cook and are abstained to worship and to go to *tondi* (crop watch tower). A woman always avoids her elder brother-in-law, father-in-law and a man also avoids his younger brother's wife, father-in-law, mother-in-law and, elder-sister-in-law. A woman participates in all indoor and outdoor economic activities like their men whereas male members of the family enjoy decision-making power.

Muria's life revolves round the ghotul (youth dormitory). The importance of this institution is manifested in all settings of Muria culture like agriculture, food-gathering, hunting activities, ritual and socio-cultural performances. It is a holy institution, tracing its origin to Lingo Pen, a famous cult-hero of the Gond. It is in ghotul that the people learn all types of activities which is essential to lead community life. The boys (*chelik*) and girls (*motiari*) learn dance, song, and ritual performance and process of socialization etc. Each member has special role to play while leaders are appointed to supervise, organize and maintain discipline among them. They strictly follow their ghotul laws more faithfully than other governmental laws because they them selves planned the laws.

Boys and girls along with their household work take care of the village guests. During urgency they also serve in agricultural and other activity especially in marriage and other lifecycle rituals by cooking food, fetching water, serving food to the guest etc., act as crop watcher, take active participation in village level festivals, rituals and other occasions. Dance and song are the essential part of Muria culture. During some occasions wearing their traditional dress and ornaments along with their traditional musical instruments namely *dhol, hakum, mandar, paijna, solor, hakum, jhikar, sulur, nissan, goga dhol, parrang, turburi, sarangi, dhusir, toheli,* etc they perform dance and song. The meaning of the songs reflects the origin of gods, goddess, myths, socio-economic practices, natural elements, folktales, riddles, etc. They also visit other villages during *madai* (festival) for various expeditions and perform *pus kolang, pen kolang, mahua dander, diwali, hulki and chherta* dance.

For socio-economic well being and security from diseases and scarcity of food they worship Talurmutte (the earth goddess), Lingo pen (cult-hero), Budha deo, Danteswari, Bhimul pen (god of rain), Mata, Anga (pen or pat deo), Dulha deo (god of marriage), Kondi deo, Dokara deo, totems, soul of their ancestors etc. Ritual worship and sacrifice of animal are very common practice to them. They perform different types of songs and dances, like *geri, mandri* etc in various occasions. They believe in soul (*jiwa*), rebirth concept and black magic. *Gunia* (traditional healer) protects them from evil eye.

The life of Muria revolves around the observance of several ritual such as kare pandum in February in the name of Tallur Muttai previous clearing of field, *irpu pandum* in February-March as first *mahua* fruits eating ritual, *marka pandum* in March as first mango fruits eating ritual, *wijja pandum* in between April to June before the seed can be sown, *hariyali* in July , *kurum pandum* first millet eating ritual, *korta* or *puna pandum* in September month for the first new rice eating ritual, *cheru* or *nuka nordana pandum* in October before which washing of rice is forbidden, *bhimul pandum*, the festival of rain god and *jata* or *pupul pandum* in December-January as first eating of pulses and beans.

There was Traditional Tribal Council which consists of village elders, *kotwar* (messenger) and headed by *manjhi* (Paragona chieftain) or *patel* (village head man), settled all types of village level disputes including inter-community conflict, land disputes, disobeying the customary law, assault of women or elders or religious, violation of religious rules and social norms, theft, mischief and other socio-economic issues. They impose fine in kind, cash or a community feast for minor mistake and rarely excommunicate for blunders. *Gaita (village priest)*, *mati pujari* (priest of earthen goddess) and *sirha* (diviner) play important role in discussion making in ritual performances.

Present situation of Murias

India gained independence shortly after Elwin's work. Since then, the Muria community has passed through various socio-economic events. They lost their right over their forest resources, exploitation by middlemen, trap of moneylender, and face the population explosion of East Bengal refugees and several non-tribal immigrants who came for business, occupation, employment and other reason. At the same time they have witnessed different types of developmental programme like infrastructural development, communication, education and health facilities, implementation of tribal development schemes etc. Hence, the peaceful, economically self-sufficient group was forced to adjust with this new situation to sustain their livelihood. They broke their shyness and came contact with the outsiders. These bring some socio-cultural and economic changes in the life of Murais. Thus, their simple way of life became complex due to interaction of cultures which is manifested in the structure of society, material culture, institutions, religious faith, values, pattern of behaviour and nature of resource utilization, technology, economy, etc. An attempt has been made to present some significant changes those have taken place in the Muria community with possible causes behind it.

House and habitat

Now most of them live in modern houses thatched by *khapra* (earthen tiles), tin, asbestos, and grasses. But still they maintain their old rectangular shape and linear pattern of house. Few of them got concrete houses under the Pradhan Mantri Awas Yojana (PMAY) and use toilets provided under Swachh Bharat Mission. Some of them have separate kitchen and cattle shades. They have a small kitchen garden within their *bari* (household land). Almost all houses have a *salphi* tree in their country yard. Now they use various types of steel and plastic articles in place of earthen and bamboo baskets. They regularly clean their house with cowdung. Almost all houses have electricity except few remote areas. Now they receive safe drinking water through bore wells.

Agriculture

Land and forest are the prime sources of Muria's livelihood. In the resent day, due to more market demand they are bound to cultivate HYV seeds in spite of the local variety with the help of modern method. Therefore, the local varieties of seeds are gradually vanished from the region. They use plough as well as tractor to till the land. Due to use of modern pesticide and chemical fertilizers in place of traditional pest control methods and manure natural characteristics of soil and fertile characteristics of land has decreased. Hence, their ageold traditional conservation methods of ecology are gradually lost. Earlier their community life was maintained by division and share of community labour but such social bondage is reducing day by day due to use of modern machineries such as tractor, harvestor, pump set, thrashing machine etc.

Occupation

Previously agriculture was their primary occupation, while hunting, fishing, and collection of NTFPs are also support their livelihood. But at present most of the male and female members are engaged as daily wage labourers in construction, agricultural work and MGNREGA (Mahatma Gandhi National Rural Employment Guaranteed). Some educated people are also engage in jobs like school teacher, peon, police and other government and private sector. Even some of them migrated in other state mainly Hyderabad and Chennai in search of job. Very few of them retain their traditional art and craft work. Therefore, art and craft work of Muria related with bamboo and wood are not so developed to the next generation.

Education

In the past they used to take informal education in the *Ghotul* which is orally transmitted. After independence through five year plans the government tries to uplift them and other SC and ST communities under different developmental and educational activities. Consequently, Ram Krishna Mission also implemented free coaching for the children and other social welfare activities like health and hygiene. But after a long duration it has been observed that some Muria children are working in various private and government sectors which attracted other students to continue their formal education.

Ghotul system

Once, ghotul was the life line of Muria community where their religious, social, political and cultural tradition flourished. This social institution helps in the process of socialization where they learn, about their customary laws, selection of mate, religious matter, folksongs and dances, etc which bound the whole community. However, it is a social school where they learn everything related to philosophy of life by mutual understanding and co-operation. Under the shadow of ghotul the Muria *cheliks* (boys) and *motiaris* (girls) developed their behaviour and leadership quality on every aspects of life which are very essential in maintaining the tradition of Muria culture.

But culture is not stagnant phenomena and changing in contemporary situation. However, the Muria way of life transformed in various ways to maintain their livelihood. Keeping in mind in the context of Ghotul the Muria youths are going to school and influenced by modernization. The youths have no time to stay at Ghotul. Due to this reason the unique Ghotulculture of Central India is gradually abolished. In 1942 there were near about 278 and 244 Muria Ghotul in Kondagaon and Narayanpur tahsil respectively. But most of those have disappeared at present. In some villages it is also observed that panchayat office, ration shop, etc are constructed in the place of Ghotul.

Language

Generally they use Gondi dialect to communicate with themselves. But, in recent days due to more contact with the outsiders during market, daily wage labour, construction work, etc. they are now habituated in speaking Hindi and Halbi dialect, the lingua-franca of Bastar. However, their children are educated through Hindi script in school and they communicate with outsiders in Hindi.

Marriage practice

Generally, the form of marriage is endogamous in nature while clan and phratry are exogamous. But at present a few inter community marriages are also happening among them due to inclination towards other religion like Hinduism, Christianity, etc. In past the acceptance of a wooden comb from a Ghotul boy by a Ghotul girl and wearing in her head as the sign of acceptance of marriage proposal in Muria community. Thus a single comb represents the opening of a new social relation between boys and girls. It also presents social right to choice a mate as life partner. Due to less existence of *ghotul* such social practices are gradually lost. Not only that due to shortage of comb's making community expert and row material of combs this traditional craft making art and social values also faded out gradually.

Dress and ornaments

The present generation of Muria preferred to use modern dresses and ornaments instead of their traditional one due to modernisation. While the old people and interior villages only follow their traditional dress pattern. They also use modern cosmetic for beautification and use soap and shampoo to clean their body. Tattooing on their body is one of their rich cultural heritages which bear the symbol of their totem, cultural and religious aspect. At present the young generations are less interested about tattooing on their body resulting their gradual decline in social-cultural and religious values and faith.

Food habit

A change in their food habits is observed due to restriction on hunting and collection of forest products. Rice becomes their staple food at present due to more importance of paddy cultivation and rice distributed through public distribution system at subsidisely rate. They take tea in the morning. Now they use various types of oils such as *mahua*, mustard oil, refined oil and spices which are purchased from the local markets due to impact of neighbouring communities and improvement of economic condition. They celebrate their happy moment out of drinking traditional as well as foreign liquor. As they are now dependent on market oriented economy their earlier relation with other communities under the butter system are gradually abolished. Hence, their inter-community relationships through exchange of food and labour are hampered.

Healthcare practices

In the past they were fully dependent on ethno-medicines and various religious performances of some sacred and religious persons like *guniya* and *sirha* to recover from diseases occurred by benevolent and malevolent spirit. Due to advancement in medical facilities they go to their nearest health centre to take the modern medical facilities. Therefore, the new generation lost their rich heritage of healthcare practices forever.

Religion

Now a days along with their indigenous deities parallelly they worship several Hindu deities and observe dasher. They observe *amush, nnawakhai, hariali, sim gani*, etc. but not in same passion like past. As per their myth, the Cult-hero Lengo Pen was expert in playing 18 types traditional of musical instrument at a time. But now a days during ritual and dance they only play very few of those namely dhol or madar, nagar, nishani, paijel, gungru. Their traditional musical instruments gradually replaced by technological innovation of musical instrument. Even some changes are also taken place in their institutional structure, process of decision-making regarding ritual observance and offering due to the impact of outsiders and process of globalization. Due to impact of other religions (Christianity, Hinduism, etc.) and increasing population their traditional value regarding the conservation of environment through sacred groves, sacred places, use of natural and common property resources has changed. The interest of dancing expedition to other villages also squeezes in to some festival and occasion. The folktales regarding their gods and goddesses, origins, religion, and social customs etc. which were orally transmitted from one generation to other. Those are now gradually abolished as there are no written records. Due to this reason their ecological and cosmological values are also steadily eroded.

Recreation

In the past the villagers used to spend their time with joking, playing more than 50 games, hunting, dancing, and singing song at leisure time. These helped them to spend their leisure as well as to share their views, leadership quality, maintaining their customary laws, and united them. But now-a-days the youths are busy in modern gadgets such as TV, radio, mobile etc. that create burden to exchange their views which are very essential to lead a community life. Even the people are so busy to raise their income that after returning from work they have no time to spend to do dancing or doing something else. It is also reported by the villagers of Binjli that once their ghotul and their dance was famous in this region but now-a-days they call dance party of other village to perform in their socio-cultural occasion.

Political system

After independence due to implementation of Panchayat Raj at village level their traditional council now slowly merged with modern political system. The voice of common people regarding decision making in village affairs now suppressed and the traditional political head gradually lost their decision-making power in village and community level affairs.

Conclusion

The Muria culture and their traditional way of life as described by V. Elwin is gradually transforming now due to impact of modernization, globalization, development interventions, education, contact with outsiders, inclined towards other religions, etc. Although they still retain their past cultural tradition somehow. So, immediate need to preserve the rich socio-cultural heritage of Muria community before being lost for ever through various cultural development programmes by collaborating the Central Government, the State Government, welfare agencies, NGO, SHGs and local community.

Acknowledgement

Author is thankful to K.M. Sinha Roy, SA (Cultural) and Subrata Roy, RA (Cultural), AnSI, Kolkata for their valuable suggestions and guidance to complete this paper. Author is also grateful to the villagers for providing necessary help during the study.

References

Elwin Verrier, 1947, "The Muria and Their Ghotul", Geoffrey Cumberlege, Oxford University Press, Bombay.

Chapter - 19

Ghotul as Shrine and Social Education Hub for Muriya/Madiya: An Observational Study at Abujhmad, Narayanpur District of Chhattisgarh

Swapan Kumar Kolay

Introduction

There is no other word for "Ghotul" but we can elaborate it as commune, dormitory, social education hub and night club. The Muriya tribe would not stand out if it has not the institution of Ghotul. When we think of India, nobody can think of casual sex or open sexuality, especially pertaining to the unmarried youth. Sex in India is not the subject of open discussion where Ghotul stand for it also.

When we discuss about the defining meaning of Ghotul, Roy (2006) mentioned that the word dormitory was derived from the Latin word dormitorium. It signifies the collective or communal sleeping house. Roy compared the youth dormitory with Gurukul and Ashram tradition of non-tribal Hindus, which can be traced from 4000 BC to 1000 BC. During this period the youth used to come at the Ashram when they were taught Veda, Upanishad etc through oral tradition. They were also taught various aspects of economic life, social system, war and the techniques to fight against the enemy. In Gurukul, they had to stay away from their family.

The Ghotul is similar to the Gurukul or Ashram. Since Gurukul were more elaborated with a figure head called Guru, the life was strictly Spartan, regimented devoid of the freedom of self governance as exhibited in the tribal dormitories and this establishes the fact that the ancient sages had modified and transformed the Nokpante and Ghotul to Ashramshala (Gritfith Ralph, T.S., 1963).

In Valmiki Ramayana, the author gives details of behavioural characteristics of forest dwellers specifically of tribes living in Dandankaranya forest. During the search of Sita's where about' the youths used to wander the whole day in the jungle but at night all use to gather and sleep together. This has been interpreted as habituation to sleeping under a common roof. A practice is still found amongst the Muriya tribal community in the Dandankaranya areas in the form of Ghotul (Shukl, Hiralal, 1977).

The Ghotul is one of the most important social institution in Madiya society where no major social activity could happen without participation of Ghotulmembers. The boys act as acolytes at festivals, the girls as brides maids at weddings (Patel, M.L., 1969). This participation continues until death ceremonies in the society. With boys telling stories, asking riddles, reporting daily affairs, planning expeditions and allotment of duties, the Ghotulis a place embedded in and nurtured by the larger socio-religious landscape of the Gond society, a sacred place where no wrongs can be committed (Behar, Ram Kumar and Baghel, Vijay Kumar, 1992). The Madiya Gond Ghotul is different from the Bastar Ghotul in that boys and girls return to their homes to sleep. Elwin had recorded two types of Ghotul: first, where fidelity to a single partner during Ghotul period. They married and divorce which was allowed and in fidelity was punish; second, attachment between Ghotul boys and girls was forbidden and bringing together beyond three days was punished (Elwin, Verrier, 1964). He stated: "The message of the Ghotul that youth must be served, that freedom and happiness are more to be treasured than any material gain, that friendliness and sympathy, hospitality and unity are of the first importance and above all that human love and its physical expression, is beautiful, clean and precious, is typically Indian" (Elwin, Verrier, 1936).

Abujhmad a Destination: Our Journey

Our research project work brought us to Narayanpur district for collection of data. We all know that mere tricious beauty of city which never nurture our soul. While planning we were happy to go to see natural beauty of the village. When we think about Narayanpur district a certain question come to mind about Abujhmad (Orcha). We can classify the word Abujhmad into Abujh and Mad where Abujh means Unknown and Mad means Hill that meant by the unknown hill for others. It's also meant that the people and land, themselves are unknown for alien groups. We can certainly think that, *Is anything really unknown for anyone?* and our intuition said that be the witness by visiting the Narayanpur and Abujhmad then only you are able to define Abujhmad (Orcha).

Full with adventure, enthusiasm and trepidation we reached to Narayanpur, the district head quarter. The central attraction of the Narayanpur district is Ramakrishna Mission Ashram which was established here 30 years ago and playing vital role for the local tribal people of the district in the field of health and education. Apart from health and education this institution is executing their various activities of development. The mission is conducting allied activities of agriculture like poultry, fisheries, animal husbandry, infrastructure development as well as info-tech like Science Park and other subsidiary activities like *Kisan Mela*, farmers, awareness campaigning and health day etc. for multidimensional development villagers.

The peaceful environment and humble hospitality of the Ashram's sages, monks and workers fascinate outsiders. Our exertion and appetite were extinct to eat delicious food which were cooked and served by the cook of the Ashram. We observed that entire world was centralized in the form of peace and kindness.

After the delicious dinner we went to meet the district collector in order to obtain some information regarding project research work. The district collector Shri Taman Singh Sonwani was an attractive personality with very humble nature. He shared his valuable experiences about Narayanpur and Abujhmad (Orcha) block. Actually, Narayanpur district is constituted by two blocks; Narayanpur and Abujhmad (Orcha). Abujhmad (Orcha) is unserveyed area where there is no revenue land. The government does not have the maps of the places of Abujhmad. This fact can very well establish the strength of Maoists in the region.

When we heard that Abujhmad is unserveyed area then really we got scared and our mind started to imagine and predict about Abujhmad. We consider that this is not our fear but the Maoist activities in this area is the major reason playing a role as a catalyst to keep the outsiders away from this place. Abujhmad is said to be in the hold of Maoist. Naxals have their own government in this "Liberated Area" ruled by the Janatana Sarkar or people's government.

But we decided to take risk because we wanted to know the indigenous cultures that are radiant for many years, if it would be not possible for any reason, we would feel regret. We are thankful to Dy. Collector C. K. Kaushik who inspired and guided us throughout our visit of village and journey. We admit that Dy. Collector boasted us which became cater for an adventurous journey including paramount serenity and spell binding panorama.

Now we were ready to go Abujhmad, our destination. The unconstructed Kuccha roads were challenging for us but the beauty of the village inspired us to go ahead. We had seen that dense forests with tall timber trees were the speciality, but why we were not hearing the chirping sound of birds. At the sametime Dy. Collector asked to us, can you hear the sound of birds. And we replied to him, No. When he again asked about the reason then we thought that tribals are the hunter gatherer and their main occupation is hunting, *"Is it the main reason or any other ecological problems are persisting in this forest?"* But our observation supports that hunting is responsible for disappearing of the birds. We could see that poverty, illiteracy, health problems and poor supply of the institutional benefit are prompting in the areas of Orcha. The areas have population density of less than 10 persons per square mile, and are home to nearly 27 percent of entire tribal population of the Chhattisgarh state.

Along with hunting and gathering majority of the tribal occupation is traditional shifting cultivation or slash and burn known locally as *Penda Kheti* for six months in a year, they cultivate a small grained rice *korsa* and for the rest of the period they survive by selling the rice and forest products like *tendu* leaves and occasionally come out to the markets, *haats, bazaar* of nearby towns to sell their NTFPs.

In order to include in the main stream, the government started various development programmes to uplift them towards development as well as to motivate them to come out from their hidden place. PDS shop, *Vyapar Mela*, road construction, electricity and water supply, establishment of health and education institutions are some of them but still huge gap is there which is creating obstacle for development.

While our journey, suddenly we saw a building which has a single roof with no wall. When we asked about that, we surprisingly heard that this was the school up to middle class. There is no sanitary and water facility and even not a single black board. We were thinking, *how the ugly activity is dominating in the beautiful sky*. But maoist activity, superstitious and illiteracy in the areas are malfunctioning in the Abujhmad. It is found that prudent people moving ahead to Narayanpur block for education, livelihood and medical facility.

Our vehicle reached at our destination but we couldn't be amazed that the destination was Ghotul, an *Abujhmadiya* Ghotul. We wanted to acquire it in the form of knowledge by the colourfull attire of the locals, the powerful cultural background of the village and its rich art, craft and dance. We had a chance of experiencing Ghotul night which is great live attraction for us because yet this day we read about Ghotul in the book. Admittedly, Ghotul, a youth dormitory is a social educational institution for the Madiya/Muriya tribal community. Recently we read in the newspaper that Ghotul is diminishing because maximum researchers and scholars elaborating it badly. We observed the Ghotul not only by semi participatory method, but self observation and interview by open ended questions and got the information from youth (both boys and girls), and older groups.

Finally the time came for arrival and we again started journey to reach our rest house. While we were on our way from Abujhmad to Narayanpur, a beautiful infrastructure fascinated us and that was *Kundla Pota Cabin*, a residential school for boys. The hostel warden cum principal of Ashram school was very simple and honest person. This was the place where the head, workers and children all were living as a family and enjoying their daily routine happily without their family members. It may be biased if we do not talk about the wall of the Ashram school. The beautiful wall was made by bamboo (mat) and looked like a small traditional cottage which created the picture of heritage resort which we ever seen in the movies. One question was striking in our mind "*why the Ashram school is better as compared to the other school in this area, why the local people are not developed inspite of lot of development programmes, why they spurned to other and from others too?*" We know there is no answer but so much whammy.

To see the bad or good and hidden or visual part of the Abujhmad, we were thinking about visual explanation. We admit that the tribals are prudent people as well as expert in the art and craft in their own ecology where the survival in any condition is markable but it has been seen, when the opportunities knocked at their door and they heard the outsiders, they do not want to narrate their experience barring few because local media blacked them out sometimes. This is important to note because apart from everything else appear, multidimensional badly presented stories in the news many time creating fencing from external world. Neither the journalist organisation nor the editors guild have shown any concern for the working rights of those conflict areas, especially when they come under attack. Finally this is the concerning matter for government and also for local tribal people.

With above flow of thinking we reached at Ramakrishna Mission Rest House around 11 pm. In our exerted body, our mind and heart were happy and nourished after getting the traditional heritage Ghotul and definitely we are going to share our experiences to all. We just want the readers feel the Ghotul with our eyes.

Origination of Ghotul

Ghotul is always a fascinating point for researchers but they are never concerned about the origin and development of Ghotul. The credit of the foundation of Ghotul goes to the Lingo Dev. He had an attractive personality and huge ability to lead the community. Lingo Dev is explained as good musician, singer, dancer, healer and leader. Varrier Elwin (1947) wrote that the member of Muriya built Ghotul to tribute Lingo Dev.

It is also believed that Lingo Dev, himself stated the custom of Ghotul where he taught the Muriya children under the *Semal* tree. From this auspicious happening, the Ghotul is started in the Muriya community (Kangali, Motiram, 1986).

Another story says that Lingo Dev is youngest amongst his seven brothers. They were living together but after marriage of his elder brothers disputes arose. Thus Lingo Dev built a separate house from their brothers' house which called *Dinda Mahal* means home for bachelors and spinsters. Hence, *Dinda Mahal* is called as Ghotul at past and it is continuing at present.

According to our opinion Ghotul was started by the wild tribes as a learning centre for the youth is since they had trouble in commuting in the jungles and preferred marriages to happen in the vicinity. It also enabled the parents to keep a check on the children. These were the pods of learning where the young tribals were taught not only about daily life but also the art of hospitality, warmth of friendship and the importance of a sense of community. The coed living was an integral part of finding the right partner. Till date, the tribe feels that it is perfectly acceptable for a young man and woman to choose a life partner for themselves, with a fair choice of experiencing single and emotional relationships. Others believe that it was a great way of keeping wild animals at bay, as the Ghotul occupants dance and sing till late night. The noise would keep the wild animals away and the older generation could sleep without fear of attacks. Even now, the Ghotul are filled with its young unwedded occupants at the end of the day, after they finish their household chores and dinner. Then after, the time comes for some merriment with musical instruments with the local beverage or drinks. The members spend the night at the Ghotul, leaving the next morning to tend to their fields or go about other house hold work.

Constitution of Ghotul

The Ghotul is constituted by different members like *Sirdar, Jhariya, Mushwan, Diwan, Kotwar and Chalan, Jamadar, Chalki, Sipahi, Vaidya,*

Diwan or Mukhwan, Raniya, Sarguti and Chelik. Head of the Ghotul is very honorable person. He is known as Sardar/Sirdar or Mukhiya. The selection of the head is done by the opinion of Ghotul's members during *Karapandum* festival and *Karadangal Pooja.* A single person can be chosen many times for this position. Opinion of the *Sardar* is superior and meant as equal to God. No one can do any work without his permission. *Sardar* distributes work to the Ghotul's members.

The work of *Jhariya* is to clean the Ghotul and make it tidy as well as to collect fire wood for burning. The *Muswan* is the decorator of the Ghotul who paints the wall and draw picture. They draw it with white mud or *Khadiya*. The pictures drawn in the wall are mainly birds, mountains, flowers and other animals. *Diwan* has special work to lookafter the younger Ghotul members. He controls and watches the activities of the youth under the roof of Ghotul. They are the most intelligent members and inspect either good or bad works of members; they give them appropriate advice and bring improvement in them. The attendance of every participants of Ghotul is maintained by the *Kotwar*. If the *Kotwar* find any member is absent in the Ghotul, he takes all the information about absentee and complain to the *Sardar*. *Jamadar* similarly watch is that any girl cannot come to Ghotul without comb. The distribution of tobacco to all the members of Ghotul and organizing the festival time to time, is supervised by *Chalki* and *Sipahi* who take care of the crops and villagers from criminal activities. *Vaidya* treats the ill or injured members of Ghotul by herbs and shrubs. Along with traditional medicine he also heals with magic *mantras* and *tantras*, by this process, it is believe that he save the ill person against ghost or evil spirits. Few girls of Ghotul are given the post of queen (*Raniya*). Their work is to keep the Ghotul cleaned, decorated and make leaves' bowls which they use for taking meals. Every girl of Ghotul is called *Sarguti* (*Saheli*). Each *Sarguti* can share their feelings and emotions to other *Sarguti*. *Motiyari* is another name of the participatory girls in the Ghotul and the boy is known as *Chelik.*

Customs (*Pratha*) of Ghotul

The base of any social organisation is the belief and customs of the people of the communities. So if we want to know any community than it is pertinent to read about their customs and it is another name of the culture of the community. The importance of the customs is taught by the elder members of Ghotul. It is significant that their customs are orally communicated to youngsters. There is no written document or any archieves of the traditions but the vital duties of elders to transfer their precious and unique old culture to next generation. Here we have mentioned the different customs of Ghotul which are taught by *Sardar* and other elder members of Ghotul. Here some major Ghotul customs are elaborated below:

Narayandeva Pooja Pratha

Narayandeva is main God of Ghotul and his position is superior in position amongst all Gods and Goddesses of Ghotul. The main priest of this God is Sirha which is also known as traditional healer. It is the belief of the members of Ghotul as well as other community members that this worship saves the village and villagers from evil eyes and other calamities.

Dudh Lautani Pratha

This is the specific rule of marriage custom which is similar to the cross cousin marriage when one girl marry to another Gotra then the Gotra of boy becomes borrower and it is compensated when the girl of boy's Gotra, marry in the Gotra of girl.

Landa Pratha

Landa is a famous beverage/liquor of Bastar. Almost all the tribal communities use it in all the occasions. *Landa* is not only the beverage but it is also one of the materials of worship and other social activities like marriage, birth and death. The youth is learning about the uses of *landa* and how they can make it and when they can use it.

Diwari Pratha

In this custom members of the village and neighbouring villages come to the Ghotul to see the dance of *Motiyarins*. These *Motiyarins* are not only dancer under Ghotul roof but also pray for the village and villagers. Thus this custom bind the inter village people and the youth learn how to live integrated to other people.

Lamjhena Pratha

Poverty is a severe problem for tribal community where the land alienation and indebtedness playing an essential role to put them from surviving to non-surviving life. When the groom cannot pay the bride prize then the father of bride decide to keep the boy as servant in his home for few years or months. The time period is decided by the elder members of the community. In this period the girl's father observe the character of boys, working style and behave so during this is the period where the suitability of the boy is examined by the father of girl. Here the boy also observes how the girl favour him in her home. By this custom the elders want to teach how the boy and girl could be judges or examine each other and how they can play a beneficial role for each other.

Akhet Pratha

After worship, singing, dancing and hunting is the important custom of the community because forest dweller people not only live in the forest but also they breathe only in the forest. Forest ecology is the supra-survival place for tribals. The constituent members of the Ghotul teach the younger boys when they can go for hunting and who would become the leader of the hunting group. Generally the younger members of the Ghotul go in the *Falgun* month for hunting. The varieties and quantities of the hunting material decide that who one is the powerful *chelik* in the Ghotul and maximum time this *Chelik* is awarded by the Ghotul *Sirdar/Sardar*.

Present situation of Ghotul

A typically spacious tribal huts surrounded by earthen or wooden wall, Ghotul is an integral part of Muria Gond tribal life in Bastar region of Chhattisgarh. It plays a vital role in developing the life and culture of Muria Gond tribal groups. Typically known as dormitory, this autonomous institution speaks a lot of the moral messages of freedom and happiness; friendliness and sympathy; hospitality and unity. The institution is taken care by mutual understanding among both male and female individuals. Boys and girls at their tender age of six year are entitled with its membership and social responsibilities. Girl members of the Ghotul are called as '*Motiaris*' with a leader '*Belosa*' and boy members are called '*Cheliks*' with a leader '*Siredar*'. One interesting fact lies the development concerning the women-folk. Besides participating actively in decision making policies, women are assigned with the administrative task at the Ghotul. Unlike other traditional societies the women are not bound to the hard and fast rule of spouse selection, arrange marriage and pre-marital conditions. The institution also aims at teaching the skilful activity of leaf weaving, about festival organisation, hunting and gathering, about customary law, vegetable growing, ash cleaning and wood carving.

At last we would consider that, under one roof in the Ghotul the youths come together to participate in traditional storytelling, dance, singing and of course sex. Older members help and guide the younger members how to behave and engage in sexual practices and what is the law and limitation is this relationship. While this may seem like a sexual freeness for all but it is not true. There are many guidelines that one must follow in the sacred Ghotul hut.

Conclusion

The main features of the Ghotul atmosphere is to eliminate jealously and possessiveness to inculcate the sense of communal property and action. It was imperative for all the unmarried girls and boys to be members of Ghotul. The Ghotul was an independent, autonomous children's republic, where the married grownups were not allowed. The grownups were unable to manage any communal village affairs without their intervention. The aims of the Ghotul are; to teach the young boys and girls about their custom and culture like hunting, agriculture, dancing, singing and worship; this is the place where local dispute is solved by the elder members of the Ghotul. By this the youth also learn about their political customary laws; young boys and girls learn their duties in the community in their different stages of life as well as they learn about sexual education and marriage custom. Hence, the Ghotul gives a platform to choose the life partner but it is possible for whom their parents are agreed.

In this way the social education system is witnessed, which within the given social milieu is inculcated in each individual through games, recreations, folktales, fables, fantasies, concept of their existence where their origin, emergence, spread and standard, value orientation are dictated which are passed on from one generation to the other, religious beliefs and concepts theories regarding diseases and sufferings.

All the above features go into shaping the personality of the individuals in the early stages of his life and that is done in the tribal dormitory.

References

Behar, Ram Kumar and Baghel, Vijay Kumar (1992) 'Muriya Ghotul: Kal, Aaj and Kal', Bastar Ek Adhyayan, (Edit Ram Kumar Behra), Madhya Pradesh Hindi Granth Academy, Bhopal, p. 48-52.

Elwin, Verrier (1936) Leaves From the Jungle: Life in a Gond Village, Oxford University, Press.

Elwin, Verrier (1947) 'The Muriya and Their Ghotul", Oxford University Press, London.Elwin, Verrier (1964) The tribal world of Verrier Elwin; an autobiography, Oxford University, Press.

Gritfith Ralph, T.S. (1963) Vedas (cf.) *Search of Roots- A Study in Ethno Genesis,* S.H.M Rizvi and Shibani Roy. New Delhi: BRPC.

Kangali, Motiram (1986) 'Gondi Sagadevo Ki Mata Kangali', Gondwana Saga, August, Nagpur.

Roy, Shibani (2006) Tribal Youth Dormitory: A Hiatus or Heuristic? in *Journal of Tribes and Tribals*, Vol. 4, No. 1.

Shukl, Hiralal (1977) *Lanka Ki Khoj*, Rachana Prakashan.

Patel, M.L. (1969) *Ghotul Form Co-operative,* People Publishing House, Delhi.

Chapter - 20

Gondi Dialects of Bastar

Shashi Pandey

In India, the Gonds outnumber the rest of the tribes, population-wise and occupy substantial geographical area in five states, namely: Madhya Pradesh, Chhattisgarh, Maharashtra and Andhra Pradesh in different geo-physical setting. This is why there are apparent variations in their speech forms and as well culture too. This phenomenon has drawn the attention of eminent anthropologists and linguists towards them.

Undivided Bastar, now in newly formed state of Chhattisgarh is predominantly populated by various ethnic groups of the Gond tribe, locally known as Dandami Marias, Abujhmarias, Murias and Dorlas from time immemorial. However all these people call themselves Koytor in their speech. Dandami Marias call their language as Kôyâ mâtâ; the Abujhmarias as Koye Polin and the Murias as Koytor polloy. The Dorlas earlier called their speech as Koyan but now prefer to call it as Dorli.

The Muria Gondi is spoken in the northern area of Bastar excluding the Abujhmar hill tract. The Abujhmaria dialect is spoken in the north-western Bastar. The Dandami Maria is prevelant in the south-eastern Bastar. The last variety Dorli is used in the south-western Bastar bordering with Andhra Pradesh. There are also transitional areas between two dialects where they share the features of both the speech forms. S. Bhattacharya (1968) has found two regional varities of Muria Gondi. He has named them as Muria (east) and Muria (west). Muria (west) is mostly spoken in Narayanpur area. Data for Muria (east) has been collected in Farasgaon. A detailed survey is necessary to ascertain the exact boundaries dividing these sub dialects in future. Most of the differences are noticed between /r/ and /r/. Muria Gondi (east) uses /r/ whereas Muria Gondi (west) uses /r/ in most of the words.

Linguistically, the above mentioned dialects belong to Gondi language. Gondi has been included in the Central Dravidian sub-group. Along with Gondi, the other major languages of this division such as Telugu, Konda, Pengo, Manda, Kui and Kuvi are very closely related to Gondi. Excluding Telugu, the rest of the languages are mostly in spoken form and used by the tribal people. W.V. Grigson (1938), Verrier Elwin (1947), Edward Jay (1970), and D. Hajra (1970) of the Anthropological Survey of India have studied these tribes in details and produced monographs which are immensely useful to understand their culture. W.V. Grigson also made important references about the speech forms of the Dandami or Bison-horn Marias and Abujhmarias, whom he has named as the Hill Marias. Various attempts have also been made to study their speech forms by different scholars from time to time. We find references also made by George Grierson in his Linguistic Survey of India about these dialects but noted that he was not satisfied with the material sent to him from Bastar. A.N. Mitchell also published 'A Grammar of Maria Gondi as spoken by the Bison-horn or Dandami Marias of Bastar State in 1942. This sketchy grammar contains many erroneous statements. Apart from this, in the introduction, he observed that the speech of Dandami Maria is almost identical with the Gondi spoken by the Hill Marias in the north-west and Murias and Jhorias of the north of the state. It is clear that this statement is very misleading.

G.U. Rao (2008), has made a detailed comparative study of all the ten subgroups of Gondi spoken in India as a whole. He has given separate status of four dialects to these speech forms. Though these dialects share many common features, they also have variations on many counts. Here I would like to discuss some of them briefly.

Phonology

All the above four dialects contain five short vowel phonemes /a, i, u, e and o/ along with there long counterparts such as /â, î, û, e and ô/. They also have in common the consonants /p, b, m, t, d, n, s, l, t, d, c, j, k and g. Besides these they have a flap /r/ and retroflex /r/.

On the other hand the consonants /n/, /n/, /h/, /1/ and have limited distribution.

(i) /n/ is a retroflex nasal. It is attested only in Abujhmaria and Dorli dialects in medial position only.

Abujhmaria	**Dorli**	
tanki	tanki	liver
konda	kandu	eye
gunda	gunda	powder

(ii) /n/ is a velar nasal. It occurs in Abujhmaria and Muria Gondi in medial and final position. So far I have noticed, it occurs as an allophone of /n/ followed by a /k/ or /g/ in Dandami Maria and Dorli.

Abujhmaria	**Muria**	**D.Maria/Dorli**	
ane	ane	ange	'sister-in law'
rena	rena	renga	'plum'
piten	piten	pite	'birds'
âkin	âkin	âki	'leaves'

(iii) /h/ is a glottal fricative. It does not occur in Dorli and Abujhmaria at all. In Dandami Maria it is absent in word-initial position. It occurs in Muria initially, medially and finally.

D.maria	**Abujhmaria**	**Muria**	
uskar	uskar~uskand	huskar	'sleep'
epur	epo	hepur	'broom'
arng	ani	harn	'sal tree'
ât	âtum	hâtum	'market'

(iv) /?/ is a glottal stop. It occurs word-medially in Abujhmaria only. It corresponds with Muria /h/.

Muria	**Abujhmaria**	
kôhk	kô?k	'horns'
tôha	tô?a	'show (imp)

(v) /l/ is retroflex lateral, occurring only in Abujhmaria in certain regions in free variation with /l/.

Muria	**Abujhmaria**	
kale	kale ~ kale	'thief'
kal	kalu ~ kalu	'liquor'
pula	pula ~ pula	'sour recipe'
talur	talori ~ talori	'mother of an animal'

(vi) // is a uvular trill found to occur in Abujhmaria in word-medial and final position.

Muria	**Abujhmaria**	
er	e	'water'
nâr	na	'village'
mari	mari	'son'
âru	âu	'six (n.m.)'

Grammar

Nouns are divided in masculine and non-masculine groups. The masculine group contains only human masculine nouns. The rest of the nouns (animals, neuter and feminine) are known as non masculine nouns. This division is common in Gondi everywhere. Pluralization of nouns share many common features. However the non-masculine nouns ending in a vowel in Dandami Maria and Dorli lengthen their short vowels into long ones, whereas the Abujhmaria and Muria dialects pluralize such vowel ending nouns by the marker /n/.

Among pronouns the first person (inclusive) plural pronoun is noticed in Dandami Maria and Dorli but not in the Abujhmaria or Muria dialects. The forms are as such:

Dandami Maria	manal	'we two'
Dorli	manar	'we two'

The third person masculine pronouns (distal) bear many variations dialect-wise.

Muria (east)	ôr	'he'	ôr	'they'
Muria (west)	ôr	he	ôr-lor	'they'
Abujhmaria	ô	'he'	oru	'they'
Dandami Maria	ôr	'he'	or	'they
'Dorli	ôndu	'he'	oru	'they'

There are two separate forms showing the present and future tenses separately in Muria and Abujhmaria but in Dandami Maria and Dorli the present and future tenses are indicated by a single form designated as non-past tense.

Dandami Maria/Dorli	**Abujhmaria/Muria**
dâtan 'I go./I will go.	dâkan 'I will go.'

There are some instances where the non-past verbal form of Dandami Maria becomes the past tense form in Muria and Abujhmaria.

D. Maria	**Muria/Abujhmaria**
ad vâta 'She will come'	ad vâta 'she had come'.

There are many examples of lexical differences in these dialects for examples:

Muria	**Abujhmaria**	
poroy	peder	'name'
menj	garbom	'egg'

mîn	kîke	'fish'
marmin	pendul	'marriage'
pir	musur	'rains'
D. Maria	**Dorli**	
pande	kape	'frog'
pendul	peli	'marriage'
akum	kom	'blowing horn'
kamka	paspu	'turmeric'
kac	inp~inm	'iron'

Above some variations were noted. These are not exhaustive. Though the grammars of these dialects have been written by many scholars, there remains much to be done. These unwritten speeches abound in oral literature. They are the treasures of indigenous knowledge. Many aspects of culture cannot be studied without knowing their speeches properly. T. Burrow and M.B. Emeneau (1961) had hoped, "Much that characterizes all India as a linguistic area will only be appreciated correctly when Central India is better known than it is now".

References

Bhattacharya S. (1968) *Muria Morphology* Bulletin of the Anthropological Survey of India. *Vol. xvii No 3.*

Burrow T. and M. B. Emeneau. (1961) *Dravidian Etymological Dictionary.* Oxford: Oxford University Press.

Elwin, V. (1947) *The Muria and their Ghotul.* London: Oxford University Press.

Grierson, G.A. (1906) *Linguistic Survey of India. Vol. iv*. Calcutta.

Hajra, D. (1970) *The Dorla of Bastar*. Calcutta: Anthropological Survey of India.

Uma Maheshwara Rao, G. (2008) *A Comparative Grammar of the Gondi Dialects*. Kuppam: Dravidian University.

Photographs

Ghotul along with wooden boundary – locally called Aawar

Ghotul at Gadbengal Village

Ghotul ***at Devgaon Village***

Ghotul ***Dance – (locally called*** **Mandri Nacha*)***

Ghotul ***Dance – (locally called*** **Rela*)***

Layaa – ***preparing for Dance***

Layaa - ***ready for Dance***

List of V. Elwin visited villages of Baster Region Kondagaon District

1. Darli near Amaravati
2. Bamhani
3. Chimari
4. Alore
5. Bade donger
6. Bedma
7. Bisrampuri
8. Dongripura
9. Kokodi
10. Madhera (East Kondagaon)
11. Palati
12. Pendravand
13. Siddhavand
14. Ulera
15. Amgaon
16. Almer
17. Binjhe
18. Chandabeda
19. Chaniagaon
20. Dhanora
21. Gorma
22. Jhakati
23. Kanhargaon
24. Kongud
25. More bedma (Near Kanhargaon)
26. Fouda (Near Dongriguda)
27. Funder
28. Todosi
29. Baghbeda (East Kondagaon)
30. Randhana
31. Asalnar
32. Rengagondi
33. Bhanpuri
34. Jugani

35. Sirsi
36. Sirpur
37. Baniagaon
38. Dahikonga
39. Hathipakna
40. Jaitpuri
41. Kabonga
42. Kachora
43. Keravahi
44. Kondagaon (Jamkotpara)
45. Lanjoda
46. Malakot
47. Masora
48. Palli
49. Pipra

Narayanpur District

1. Amsara
2. Borpal
3. Devgaon
4. Edka
5. Gavari
6. Khurpai
7. Arpal
8. Chandagaon
9. Kalepal
10. Malingnar
11. Metavand
12. Nayanar
13. Panigaon
14. Remavand
15. Turtha
16. Aturgaon
17. Kongera
18. Rajpur

19. Taragaon
20. Toynar
21. Binjali
22. Dugabengal
23. Garhbengal
24. Palki
25. Bandopal
26. Amgaon
27. Bakulvahi
28. Bangal
29. Halami Munjmeta
30. Kapsi
31. Markabeda
32. Timnar

Kanker District (Antagarh Tehsil)

1. Semurgaon
2. Chikhali
3. Lohatter
4. Penjori
5. Fupgaon
6. Kalgaon
7. Karikhodara
8. Lamkanar

Index

F

G

H

I

N

O

P